RUSSIAN

PHRASEBOOK & DICTIONARY

Contacting the Editors

Every effort has been made to provide accurate information in this publication, but changes are inevitable. The publisher cannot be responsible for any resulting loss, inconvenience or injury. We would appreciate it if readers would call our attention to any errors or outdated information. We also welcome your suggestions; if you come across a relevant expression not in our phrase book, please contact us at: **hello@insightguides.com**

All Rights Reserved
© 2016 Apa Digital (CH) AG and Apa Publications (UK) Ltd.

First Edition: 2016
Printed in China

Cover & Interior Design: Pawel Pasternak
Production: AM Services
Production Manager: Vicky Glover
Cover Photo: iStock (front), Shutterstock (back)

Interior Photos: Shutterstock

CONTENTS

FOOD & DRINK

GOING OUT

DICTIONARY

PRONUNCIATION

This section is designed to make you familiar with the sounds of Russian using our simplified phonetic transcription. You'll find the pronunciation of the Cyrillic (Russian) letters explained below, together with their 'imitated' equivalents. To use this system, found throughout the phrase book, simply read the pronunciation as if it were English, noting any special rules in the tables that follow.

Keep in mind that stress in Russian is irregular. In this phrase book, the stress is indicated with an underline.

CONSONANTS

Letter	Approximate Pronunciation	Symbol	Example	Pronunciation
б*	like b in bit	b	был	*bihl*
в	like v in vivid	v	ваш	*vahsh*
г	like g in go	g	город	*goh • raht*
д	like d in do	d	да	*dah*
ж	like s in pleasure	zh	жаркий	*zhahr • keey*
з	like z in zoo	z	завтра	*zahf • trah*
к	like k in kitten	k	карта	*kahr • tah*
л	like l in lily	l	лампа	*lahm • pah*
м	likew m in my	m	масло	*mahs • lah*
н	like n in not	n	нет	*nyet*
п	like p in pot	p	парк	*pahrk*
р	trilled r	r	русский	*roos • keey*
с	like s in see	s	слово	*sloh • vah*
т	like t in tip	t	там	*tahm*
ф	like f in face	f	ферма	*fyer • mah*
х	like ch in Scottish loch	kh	хлеб	*khlyep*
ц	like ts in sits	ts	цена	*tsih • nah*
ч	like ch in chip	ch	час	*chahs*

| ш | like sh in shut | **sh** | ваша | _vah_ • shah |
| щ | like sh followed by ch | **shch** | щи | shchee |

Capital **б** in writing appears as **Б**.

> (i)
>
> The pronunciation of Russian consonants can be either hard or soft. Consonants are soft when followed by the vowels **я**, **е**, **и**, **ё**, **ю** and the soft sign, **ь**. In the Russian phonetic transcription system, when a letter is soft it is generally followed by y + a vowel (as in **нет** nyet), or by an apostrophe (for example, **сколько** _skol'_ • kah). The apostrophe, included in the phonetics, is commonly used to represent the soft sign when Russian is written in the Latin alphabet. When the letter **ъ**, known as the hard sign, is used, it precedes a vowel and is pronounced like the y in yet. It indicates that the preceding consonant is hard.

VOWELS

Letter	Approximate Pronunciation	Symbol	Example	Pronunciation
а	between a in cat and u in cut	**ah**	как	kahk
е	like ye in yet	**ye/yeh**	где	gdyeh
ё*	like yo in yonder	**yo/yoh**	мёд	myot
и	like ee in see	**ee**	синий	_see_ • neey
й	like y in boy	**y**	бой	boy
о	like o in hot	**o/oh**	стол	stol
у	like oo in boot	**oo**	улица	_oo_ • lee • tsah
ы	like i in ill	**ih**	вы	vih
э	like e in met	**e/eh**	эта	_eh_ • tah
ю	like you in youth	**yoo**	юг	yook
я	like ya in yard	**yah**	мясо	_myah_ • sah

*Capital **ё** in writing appears as **Ё**.

ⓘ

The vowels **o**, **e**, **a** and **я** are pronounced differently depending on whether or not they are stressed. This explains why a given vowel is not always represented the same way in phonetic transcription.

VOWEL COMBINATIONS

Letter	Approximate Pronunciation	Symbol	Example	Pronunciation
ай	like y in my	**ie**	**май**	*mie*
яй	like y in my, preceded by y in yes	**yie**	**негодяй**	*nee•gah•<u>dyie</u>*
ой	like oy in boy	**oy**	**вой**	*voy*
ей	like ey in obey, preceded by y in yes	**yey**	**соловей**	*sah•lah•<u>vyey</u>*
ий	like ee in see, followed by y in yes	**eey**	**ранний**	*<u>rahn</u>•neey*
ый	like i in ill, followed by y in yes	**iy**	**красивый**	*krah•<u>see</u>•viy*
уй	like oo in good, followed by y in yes	**ooy**	**дуй**	*dooy*
юй	as уй above, preceded by y in yes	**yooy**	**плюй**	*plyooy*

ⓘ

Like most of the languages of Eastern Europe, Russian is a Slavic language. It uses the Cyrillic alphabet.

HOW TO USE THE APP

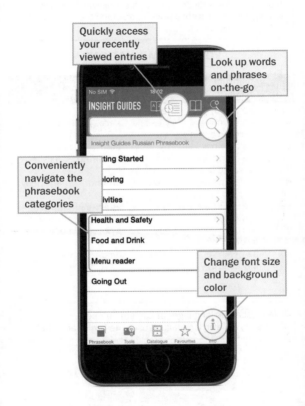

Quickly access your recently viewed entries

Look up words and phrases on-the-go

Conveniently navigate the phrasebook categories

Change font size and background color

Save the most useful
everyday words and
phrases to your Favorites

Use the Flash
Cards Quiz to learn
and memorize new
words easily

Take all digital
advantages of the app:
listen to words and
phrases pronounced
by native speakers

To learn how to
activate the app,
see the inside
back cover of this
phrasebook.

GRAMMAR

VERBS

The infinitive of most verbs ends in **–ть**. Russian verbs follow two conjugation patterns in the present and future tenses; following are the patterns for the verbs **жить** zhiht' (to live) and **говорить** gah • vah • reet' (to speak):

ЖИТЬ (TO LIVE)		PRESENT	FUTURE
I	я	**живу**	**буду жить**
you (sing.)	ты	**живёшь**	**будешь жить**
he/she/it	он/она/оно	**живёт**	**будет жить**
we	мы	**живём**	**будем жить**
you (pl.)	вы	**живёте**	**будете жить**
they	они	**живут**	**будут жить**

ГОВОРИТЬ (TO SPEAK)		PRESENT	FUTURE
I	я	**говорю**	**буду говорить**
you (sing.)	ты	**говоришь**	**будешь говорить**
he/she/it	он/она/оно	**говорит**	**будет говорить**
we	мы	**говорим**	**будем говорить**
you (pl.)	вы	**говорите**	**будете говорить**
they	они	**говорят**	**будут говорить**

Some verbs have a mixed conjugation, combining the first and second patterns.

The past tense is formed by removing the **–ть** of the infinitive and adding:

–л (l)   masculine ending
–ла (lah)   feminine ending
–ло (loh)   neuter ending
–ли (lee)   plural ending

It is the gender and number of the subject that control the ending, for example:

ГОВОРИТЬ (TO SPEAK)		PAST
I	я	**говорил**
you (sing.)	ты	**говорил**
he	он	**говорил**
she	она	**говорила**
it	оно	**говорило**
we	мы	**говорили**
you (pl.)	вы	**говорили**
they	они	**говорили**

There are no irregular verbs in the Russian language.

WORD ORDER

In the Russian language, word order is rather flexible. Though the Russian sentence is generally arranged subject-verb-object, grammar rules allow virtually any combination of subject, verb and object within the sentence.

You can form a simple question in Russian by adding an interrogatory intonation (letting the voice rise at the end of the sentence).

Счёт включает обслуживание.　　　　Service is included.
shchot fklyoo • chah • eet
ahp • sloo • zhih • vah • nee • yeh

Счёт включает обслуживание?　　　　Is service included?
shchot fklyoo • chah • eet
ahp • sloo • zhih • vah • nee • yeh

NEGATION

To form a negative sentence, add **не** *nee* (not) before the verb.
Example:

Мы курим. *mih <u>koo</u>•reem*	We smoke.
Мы не курим. *mih nee <u>koo</u>•reem*	We don't smoke.

IMPERATIVES

Imperative sentences, or sentences that are commands, are
formed by adding the appropriate ending to the stem of the verb
(i.e. the verb in the infinitive without the **–ть, –сь, –ся** ending).
Example: Speak!

you (sing.)	**Говори!** *gah-vah-<u>ree</u>*
you (pl.)	**Говорите!** *gah-vah-<u>ree</u>-tee*

NOUNS

There are three genders in Russian: masculine, feminine and
neuter. The endings of nouns vary according to their role in
the sentence. There are six different cases (roles) in both the
singular and plural. Adjectives agree in number and gender with
the noun they modify. There are no articles in Russian.

ADJECTIVES

Adjectives agree in number and gender with the noun they
modify.

masculine ending	**–ый, –ой, –ий**
feminine ending	**–ая**
neuter ending	**–ое**

Example:

красный m <u>krahs</u> • niy	red
красная f krahs • nah • yah	red
красное n <u>krahs</u> • nah • yeh	red

COMPARATIVES & SUPERLATIVES

The comparative may be formed by adding **более** <u>boh</u> • lee • yeh (more) or **менее** <u>myeh</u> • nee • yeh (less) before the adjective or adverb. However, more often these are formed with the help of the endings **–e** and **–ee** which are added to the stem.
The superlative is formed by adding **самый** sah • miy (the most) and **наимение** nah • ee • myeh • nee • yeh (the least) before the adjective.

большой bahl' • <u>shoy</u>	big
больше bol' • <u>sheh</u>	bigger
самый большой <u>sah</u> • miy bahl' • <u>shoy</u>	biggest
дорогой dah • rah • <u>goy</u>	expensive
менее дорогой <u>myeh</u> • nee • yeh dah • rah • <u>goy</u>	more expensive
наименее дорогой nah • ee • <u>myeh</u> • nee • yeh dah • rah • <u>goy</u>	most expensive

ADVERBS & ADVERBIAL EXPRESSIONS

Many adverbs are formed by adding **–o** to the stem of an adjective.

хороший khah • <u>roh</u> • shiy	good	**хорошо** khah • rah • <u>shoh</u>	well
красивый krah • <u>see</u> • viy	beautiful	**красиво** krah • <u>see</u> • vah	beautifully

GETTING STARTED

THE BASICS

NUMBERS

NEED TO KNOW

0	**ноль**	*nol'*
1	**один**	*ah • <u>deen</u>*
2	**два**	*dvah*
3	**три**	*tree*
4	**четыре**	*chee • <u>tih</u> • ree*
5	**пять**	*pyaht'*
6	**шесть**	*shest'*
7	**семь**	*syem'*
8	**восемь**	*<u>voh</u> • seem'*
9	**девять**	*<u>dyeh</u> • veet'*
10	**десять**	*<u>dyeh</u> • seet'*
11	**одиннадцать**	*ah • <u>dee</u> • nah • tsaht'*
12	**двенадцать**	*dvee • <u>nah</u> • tsaht'*
13	**тринадцать**	*tree • <u>nah</u> • tsaht'*

14	**четырнадцать**
	chee • tihr • nah • tsaht'
15	**пятнадцать**
	peet • nah • tsaht'
16	**шестнадцать**
	shihs • nah • tsaht'
17	**семнадцать**
	seem • nah • tsaht'
18	**восемнадцать**
	vah • seem • nah • tsaht'
19	**девятнадцать**
	dee • veet • nah • tsaht'
20	**двадцать**
	dvah • tsaht'
21	**двадцать один**
	dvah • tsaht' ah • deen
22	**двадцать два**
	dvah • tsaht' dvah
30	**тридцать**
	tree • tsaht'
31	**тридцать один**
	tree • tsaht' ah • deen
40	**сорок**
	soh • rahk
50	**пятьдесят**
	peet' • dee • syaht
60	**шестьдесят**
	sheez' • dee • syaht
70	**семьдесят**
	syem' • dee • seet
80	**восемьдесят**
	voh • seem' • dee • seet
90	**девяносто**
	dee • vee • nos • tah

100	**сто**
	stoh
101	**сто один**
	stoh ah • deen
200	**двести**
	dvyes • tee
500	**пятьсот**
	peet • sot
1,000	**тысяча**
	tih • see • chah
10,000	**десять тысяч**
	dyeh • seet' tih • seech
1,000,000	**миллион**
	mee • lee • on

ORDINAL NUMBERS

first	**первый**
	pyer • viy
second	**второй**
	ftah • roy
third	**третий**
	tryeh • teey
fourth	**четвёртый**
	cheet • vyor • tiy
fifth	**пятый**
	pyah • tiy
once	**один раз**
	ah • deen rahs
twice	**два раза**
	dvah rah • zah
three times	**три раза**
	tree rah • zah

Один ah • <u>deen</u> (one) has three gender forms: **один** *m*
ah • <u>deen</u>, **одна** *f* ahd • <u>nah</u> and **одно** *n* ahd • <u>noh</u>.
Два *dvah* (two) has two forms: **два** *dvah* for both masculine
and neuter and **две** *dveh* for feminine.
Ordinal numbers follow the pattern of adjectives.

TIME

NEED TO KNOW

What time is it?	**Который час?** *kah • <u>toh</u> • riy chahs*
It's noon [midday].	**Сейчас полдень.** *see • <u>chahs</u> pol • deen'*
At midnight.	**В полночь.** *f pol • nahch*
From nine o'clock to five o'clock.	**С девяти до пяти часов.** *s dee • vyah • <u>tee</u> dah pyah • <u>tee</u> chah • <u>sof</u>*
Twenty after [past] four.	**Двадцать минут пятого.** *<u>dvah</u> • tsaht'mee • <u>noot</u> pyah • tah • vah*
A quarter to nine.	**Без четверти девять.** *byes <u>chet</u> • veer • tee dyeh • veet'*
5:30 a.m./p.m.	**Пять тридцать утра/вечера.** *pyaht'<u>tree</u> • tsaht' oot • <u>rah</u>/ <u>vyeh</u> • chee • rah*

Russians have a different way of thinking about and expressing time. For them, the hour between 12 and 1 is the 'first hour,' the hour between 1 and 2 is the 'second hour,' etc. Up until half past the hour, time is expressed by stating how many minutes into the given hour it is.

Example: **десять минут третьего** _dyeh_ • _seet' mee_ • _noot tryey_ • _tee_ • _vah_ (ten after two) would be 'ten minutes of (into) the third (hour)'.

After half past the hour, time is expressed by using **без** _byez_ (without) and the number of minutes remaining until the next hour.

Example: **без двадцати восемь** _byez dvah_ • _tsah_ • _tee voh_ • _seem'_ (twenty to eight) would be 'eight without twenty'.

DAYS

NEED TO KNOW

Monday	**понедельник** _pah_ • _nee_ • _dyel'_ • _neek_
Tuesday	**вторник** _ftohr_ • _neek_
Wednesday	**среда** _sree_ • _dah_
Thursday	**четверг** _cheet_ • _vyerk_
Friday	**пятница** _pyaht_ • _nee_ • _tsah_
Saturday	**суббота** _soo_ • _boh_ • _tah_
Sunday	**воскресенье** _vahs_ • _kree_ • _syen'_ • _yeh_

DATES

yesterday	**вчера**
	fchee • rah
today	**сегодня**
	see • vod • nyah
tomorrow	**завтра**
	zahf • trah
day	**день**
	dyen'
week	**неделя**
	nee • dyeh • lyah
month	**месяц**
	myeh • seets
year	**год**
	got

It is standard practice to write dates with the day
of the month first followed by the month and then
the year. Periods [full stops] are often used to separate the
numbers (forward slashes are less common and hyphens
are never used). So June 7, 2008 would be expressed as
07.06.08 or 07/06/08.

MONTHS

January	**январь**
	yeen • vahr'
February	**февраль**
	feev • rahl'
March	**март**
	mahrt

April	**апрель**
	ahp • ryel'
May	**май**
	mie
June	**июнь**
	ee • yoon'
July	**июль**
	ee • yool'
August	**август**
	ahf • goost
September	**сентябрь**
	seen • tyahbr'
October	**октябрь**
	ahk • tyahbr'
November	**ноябрь**
	nah • yahbr'
December	**декабрь**
	dee • kahbr

SEASONS

spring	**весна**
	vees • nah
summer	**лето**
	lyeh • tah
fall [autumn]	**осень**
	oh • seen'
winter	**зима**
	zee • mah

HOLIDAYS

| January 1, New Year's Day | **Новый Год** |
| | *noh • viy got* |

January 7, Christmas Day	**Рождество** *razh • dyes • <u>tvoh</u>*
March 8, International Women's Day	**Международный Женский День** *myezh • doo • nah • <u>rohd</u> • nihy'* *<u>zhen</u> • skeey dyen*
May 1, May Day/ Labor Day	**1-е мая** *<u>pyer</u> • vah • yeh <u>mah</u> • yah*
May 9, Victory in Europe Day	**День Победы** *dyen' pah • <u>byeh</u> • dih*
June 12, Independence Day	**День Независимости России** *dyen'* *nyeh • zah • <u>vee</u> • see • mahs • tee* *rahs • <u>see</u> • ee*
November 4, Day of National Unity	**День Национального Единства** *dyen'* *nah • tsih • ah • <u>nahl'</u> • nah • vah* *yeh • <u>deen</u> • stvah*
December 12, Constitution Day	**День Конституции** *dyen' kahn • stee • <u>too</u> • tsee • ee*
Movable Dates: Easter	**Пасха** *<u>pahs</u> • khah*

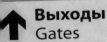
ARRIVAL & DEPARTURE

NEED TO KNOW

I'm here on vacation [holiday]/business.	**Я здесь в отпуске/по делам.** *yah zdyehs' v <u>ot</u> • poos • kee/pah dee • <u>lahm</u>*
I'm going to…	**Я еду в…** *yah <u>yeh</u> • doo v…*
I'm staying at the…Hotel	**Я живу в гостинице…** *yah zhih • <u>voo</u> v gahs • <u>tee</u> • nee • tseh…*

YOU MAY HEAR…

Ваш билет/паспорт, пожалуйста. *vahsh bee • <u>lyet</u>/pahs • pahrt pah • <u>zhahl</u> • stah*	Your ticket/ passport, please.
Цель Вашего визита? *tsel' <u>vah</u> • shee • vah vee • <u>zee</u> • tah*	What's the purpose of your visit?
Где вы остановились? *gdyeh vih ahs • tah • nah • <u>vee</u> • lees'*	Where are you staying?

Сколько вы пробудете здесь?
skol' • ka vih prah • <u>boo</u> • dee • tee zdyes'

How long are you staying?

С кем вы приехали?
s kyem vih pree • <u>yeh</u> • khah • lee

Who are you with?

BORDER CONTROL

YOU MAY HEAR...

Есть ли у Вас вещи, подлежащие декларированию?
yest' lee oo vahs <u>vyeh</u> • shchee
pahd • lee • <u>zhah</u> • shchee • yeh
dee • klah • <u>ree</u> • rah • vah • nee • yoo

Do you have anything to declare?

Вам надо оплатить пошлину.
vahm <u>nah</u> • dah ah • plah • <u>teet'</u>
<u>posh</u> • lee • noo

You must pay duty on this.

Откройте эту сумку.
aht • <u>kroy</u> • tee eh • too <u>soom</u> • koo

Please open this bag.

I'm just passing through.

Я проездом.
yah prah • <u>yez</u> • dahm

I would like to declare...

Я хочу предъявить...таможне.
yah khah • <u>choo</u> pree • dyah • <u>veet'</u>...
tah • <u>mozh</u> • nyeh

I have nothing to declare.

Мне нечего декларировать.
mneh <u>nyeh</u> • chee • vah
dee • klah • <u>ree</u> • rah • vaht'

YOU MAY SEE...

ТАМОЖНЯ	customs
tah • _mozh_ • nyah	
ТОВАРЫ БЕЗ ПОШЛИНЫ	duty-free goods
tah • _vah_ • rih byez _posh_ • lee • nih	
ТАМОЖЕННЫЙ ДОСМОТР	goods to declare
tah • _moh_ • zhih • niy dah • _smotr_	
СВОБОДНЫЙ КОРИДОР	nothing to
svah • _bod_ • niy kah • ree • _dor_	declare
ПАСПОРТНЫЙ КОНТРОЛЬ	passport control
pahs • pahrt • niy kahnt • _rol'_	
МИЛИЦИЯ	police
mee • _lee_ • tsih • yah	

MONEY

AT THE BANK

Can I exchange foreign currency here?	**Можно обменять валюту здесь?**
	mozh • nah ahb • mee • _nyaht'_
	vah • _lyoo_ • too zdyes'
What's the exchange rate?	**Какой курс?**
	kah • _koy_ koors
How much is the fee?	**Сколько процентов комиссионный сбор?**
	skol' • kah prah • _tsen_ • tahf
	kah • mees • see • _on_ • niy zbor
I think there's a mistake.	**Я думаю, здесь ошибка.**
	yah du • _ma_ • yoo zdes' ash • _eeb_ • kah

NEED TO KNOW

Where's...?	**Где...?**
	gdyeh...
the ATM	**банкомат**
	bahn • kah • maht
the bank	**банк**
	bahnk
the currency exchange office	**обмен валюты**
	ahb • myen vah • lyoo • tih
What time does the bank open/close?	**Во сколько открывается/ закрывается банк?**
	va skol' • kah aht • krih • vah • ee • tsah/ zah • krih • vah • ee • tsah bahnk
I'd like to change dollars/pounds into rubles.	**Я хотел m /хотела f бы обменять доллары/фунты на рубли.**
	yah khah • tyel/khah • tyeh • lah bih ahb • mee • nyaht' dol • lah • rih/ foon • tih nah roob • lee
I want to cash some traveler's checks.	**Я хочу обменять дорожные чеки.**
	yah khah • choo ahb • mee • nyaht' dah • rozh • nih • ee cheh • kee

I've lost my traveler's checks [cheques].	**Я потерял m /потеряла f дорожные чеки.**
	yah pah • tee • ryahl/pah • tee • ryah • lah dah • rozh • nih • ee cheh • kee
My card was lost.	**Я потерял m /потеряла f свою карточку.**
	yah pah • tee • ryahl/pah • tee • ryah • lah svah • yoo kahr • tahch • koo

My credit cards have been stolen.	**У меня украли кредитные карточки.**
	oo mee • nyah ook • rah • lee kree • deet • nih • ee kahr • tahch • kee
My card doesn't work.	**Моя карточка не работает.**
	mah • yah kahr • tahch • kah nee rah • boh • tah • eet
The ATM ate my card.	**Банкомат забрал мою карту.**
	bahn • kah • maht zahb • rahl moh • yoo kahr • toot

For Numbers, see page 18.

Contact your travel agent or the Russian embassy before your trip to determine the latest regulations regarding how much foreign currency you can bring into the country. In major towns and cities, currency exchange offices can be found in banks, hotels, stores and even street kiosks. Some operate 24 hours a day.

Others are open from early morning to late evening, with a break for lunch. All currency exchange offices accept U.S. dollars and euro, and some pounds sterling; however, notes that are not clean and crisp are often rejected and you may be required to show your passport. You may have difficulty changing notes issued before 1993. For other currencies and traveler's checks, it's best to use banks and large hotels.

Warning: You may be approached by someone on the street offering attractive exchange rates. It is highly inadvisable to take up such offers.

YOU MAY SEE...

ВСТАВЬТЕ КАРТУ	insert card
fstahf' • tyeh kahr • too	
ОТМЕНИТЬ´	cancel
aht • mee • neet	
ОЧИСТИТЬ	clear
ah • chees • teet'	
ВВОД	enter
vvot	
ПИН-КОД	PIN
peen • kot	
СНИМАТЬ	withdraw funds
snee • maht'	
С ТЕКУЩЕГО СЧЕТА	from checking
s tee • koo • shchee • vah shchoh • tah	[current] account
СО СБЕРЕГАТЕЛЬНОГО СЧЕТА	from savings
sah zbee • ree • gah • teel' • nah • vah	account
shchoh • tah	
ЧЕК	receipt
chehk	

YOU MAY SEE...

The monetary unit is the ruble (**рубль** *roobl'*), which is divided into 100 kopecks (**копеек** *kah • pyeh • yek*).
Coins: 1, 5, 10, 50 **kopecks**; 1, 2, 5 **rubles**
Notes: 10, 50, 100, 500, 1000 **rubles**

CONVERSATION

NEED TO KNOW

Hello./Hi!	**Здравствуйте./Привет!** _zdrah_ • stvooy • tee/pree • _vyet_
How are you?	**Как дела?** _kahk dee_ • _lah_
Fine, thanks.	**Спасибо, хорошо.** spah • _see_ • bah khah • rah • _shoh_
Excuse me!	**Извините!** eez • vee • _nee_ • tee
Do you speak English?	**Вы говорите по-английски?** vih gah • vah • _ree_ • tee pah ahn • _gleey_ • skee
What's your name?	**Как Вас зовут?** kahk vahz zah • _voot_
My name is...	**Меня зовут...** mee • _nyah_ zah • _voot_...
Pleased to meet you.	**Очень приятно.** _oh_ • cheen' pree • _yaht_ • nah
Where are you from?	**Откуда вы приехали?** aht • _koo_ • dah vih pree • _yeh_ • khah • lee
I'm from the U.S./U.K.	**Я из США/Великобритании.** yah ees seh sheh _ah_/ vee • lee • kah • bree • _tah_ • nee • ee
What do you do?	**Ваша профессия?** _vah_ • shah prah • _fyeh_ • see • yah
I work for...	**Я работаю в...** yah rah • _boh_ • tah • yoo v...
I'm a student.	**Я студент.** yah stoo • _dyehnt_

I'm retired.	**Я на пенсии.**
	yah nah pyehn • see • ee
Do you like…?	**Вы любите…?**
	vih lyoo • bee • tee…
Goodbye.	**До свидания.**
	dah svee • dah • nee • yah
See you later.	**Увидимся.**
	oo • vee • deem • syah

LANGUAGE DIFFICULTIES

Do you speak English?	**Вы говорите по-английски?**
	vih gah • vah • ree • tee pah ahn • gleey • skee
Does anyone here speak English?	**Кто-нибудь говорит по-английски?**
	ktoh nee • bood' goh • voh • reet poh ahn • gleey • skee
I don't speak Russian.	**Я не говорю по-русски.**
	yah nyeh gah • vah • ryoo pah • roos • kee
I don't speak much Russian.	**Я плохо говорю по-русски.**
	yah ploh • khah gah • vah • ryoo pah • roos • kee
Speak slowly, please.	**Говорите медленнее, пожалуйста.**
	gah • vah • ree • tee myed • lee • nee • yeh pah • zhahl • stah
Repeat that, please.	**Повторите, пожалуйста.**
	pahf • tah • ree • tee pah • zhahl • stah
Excuse me?	**Простите?**
	prah • stee • tee
What was that?	**Что такое?**
	shtoh tah • koh • yeh
Can you spell it?	**Вы можете это написать?**
	vih moh • zheh • teh eh • toh nah • pee • saht'

Write it down, please.	**Напишите, пожалуйста.** *nah • pee • <u>shih</u> • tee pah • <u>zhahl</u> • stah*
Translate this for me, please.	**Переведите мне это, пожалуйста.** *pee • ree • vee • <u>dee</u> • tee mnyeh eh • tah* *pah • <u>zhahl</u> • stah*
What does this/that mean?	**Что это/то значит?** *shtoh <u>eh</u> • tah/toh znah • cheet*
I (don't) understand.	**Я (не) понимаю.** *yah (nee) pah • nee • <u>mah</u> • yoo*
Do you understand?	**Вы понимаете?** *vih pah • nee • <u>mah</u> • ee • tee*

It is polite to address people you know by their first name and patronymic, derived from the father's name. So, Nikolay, whose father's name is Ivan, would be called Nikolay Ivanovich; Natalia, whose father's name is Alexander, would be called Natalia Alexandrovna.
Like many other languages, Russian has two forms of the pronoun you: the informal (singular) **ты** *tih* and the formal (plural) **вы** *vih*. **Ты** is used between members of the same family, close friends and to address young children; **вы** *vih* is the polite form of address when you are talking to a person you do not know well or who is older or senior to you. When you are addressing more than one person, **вы** must always be used.
The pre-revolutionary **господин** *gahs • pah • <u>deen</u>* (Mr.) and **госпожа** *gahs • pah • <u>zhah</u>* (Mrs. or Miss) has re-entered usage in Russia.

MAKING FRIENDS

Hello./Hi!	**Здравствуйте./Привет!** *zdrah • stvooy • tee/pree • <u>vyet</u>*
Good morning.	**Доброе утро.** *<u>doh</u> • brah • yeh <u>oot</u> • rah*
Good afternoon.	**Добрый день.** *<u>doh</u> • briy dyen'*
Good evening.	**Добрый вечер.** *<u>doh</u> • briy <u>vyeh</u> • cheer*
My name is…	**Меня зовут…** *mee • <u>nyah</u> zah • <u>voot</u>…*
What's your name?	**Как Вас зовут?** *kahk vahz zah • <u>voot</u>*

I'd like to introduce you to...	**Хочу познакомить Вас с...**
	khah • <u>choo</u> pah • znah • <u>koh</u> • meet' vahs s...
Nice to meet you.	**Очень приятно.**
	<u>oh</u> • cheen' pree • <u>yaht</u> • nah
How are you?	**Как дела?**
	kahk dee • <u>lah</u>
Fine, thanks.	**Спасибо, хорошо.**
	spah • <u>see</u> • bah khah • rah • <u>shoh</u>
And you?	**А как вы?**
	ah kahk vih

(i)

At first meeting **Здравствуйте!** <u>zdrah</u> • stvooy • tee
(Hello!) is the preferred greeting; you can use the
informal **Здравствуй!** <u>zdrah</u> • stvooy to address children.
Привет! pree • <u>vyet</u> (Hi!) is less formal and may sound rude
if used in the wrong context.

TRAVEL TALK

I'm here...	**Я здесь...**
	yah zdyes'...
on business	**в командировке**
	f kah • mahn • dee • <u>rof</u> • kyeh
on vacation [holiday]	**в отпуске**
	v <u>ot</u> • poos • kyeh
studying	**учусь**
	oo • <u>choos'</u>
I'm staying for...	**Я здесь на...**
	yah zdyes' nah...
I've been here...	**Я здесь уже...**
	yah zdyes' oo • <u>zheh</u>...
a day	**день**
	dyen'

a week	**неделю**
	nee • _dyeh_ • lyoo
a month	**месяц**
	myeh • syahts
Where are you from?	**Откуда вы?**
	aht • _koo_ • dah vih
I'm from...	**Я из...**
	yah eez...

For Numbers, see page 18.

PERSONAL

Who are you with?	**С кем вы?**
	s kyem vih
I'm on my own.	**Я один** m **/одна** f .
	yah ah • _deen_/ahd • _nah_
I'm with...	**Я с...**
	yah s...
my husband/wife	**моим мужем/моей женой**
	mah • _eem_ moo • zhihm/mah • _yey_
	zhee • _noy_
my boyfriend/ girlfriend	**моим другом/моей подругой**
	mah • _eem_ _droo_ • gahm/mah • _yey_
	pah • _droo_ • gie
I'm with...	**Я с...**
	yah s...
a friend/friends	**другом/друзьями**
	droo • gahm/drooz' • _yah_ • mee
a colleague/ colleagues	**коллегой/коллегами**
	kah • _lyeh_ • gie/kah • _lyeh_ • gah • mee
When's your birthday?	**Когда Ваш день рождения?**
	kahg • _dah_ vahsh dyen'
	rahzh • _dyeh_ • nee • yah
How old are you?	**Сколько Вам лет?**
	skol' • kah vahm lyet

I'm…	**Мне…**
	mnyeh…
I'm…	**Я…**
	yah…
single	**холост** *m* /**не замужем** *f*
	yah <u>khoh</u> • lahst/nee <u>zah</u> • moo • zhihm
in a relationship	**с партнёром**
	s pahrt • <u>nyoh</u> • rahm
engaged	**помолвлен** *m* /**помолвлена** *f*
	pah • <u>mohl</u> • vlen/pah • <u>mohl</u> • vle • nah
married	**женат** *m* /**замужем** *f zhih • <u>naht</u>/*
	<u>zah</u> • moo • zhihm
divorced	**разведён** *m* /**разведена** *f*
	rahz • vee • <u>dyon</u>/rahz • vee • dee • <u>nah</u>
separated	**не живу с женой** *m* /**мужем** *f*
	nee zhih • <u>voo</u> s zhih • <u>noy</u>/moo • zhihm
I'm widowed.	**Я вдовец** *m* /**вдова** *f.*
	yah vdah • <u>vyets</u>/vdah • <u>vah</u>
Do you have children/ grandchildren?	**У Вас есть дети/внуки?**
	oo vahs yest' <u>dyeh</u> • tee/<u>vnoo</u> • kee

WORK & SCHOOL

What do you do?	**Ваша профессия?**
	<u>vah</u> • shah prah • <u>fyeh</u> • see • yah
What are you studying?	**Что вы изучаете?**
	shtoh vih ee • zoo • <u>chah</u> • ee • tee
I'm studying…	**Я изучаю…**
	yah ee • zoo • <u>chah</u> • yoo…
I…	**Я…**
	yah
work full-/ part-time	**работаю полный/неполный день**
	rah • <u>boh</u> • tah • yu pohl • niy/ neh • <u>pohl</u> • niy dehn'

am unemployed	**безработный** *m* **/безработная** *f* *yah bez • rah • boht • nee/ bez • rah • boht • na • yah*
work at home	**работаю дома** *rah • boh • tah • yu doh • mah*
Who do you work for?	**Где вы работаете?** *gdyeh vih rah • boh • tah • ee • tee*
I work for…	**Я работаю в…** *yah rah • boh • tah • yoo v…*
Here's my business card.	**Вот моя визитка.** *vot mah • yah vee • zeet • kah*

WEATHER

What is the weather forecast?	**Какой прогноз погоды?** *kah • koy prahg • nos pah • goh • dih*
What beautiful/ terrible weather!	**Какая чудесная/ужасная погода!** *kah • kah • yah choo • dyes • nah • yah/ oo • zhahs • nah • yah pah • goh • dah*
It's cool./warm.	**Прохладно./Тепло.** *prah • khlahd • nah/teep • loh*
It's hot./cold.	**Жарко./Холодно.** *zhahr • kah/hoh • lahd • nah*
It's rainy./sunny.	**Дождливо./Солнечно.** *dahzh • dlee • vah/sol • neech • nah*
It's snowy./icy.	**Идёт снег./Гололёд.** *ee • dyot snyek/gah • lah • lyot*
Do I need a jacket?	**Нужно надевать куртку?** *noozh • nah nah dee • vaht' koort • koo*
Do I need an umbrella?	**Нужно брать зонт?** *noozh • nah braht' zont*

For Seasons, see page 24.

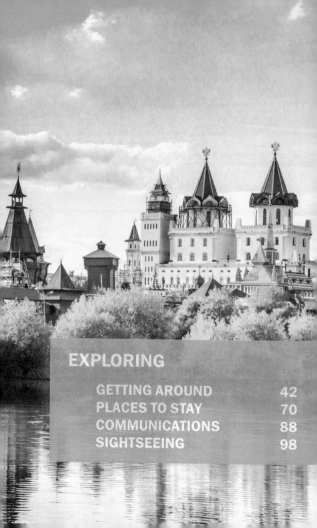

EXPLORING

GETTING AROUND

NEED TO KNOW

How do I get to town?	**Как мне добраться до города?** kahk mnyeh dah • _brah_ • tsah dah goh • rah • dah
Where's…?	**Где…?** gdyeh…
the airport	**аэропорт** ah • eh • rah • _port_
the train [railway] station	**вокзал** vahg • _zahl_
the bus station	**автовокзал** ahf • tah • vahg • _zahl_
the metro station [underground]	**станция метро** _stahn_ • tsih • yah mee • _troh_
How far is it?	**Как далеко это отсюда?** kahk dah • lee • _koh eh_ • tah aht • _syoo_ • dah
Where can I buy tickets?	**Где можно купить билеты?** gdyeh _mozh_ • nah koo • _peet'_ bee • _lyeh_ • tih

A one-way [single]/ return-trip ticket.	**Билет в один конец/туда и обратно.**
	bee • lyet v ah • deen kah • nyets/ too • dah ee ahb • raht • nah
How much?	**Сколько?**
	skol' • kah
Are there any discounts?	**Есть какая-нибудь скидка?**
	yehst' kah • kah • yah • nee • boot' skeet • kah
Which gate/line?	**Какой выход/путь?**
	kah • koy vih • khaht/poot'
Which platform?	**Какая платформа?**
	kah • kah • yah plaht • for • mah
Where can I get a taxi?	**Где можно взять такси?**
	gdyeh mozh • nah vzyaht' tahk • see
Please take me to this address.	**Пожалуйста, отвезите меня по этому адресу.**
	pah • zhahl • stah aht • vee • zee • tee mee • nyah pah eh • tah • moo ahd • ree • soo
Where can I rent a car?	**Где можно взять машину напрокат?**
	gdyeh mozh • nah vzyaht' mah • shih • noo nah • prah • kaht
Could I have a map?	**Можно мне карту?**
	mozh • nah mnyeh kahr • too

TICKETS

When's...to Moscow?	**Когда...в Москву?**
	kahg • dah...v mahs • kvoo
the (first) bus	**(первый) автобус**
	(pyer • viy) ahf • toh • boos

the (next) flight	**(следующий) рейс**
	(slyeh • doo • yoo • shcheey) reys
the (last) train	**(последний) поезд**
	(pahs • lyed • neey) poh • eest
Where can I buy tickets?	**Где можно купить билеты?**
	gdyeh mozh • nah koo • peet' bee • lyeh • tih
One ticket/Two tickets, please.	**Один билет/Два билета, пожалуйста.**
	ah • deen bee • lyet/dvah bee • lyeh • tah pah • zhahl • stah
For today/tomorrow.	**На сегодня/завтра.**
	nah see • vod • nyah/zahf • trah
A first/economy class ticket.	**Билет на первый/туристический класс.**
	bee • lyet nah pyer • viy/ too • rees • tee • chees • keey klahss
A...ticket.	**Билет...**
	bee • lyeht
one-way	**в один конец**
	v ah • deen kah • nyets
return trip	**туда и обратно**
	too • dah ee ahb • raht • noh
business class	**бизнес-класс**
	biz • nes klahss

How much?	**Сколько?**
	skol' • kah
Is there a discount for...?	**Есть скидка...?**
	yest' skeet • kah...
children	**на детей**
	nah dee • tyey
students	**студентам**
	stoo • dyen • tahm
senior citizens	**пенсионерам**
	peen • see • ah • nyeh • rahm
tourists	**туристам**
	too • rees • tahm
I have an e-ticket.	**У меня электронный билет.**
	oo mee • nyah ee • leek • tron • niy bee • lyet
Can I buy a ticket on the bus/train?	**Я могу купить билет в автобусе/поезде?**
	yah mah • goo koo • peet' bee • lyet v ahf • toh • boo • see/poh • eez • dee
Do I have to stamp the ticket before boarding?	**Нужно ли перед посадкой компостировать билет?**
	noozh • nah lee peret pah • saht • koy kam • pas • tee • ro • vat' bee • lyet
How long is this ticket valid?	**Как долго действителен билет?**
	kahk dol • go dey • stvee • tee • lyen bee • lyet
Can I return on the same ticket?	**Могу я вернуться по этому билету?**
	mah • goo yah vyer • noo • tsah poh yeh • tah • moo bee • lye • too
I'd like to...my reservation.	**Я хотел *m* /хотела *f* бы...свой предварительный заказ.**
	yah khah • tyel/khah • tyeh • lah bih...svoy preed • vah • ree • teel' • niy zah • kahz
cancel	**отменить**
	aht • mee • neet'

change	**изменить**
	eez • mee • neet'
confirm	**подтвердить**
	paht • tveer • deet'

For Days, see page 22.

AIRPORT TRANSFER

YOU MAY HEAR...

Рейсом какой авиакомпании вы летите?
rey • sahm kah • koy
ah • vee • ah • kahm • pah • nee • ee
vih lee • tee • tyeh

What airline are you flying?

Внутренний или международный?
vnoot • reen • neey ee • lee
meezh • doo • nah • rod • niy

Domestic or International?

Какой терминал?
kah • koy teer • mee • nahl

What terminal?

YOU MAY SEE...

ПРИБЫТИЕ	arrivals
pree • <u>bih</u> • tee • yeh	
ОТПРАВЛЕНИЕ	departures
aht • prahv • <u>lyeh</u> • nee • yeh	
ВЫДАЧА БАГАЖА	baggage claim
<u>vih</u> • dah • chah bah • gah • <u>zhah</u>	
ВНУТРЕННИЕ РЕЙСЫ	domestic flights
<u>vnoo</u> • treen • nee • yeh <u>rey</u> • sih	
МЕЖДУНАРОДНЫЕ РЕЙСЫ	international
meezh • doo • <u>nah</u> • rod • nih • yeh <u>rey</u> • sih	flights
РЕГИСТРАЦИОННАЯ СТОЙКА	check-in desk
ree • gee • strah • tsih • <u>on</u> • nah • yah	
<u>stoy</u> • kah	
РЕГИСТРАЦИЯ ЭЛЕКТРОННЫХ	e-ticket check-in
БИЛЕТОВ	
ree • gee • <u>strah</u> • tsih • yah	
ee • leek • <u>tron</u> • nihkh bee • <u>lyeh</u> • tahf	
ВЫХОД НА ПОСАДКУ	departure gates
<u>vih</u> • khaht nah pah • <u>saht</u> • koo	

How much is a taxi to the airport?	**Сколько стоит такси в аэропорт?** <u>skol'</u> • kah <u>stoh</u> • eet tahk • <u>see</u> v ah • eh • rah • <u>port</u>
To...Airport, please.	**В аэропорт..., пожалуйста.** v ah • eh • rah • <u>port</u>... pah • <u>zhahl</u> • stah
My airline is...	**Я лечу самолётом авиакомпании...** yah lee • <u>choo</u> sah • mah • <u>lyoh</u> • tahm ah • vee • ah • kahm • <u>pah</u> • nee • ee...
My flight leaves at...	**Мой рейс отправляется в...** moy reys aht • prahv • <u>lyah</u> • ee • tsah v...

I'm in a rush.	**Я спешу.**
	yah spee • shoo
Can you take an alternate route?	**Вы можете поехать другим путём?**
	vih moh • zhih • tee pah • yeh • khaht' droo • geem poo • tyom
Can you drive faster/slower?	**Не могли бы вы ехать быстрее/медленнее?**
	nee mahg • lee bih vih yeh • khat' bihs • tryeh • yeh/myed • leen • nee • yeh

For Time, see page 21.

CHECKING IN

Where is check-in?	**Где регистрация?**
	gdyeh ree • gees • trah • tsih • yah
My name is...	**Меня зовут...**
	mee • nyah zah • voot...
I'm going to...	**Я лечу в...**
	yah lyee • choo v...
I have...	**У меня есть...**
	oo mye • nyah yest'
one suitcase	**один чемодан**
	ah • deen chee • mah • dahn

YOU MAY HEAR...

Следующий!   Next!
slyeh • _doo_ • _yoo_ • _shcheey_

Ваш билет/паспорт, пожалуйста.   Your ticket/
vahsh bee • _lyet_/_pahs_ • _pahrt_   passport, please.
pah • _zhahl_ • _stah_

Сколько у Вас мест багажа?   How much
skol' • _kah oo vahs myest bah_ • _gah_ • _zhah_ luggage
                          do you have?

У Вас перевес багажа.   You have excess
oo vahs pee • _ree_ • _vyes bah_ • _gah_ • _zhah_ luggage.

Этот слишком тяжёлый/большой That's too heavy/
для ручной клади.   large for a carry-
_eh_ • _taht sleesh_ • _kahm tee_ • _zhoh_ • _liy_/ on [to carry on
bahl • _shoy dlyah rooch_ • _noy klah_ • _dee_ board].

Вы сами упаковывали багаж? Did you pack
vih sah • _mee oo_ • _pah_ • _koh_ • _vih_ • _vah_ • _lee_ these bags
bah • _gahsh_   yourself?

Вас просили что-нибудь перевезти? Did anyone give
vahs prah • _see_ • _lee shtoh_ • _nee_ • _boot'_ you anything
pee • _ree_ • _vees_ • _tee_   to carry?

Выньте всё из карманов.   Empty your
vihn' • _tee fsyoh ees kahr_ • _mah_ • _nahf_ pockets.

Снимите обувь.   Take off your
snee • _mee_ • _tee oh_ • _boof'_   shoes.

Производится посадка на рейс... Now boarding
prah • _eez_ • _voh_ • _dee_ • _tsah_   flight...
pah • _saht_ • _kah nah reys..._

two suitcases	**два чемодана**
	dvah chee • mah • dah • nah
one piece of hand luggage	**одна единица ручной клади**
	od • nah yeh • dee • nee • tsa rooch • noy klah • dee
How much luggage is allowed?	**Сколько багажа разрешается провозить?**
	skol' • kah bah • gah • zhah rahz • ree • shah • ee • tsah prah • vah • zeet'
Is that pounds or kilos?	**Это в фунтах или килограммах?**
	eh • tah v foon • tah ee • lee kee • lo gram mahkh
Which gate does flight…leave from?	**У какого выхода посадка на рейс…?**
	oo kah • koh • vah vih • khah • dah pah • saht • kah nah reys…
Which terminal?	**Какой терминал?**
	kah • koy tyer • meeh • nal
I'd like a window/ an aisle seat.	**Я бы хотел *m* /хотела *f* место у окна/ прохода.**
	yah bih khah • tyel/khah • tyeh • lah myes • tah oo ahk • nah/prah • khoh • dah
When do we leave/ arrive?	**Во сколько мы вылетаем/прилетаем?**
	vah skol' • kah mih vih • lee • tah • eem/ pree • lee • tah • eem

Is there any delay on flight…? How late will it be?	**Рейс в…задерживается?** reys v… zah • <u>dyer</u> • zhih • vah • ee • tsah **На сколько задерживается?** nah <u>skol'</u> • kah zah • <u>dyer</u> • zhih • vah • ee • tsah

LUGGAGE

Where is/are…?	**Где…?** gdyeh…
the luggage trolleys	**багажные тележки** bah • <u>gahzh</u> • nih • ee tee • <u>lyesh</u> • kee
the luggage lockers	**камеры хранения** <u>kah</u> • mee • rih khrah • <u>nyeh</u> • nee • yah
the baggage claim	**выдача багажа** <u>vih</u> • dah • chah bah • gah • <u>zhah</u>
My luggage has been lost/stolen.	**У меня пропал/украли багаж.** oo mee • <u>nyah</u> prah • <u>pahl</u>/oo • <u>krah</u> • lee bah • <u>gahsh</u>
My suitcase was damaged.	**Мне повредили чемодан.** mnyeh pah • vree • <u>dee</u> • lee chee • mah • <u>dahn</u>

FINDING YOUR WAY

Where is…?	**Где…?** gdyeh…
the currency exchange office	**обмен валюты** ahb • <u>myen</u> vah • <u>lyoo</u> • tih
the car hire	**прокат автомобилей** prah • <u>kaht</u> ahf • tah • mah • <u>bee</u> • ley
the exit	**выход** <u>vih</u> • khaht

the taxis	**такси**
	tahk • see
Is there…into town?	**Есть…в город?**
	yest'…v goh • raht
a bus	**автобус**
	ahf • toh • boos
a train	**поезд**
	poh • eest
a metro [subway]	**метро**
	mee • troh

For Asking Directions, see page 65.

TRAIN

How do I get to the train station?	**Как мне добраться до вокзала?**
	kahk mnyeh dah • brah • tsah dah vahg • zah • lah
Is it far?	**Это далеко?**
	eh • tah dah • lee • koh
Where is/are…?	**Где…?**
	gdyeh…
the ticket office	**билетные кассы**
	bee • lyet • nih • ee kah • sih
the information desk	**бюро информации**
	byoo • roh een • fahr • mah • tsee • ee
the luggage lockers	**камеры хранения**
	kah • mee • rih khrah • nyeh • nee • yah
the platforms	**платформы**
	plaht • for • mih
Could I have a schedule [timetable]?	**Можно расписание?**
	mozh • nah rahs • pee • sah • nee • yeh
How long is the trip?	**Сколько длится поездка?**
	skol' • kah dlee • tsah pah • yest • kah

Is it a direct train?	**Это прямой поезд?** _eh_ • tah pryah • _moy_ _poh_ • yest
Do I have to change trains?	**Мне надо делать пересадку?** mnyeh _nah_ • dah dyeh • laht' pee • ree • _saht_ • koo
Is the train on time?	**Поезд приедет вовремя?** _poh_ • yest pree • _ye_ • dit _voh_ • vre • myah

For Tickets, see page 43.

👁

YOU MAY SEE...

К ПЛАТФОРМАМ k plaht • _for_ • mahm	platforms
ИНФОРМАЦИЯ een • fahr • _mah_ • tsih • yah	information
ЗАКАЗ БИЛЕТОВ zah • _kahz_ bee • _lyeh_ • tahf	reservations
ЗАЛ ОЖИДАНИЯ zahl oh • zhee • _dah_ • nee • yah	waiting room
ПРИБЫТИЕ pree • _bih_ • tee • yeh	arrivals
ОТПРАВЛЕНИЕ aht • prahv • _lyeh_ • nee • yeh	departures

ⓘ

An often-quoted line by the great Russian writer Nikolai Gogol (1809-1852) states that Russia's roads are one of its greatest misfortunes. While the state of Russian roads is still a source of national frustration, the excellent rail system built during the Soviet era provides a good alternative to automobile travel. Unfortunately, Russia's train stations have become less safe than they were in the past.

DEPARTURES

Which platform does the train to…leave from?	**С какой платформы отходит поезд до…?** *s kah • koy plaht • for • mih aht • khoh • deet poh • eest dah…*
Is this the track [platform] to…?	**С этой платформы поезд на…?** *s eh • tie plaht • for • mih poh • eest nah…*
Where is track [platform]…?	**Где платформа…?** *gdyeh plaht • for • mah…*
Where do I change for…?	**Где мне делать пересадку на…?** *gdyeh mnyeh dyeh • laht' pee • ree • saht • koo nah…*

ON BOARD

Can I sit here/open the window?	**Можно здесь сидеть/открывать окно?** *mo • zhno zdyes see • dyet'/at • krih • vat' ahk • noh*
Is this seat taken?	**Это место занято?** *eh • tah myes • tah zah • nee • tah*
I think that's my seat.	**Мне кажется, это моё место.** *mnyeh kah • zhih • tsah eh • tah mah • yoh myes • tah*

Here's my
reservation.

Вот моя бронь.
vot ma • <u>yah</u> brohn'

YOU MAY HEAR...

Посадка заканчивается!
pah • <u>saht</u> • kah
zah • <u>kahn</u> • chee • vah • ee • tsah

All
aboard!

Пожалуйста, предъявите билеты.
pah • <u>zhahl</u> • stah preed • yah • <u>vee</u> • tee
bee • <u>lyeh</u> • tih

Tickets, please.

Вам надо делать пересадку в...
vahm <u>nah</u> • dah dyeh • laht'
pee • ree • <u>saht</u> • koo v...

You have to
change
at...

Следующая остановка...
<u>slyeh</u> • doo • yoo • shchah • yah
ahs • tah • <u>nof</u> • kah...

Next stop...

BUS

Where's the bus
station?

Где автобусная станция?
gdyeh ahf • <u>toh</u> • boos • nah • yah
<u>stahn</u> • tsih • yah

How far is it?

Как далеко это?
kahk dah • lee • <u>koh</u> eh • tah

How do I get to...?

Как мне доехать до...?
kahk mnyeh dah • <u>yeh</u> • khaht' dah...

Does the bus stop
at...?

Этот автобус останавливается в...?
<u>eh</u> • taht ahf • <u>toh</u> • boos
ah • stah • <u>nahv</u> • lee • vah • ee • tsah v...

Could you tell me
when to get off?

Вы скажете мне, где выходить?
vih <u>skah</u> • zhih • tee mnyeh gdyeh
vih • khah • <u>deet'</u>

Do I have to change buses?	**Мне нужно делать пересадку?** mnyeh <u>noozh</u> • nah <u>dyeh</u> • laht' pee • ree • <u>saht</u> • koo
Stop here, please!	**Остановите здесь, пожалуйста!** ah • stah • nah • <u>vee</u> • tee zdyes' pah • <u>zhahl</u> • stah

For Tickets, see page 43.

YOU MAY SEE...

АВТОБУСНАЯ ОСТАНОВКА   bus stop
ahf • <u>toh</u> • boos • nah • yah ahs • tah • <u>nof</u> • kah

ОСТАНОВКА ПО ТРЕБОВАНИЮ   request stop
os • tah • <u>nov</u> • kah po <u>tree</u> • bo • vah • nee • yoo

ВХОД/ВЫХОД   enter/exit
fkhot/<u>vih</u> • khaht

ПРОКОМПОСТИРУЙТЕ ТАЛОН   stamp your
prah • kahm • pah • <u>stee</u> • rooy • tyeh tah • <u>lon</u>   ticket

---

Buses offer a standard fare no matter how far you're going but you can't change buses on the same ticket. In big cities, a system of magnetized fare cards that can be used on buses and trolleybuses (electric buses powered by two overhead wires) as well as the metro (where such cards can be purchased) is in operation. In smaller cities you will need to purchase **талоны** tah • <u>loh</u> • nih (paper tickets that you have to stamp) from a conductor on the bus or from kiosks.
A popular alternative to buses are fixed-route taxis called **маршрутные такси** mahrsh • <u>root</u> • nih • yeh tahk • see or mini-buses, **маршрутки** mahrsh • <u>root</u> • kee, that follow a fixed route, usually the same as bus routes.

METRO

Where's the nearest metro [underground] station?	**Где ближайшая станция метро?** _gdyeh blee • zhie • shah • yah_ _stahn • tsih • yah meet • roh_
Could I have a map of the metro [underground]?	**Можно мне схему метро?** _mozh • nah mnyeh_ _skhyeh • moo meet • roh_
Which line for...?	**По какой линии ехать до...?** _pah kah • koy lee • nee • ee yeh • khaht' dah..._
Which direction?	**В каком направлении?** _f kah • kom • nap • rah • vlye • nee • ee_
Where do I change for...?	**Где делать пересадку до...?** _gdyeh dyeh • laht' pee • ree • saht • koo dah..._
Is this the right train for...?	**Этот поезд идёт до...?** _eh • taht poh • eest ee • dyot dah..._
How many stops to...?	**Сколько остановок до ...?** _skol' • kah as • tah • noh • vahk doh_
Where are we?	**Где мы находимся?** _gdyeh mih nah • khoh • deem • syah_

For Finding your Way, see page 51.

МЕТРО meet • _roh_ (subway) is the fastest and most convenient way to get around town. Moscow, St. Petersburg and a few other major cities have subway systems. Moscow has the most extensive system; its older stations are sights worth visiting in their own right, featuring a blend of ornate neoclassicism and Socialist Realism.

The subway operates from 6:00 a.m. to 1:00 a.m. There is a set fare regardless of the distance traveled. If you plan to use public transit a lot, you may decide to buy a pass (**единый билет** yee • _dee_ • niy bee • _lyet_), valid for 8 days, 16 days or a month, for travel on the metro, bus, trolleybus and tram.

BOAT & FERRY

When is the ferry to…?	**Когда паром до…?** kahg • _dah_ pah • _rom_ dah…
Where are the life jackets?	**Где спасательные жилеты?** gdyeh spah • _sah_ • teel' • nih • ee zhih • _lyeh_ • tih

YOU MAY SEE...

СПАСАТЕЛЬНАЯ ШЛЮПКА   life boat
spah • <u>sah</u> • teel' • nah • yah <u>shlyoop</u> • kah

СПАСАТЕЛЬНЫЙ ЖИЛЕТ   life jacket
spah • <u>sah</u> • teel' • niy zhih • <u>lyeht</u>

TAXI

Where can I get a taxi?	**Где можно взять такси?** gdyeh <u>mozh</u> • nah vzyaht' tahk • <u>see</u>
Can you send a taxi?	**Не могли бы Вы прислать такси?** nee mogh • lee bih vih pree • <u>slat'</u> tahk • <u>see</u>
What is the number for a taxi?	**Как вызвать такси по телефону?** kahk <u>vihz</u> • vaht' tahk • <u>see</u> pah tee • lee • <u>foh</u> • noo
I'd like a taxi now/ for tomorrow at...	**Мне нужно такси сейчас/на завтра на...** mnyeh <u>noozh</u> • nah tahk • <u>see</u> see • <u>chahs</u>/ nah <u>zahf</u> • trah nah...
Pick me up at (place/time)...	**Подъезжайте за мной к/в...** pahd • yeh • <u>zhie</u> • tee zah mnoy k/v...

You'll find mainly private taxi services throughout Russia. It is common practice for Russians to hail private cars in the street, but foreigners, especially those who know little Russian and are unfamiliar with their surroundings, should exercise extreme caution. Before entering a private car, make sure that the driver understands where you want to go and agree on a price.
Warning: Never enter a car if somebody besides the driver is in it. Be especially careful after dark.

Куда?
koo • <u>dah</u>

Where to?

Какой адрес?
kah • <u>koy</u> <u>ahd</u> • rees

What's the
address?

**Здесь положен дополнительный
аэропортовый сбор/сбор за ночное
время.**
zdyes' po • <u>lo</u> • zhihn doh • pohl • <u>nee</u> • tyel' • nih
ah • eh • rah • <u>por</u> • toh • viy sbohr/sbohr za
noch • <u>no</u> • eh <u>vreh</u> • myah

There's a
nighttime/
airport
surcharge.

Please take me to...	**Пожалуйста, отвезите меня...**
	pah • <u>zhahl</u> • stah aht • vee • <u>zee</u> • tee
	mee • <u>nyah</u>...
this address	**по этому адресу**
	pah <u>eh</u> • tah • moo <u>ahd</u> • ree • soo
the airport	**в аэропорт**
	v ah • <u>eh</u> • rah • <u>port</u>
the train station	**на вокзал**
	nah vahg • <u>zahl</u>

I'm late.	**Я опаздываю.**
	yah ah • _pahz_ • dih • vah • yoo
Can you drive faster/slower?	**Не могли бы вы ехать быстрее/медленнее?**
	nee mahg • _lee_ bih vih yeh • khaht' bihs • _tryeh_ • yeh/_myed_ • leen • nee • yeh
Stop/Wait here.	**Остановитесь/Подождите здесь.**
	ah • stah • nah • _vee_ • tees'/ pah • dahzh • _dee_ • tee zdyes'
How much will it cost?	**Сколько это будет стоить?**
	skol' • kah eh • tah _boo_ • deet _stoh_ • eet'
You said…rubles.	**Вы сказали…рублей.**
	vih skah • _zah_ • lee… roob • _lyey_
Keep the change.	**Оставьте сдачу.**
	ah • _stahf'_ • tee zdah • choo
A receipt, please.	**Можно чек, пожалуйста.**
	mozh • nah chehk pah • _zhahl_ • stah

BICYCLE & MOTORBIKE

I'd like to hire…	**Я хотел** m **/хотела** f **бы взять напрокат…**
	yah khah • _tyel_/khah • _tyeh_ • lah bih vzyaht' nah • prah • _kaht_…

a bicycle	**велосипед**
	vee • lah • see • <u>pyet</u>
a moped	**мопед**
	mah • <u>pyet</u>
a motorcycle	**мотоцикл**
	mah • tah • <u>tsihkl</u>
How much per day/week?	**Сколько стоит в день/неделю?**
	<u>skol'</u> • kah <u>stoh</u> • eet v dyen'/ nee • <u>dyeh</u> • lyoo
Can I have a helmet/lock?	**Могу я получить шлем/замок?**
	mah • <u>goo</u> yah pah • loo • <u>cheet'</u> shlyem/ zah • <u>mok</u>

CAR HIRE

Where can I rent a car?	**Где можно взять машину напрокат?**
	gdyeh <u>mozh</u> • nah vzyaht' mah • <u>shih</u> • noo nah • prah • <u>kaht</u>
I'd like to rent [hire]…	**Я хотел m /хотела f бы взять напрокат…**
	yah khah • <u>tyel</u>/khah • <u>tyeh</u> • lah bih vzyaht' nah • prah • <u>kaht</u>…
a cheap/small car	**недорогую/небольшую машину**
	nih • do • ro • <u>goo</u> • yoo/ nye • bol' • <u>shoo</u> • yoo mah • <u>shih</u> • noo
a 2-/4-door car	**двух/четырёх дверную машину**
	dvookh/chee • tih • <u>ryokh dyer</u> • noo • yoo mah • <u>shih</u> • noo
an automatic/ manual car	**машину с автоматической/ручной трансмиссией**
	mah • <u>shih</u> • noo s ahf • tah • mah • <u>tee</u> • chees • koy/ rooch • <u>noy</u> trahns • <u>mee</u> • see • yey
a car with air-conditioning	**машину с кондиционером**
	mah • <u>shih</u> • noo s kahn • dee • tsih • ah • <u>nyeh</u> • rahm

a car with a car seat	**машину с детским сидением**
	mah • shih • noo s dyets • keem
	see • dyen' • yem
How much…?	**Сколько…?**
	skol' • kah…
per day/week	**в день/неделю**
	v dyen'/nee • dyeh • lyoo
per kilometer	**за километр**
	zah kee • lah • myetr
for unlimited mileage	**за неограниченный пробег**
	zah nee • ahg • rah • nee • cheen • niy
	prah • byek
with insurance	**со страховкой**
	sah strah • khof • kie
Are there any special weekend rates?	**Есть особый тариф по выходным?**
	yest' ah • soh • biy tah • reef pah
	vih • khahd • nihm

YOU MAY HEAR...

У Вас есть международное
водительское удостоверение?
oo vahs yest'
meezh • doo • nah • <u>rod</u> • nah • yeh
vah • <u>dee</u> • teel' • skah • yeh
oo • dahs • tah • vee • <u>ryeh</u> • nee • yeh

Do you have
an international
driver's license?

Ваш паспорт, пожалуйста.
vahsh <u>pahs</u> • pahrt pah • <u>zhahl</u> • stah

Your passport,
please.

Вам нужна страховка?
vahm noozh • <u>nah</u> strah • <u>khof</u> • kah

Do you want
insurance?

Нужен залог...
<u>noo</u> • zhihn zah • <u>log</u>...

There is a
deposit of...

Распишитесь здесь.
rahs • pee • <u>shih</u> • tees' zdyes'

Please sign here.

FUEL STATION

Where's the nearest
fuel station?

Где ближайшая заправочная станция?
gdyeh blee • <u>zhie</u> • shah • yah
zah • <u>prah</u> • vahch • nah • yah
<u>stahn</u> • tsih • yah

Fill it up, please.

Полный бак, пожалуйста.
<u>pol</u> • niy bahk pah • <u>zhahl</u> • stah

...liters, please.

...литров бензина, пожалуйста. ...
<u>leet</u> • rahf been • <u>zee</u> • nah
pah • <u>zhahl</u> • stah

I'll pay in cash/
by credit card.

Я заплачу наличными/по кредитной
карточке.
yah zah • plah • <u>choo</u> nah • <u>leech</u> • nih • mee/
pah kree • <u>deet</u> • nie <u>kahr</u> • tahch • kyeh

бензин А-98	super
been • zeen ah dee • vyah • nos • tah voh • seem'	
бензин А-93	regular
been • zeen ah dee • vyah • nos • tah tree	
дизельное топливо	diesel
dee • zeel' • nah • yeh top • lee • vah	

ASKING DIRECTIONS

Is this the right road to...?	**Это дорога на...?**
	eh • tah dah • roh • gah nah...
How far is it to...?	**Далеко до...отсюда?**
	dah • lee • koh dah... aht • syoo • dah
Where's...?	**Где...?**
	gdyeh...
...Street	**улица...**
	oo • lee • tsah...
this address	**этот адрес**
	eh • taht ahd • rees

the highway [motorway]	**шоссе**
	shahs • seh
Can you show me on the map?	**Можете показать мне на карте?**
	moh • zhih • tee pah • kah • zaht' mnyeh nah kahr • tee
I'm lost.	**Я заблудился** *m* /**заблудилась** *f.*
	yah zah • bloo • deel • syah/ zah • bloo • dee • lahs'

YOU MAY HEAR...

прямо	straight ahead
pryah • mah	
слева	on the left
slyeh • vah	
справа	on the right
sprah • vah	
на углу/за углом	on/around the corner
nah oo • gloo/zah oo • glohm	
напротив	opposite
nah • proh • teef	
позади	behind
pah • zah • dee	
рядом с	next to
ryah • dahm s	
после	after
pos • lee	
север/юг	north/south
syeh • veer/yook	
восток/запад	east/west
vahs • tok/zah • paht	
у светофора	at the traffic light
oo svee • tah • foh • rah	
на перекрестке	at the intersection
nah pee • ree • kryost • kee	

YOU MAY SEE...

 ОБГОН ЗАПРЕЩЕН
ahb • gon zah • pree • shchon

no passing

 СТОП
stop

stop

 ОДНОСТОРОННЕЕ ДВИЖЕНИЕ
*ahd • nah • stah • ron • nyeh • yeh
dvee • zheh • nee • yeh*

one-way
street

 УСТУПИ ДОРОГУ
oos • too • pee dah • roh • goo

yield
[give way]

 ВЪЕЗД ЗАПРЕЩЕН
zah • pree • shchon

no entry

 СТОЯНКА ЗАПРЕЩЕНА
*stah • yahn • kah
zah • pree • shchee • nah*

no parking

 ОПАСНЫЙ ПОВОРОТ
ah • pahs • niy pah • vah • rot

dangerous
curve

 ПЕШЕХОДНЫЙ ПЕРЕХОД
pee • shih • khod • niy pee • ree • khot

pedestrian
crossing

 ОГРАНИЧЕНИЕ СКОРОСТИ
*ah • grah • nee • cheh • nee • yeh
skoh • rahs • tee*

maximum
speed limit

PARKING

Parking is usually unrestricted, except in central areas of Moscow and St. Petersburg, where parking meters and no-parking zones can be found. Illegally parked cars are subject to clamping and towing.

Can I park here?	**Здесь можно поставить машину?**
	zdyes' <u>mozh</u> • nah pah • <u>stah</u> • veet'
	mah • <u>shih</u> • noo
Where is the nearest parking garage/parking lot [car park]?	**Здесь рядом есть крытая стоянка/ автостоянка?**
	zdyes' <u>ryah</u> • dahm
	yest' <u>krih</u> • tah • yah stah • <u>yahn</u> • kah/
	ahf • tah • stah • <u>yahn</u> • kah
Where's the parking meter?	**Где счётчик времени стоянки?**
	gdyeh <u>shchot</u> • cheek <u>vreh</u> • meh • nee
	stah • <u>yahn</u> • kee
How much…?	**Сколько…?**
	<u>skol'</u> • kah…
per hour	**в час**
	f chahs

per day	**в день**
	v dyen'
overnight	**за ночь**
	zah nahch

BREAKDOWN & REPAIR

My car broke down/won't start.	**У меня сломалась/не заводится машина.**
	oo mee•nyah slah•mah•lahs'/nee zah•voh•dee•tsah mah•shih•nah
Can you fix it?	**Можно починить?**
	mozh•nah pah•chee•neet'
When will it be ready?	**Когда будет готово?**
	kahg•dah boo•deet gah•toh•vah
How much will it cost?	**Сколько это будет стоить?**
	skol'•kah eh•tah boo•deet stoh•eet'
I have a puncture/ flat tyre (tire).	**У меня проколота шина/спущено колесо.**
	oo meh•nya proh•koh•loh•tah shee•nah/spoo•shchyeh•noh koh•leh•soh

For Time, see page 21.

ACCIDENTS

There has been an accident.	**Произошла авария.**
	prah•ee•zah•shlah ah•vah•ree•yah
Call an ambulance/ the police.	**Вызовите скорую помощь/милицию.**
	vih•zah•vee•tee skoh•roo•yoo poh•mahshch'/mee•lee•tsih•yoo

For Police, see page 147.

PLACES TO STAY

NEED TO KNOW

Can you recommend a hotel?	**Можете порекомендовать гостиницу?** _moh • zhih • tee pah • ree • kah • meen • dah • vaht' gahs • tee • nee • tsoo_
I have a reservation.	**У меня заказ.** _oo mee • nyah zah • kahs_
My name is…	**Меня зовут…** _mee • nyah zah • voot…_
Do you have a room…?	**У вас есть номер…?** _oo vahs yest' noh • meer…_
for one/two	**на одного/двоих** _nah ahd • nah • voh/dvah • eekh_
with a bathroom	**с ванной** _s vahn • nie_
with air- -conditioning	**с кондиционером** _s kahn • dee • tzih • ah • nyeh • rahm_
For tonight.	**На эти сутки.** _nah eh • tee soot • kee_
For two nights.	**На два дня.** _nah dvah dnyah_
For one week.	**На неделю.** _nah nee • dyeh • lyoo_
How much?	**Сколько?** _skol' • kah_
Do you have anything cheaper?	**Есть что-нибудь подешевле?** _yest' shtoh • nee • boot' pah • dee • shev • lee_

When's check-out?	**Во сколько надо освободить номер?** *vah <u>skol'</u> • kah <u>nah</u> • dah* *ah • svah • bah • <u>deet'</u> noh • <u>meer</u>*
Can I leave this in the safe?	**Можно оставить это в сейфе?** *<u>mozh</u> • nah ah • <u>stah</u> • veet' <u>eh</u> • tah f* *<u>sey</u> • fee*
Can I leave my bags?	**Можно я оставлю сумки?** *<u>mozh</u> • nah yah ah • <u>stahv</u> • lyoo* *<u>soom</u> • kee*
Can I have the bill/a receipt?	**Можно счёт/чек?** *<u>mozh</u> • nah shchot/chehk*
I'll pay in cash/by credit card.	**Я заплачу наличными/по кредитной карточке.** *yah zah • plah • <u>choo</u>* *nah • <u>leech</u> • nih • mee/ pah* *kree • <u>deet</u> • noy <u>kahr</u> • tahch • kee*

SOMEWHERE TO STAY

Can you recommend...	**Можете порекомендовать... ?** *<u>moh</u> • zhih • tee* *pah • ree • kah • meen • dah • <u>vaht'</u>*
a hotel	**гостиницу** *gahs • <u>tee</u> • nee • tsoo*
a hostel	**общежитие** *ahp • shchee • <u>zhih</u> • tee • yeh*
a campsite	**палаточный лагерь** *pah • <u>lah</u> • toch • niy <u>lah</u> • geer'*
a bed and breakfast	**гостиницу типа «ночлег и завтрак»** *gahs • <u>tee</u> • nee • tsoo tee • pah noch • <u>lyeg</u>* *ee <u>zavt</u> • rahk*

ⓘ

Because of the many rules governing foreigners in Russia, it is easiest to make travel, housing and visa arrangements through a tour or travel agency.

A Russian visa can be obtained once you have either a hotel reservation or an official invitation (**приглашение** *pree • glah • sheh • nee • yeh*) from a friend, business associate or relative in Russia.

Wherever you stay, you will need to make sure you are given an official registration paper, which you will need to relinquish when you exit the country.

If you stay in a hotel, the staff will take your passport from you while they process this registration. Be sure to obtain a receipt for your passport and carry it with you, as you can be stopped by the police and fined for not having a passport with you. If you stay with friends or relatives, you will need to obtain this registration from **ОВИР** *ah • veer* (the Department of Visas and Registration) within 72 hours of your arrival.

What is it near?	**Что находится рядом?**
	shtoh nah • khoh • dee • tsah ryah • dahm
How do I get there?	**Как туда добраться?**
	kahk too • dah dah • brah • tsah

AT THE HOTEL

I have a reservation.	**У меня заказ.**
	oo mee • nyah zah • kahs
My name is…	**Моя фамилия…**
	mee • nyah zah • voot…
Do you have a room…?	**У вас есть номер…?**
	oo vahs yest' noh • meer…

If at all possible, arrange to be met at the airport by a representative from your hotel. Some travel agencies, such as Intourist, will meet you when you exit customs. If you are not being met, try to use public transportation to get to your hotel. Be very cautious about getting into a taxi. Intourist no longer holds a monopoly on accommodations in Russia, and in major cities an increasing number of new or newly renovated hotels are now jointly operated with Western companies. These first-class ventures offer a new, if pricey, option for tourists. If you are on an Intourist package tour you can state your hotel preference, but the final arrangements rest with Intourist.

Hotels also usually have service bureaus (**бюро обслуживания** byoo • _roh_ ahp • _sloo_ zhih • vah • nee • yah) manned by multilingual staff, who provide information, arrange outings and excursions, make reservations and provide general assistance.

with a bathroom [toilet]/shower	**с ванной/душем** s _vahn_ • nie/_doo_ • shehm
with air--conditioning	**с кондиционером** s kahn • dee • tsih • ah • _nyeh_ • rahm

that's smoking/ non-smoking	**для курящих/некурящих** *dlyah koo • ryah • shcheekh/ nee • koo • ryah • shcheekh*
For…	**На…** *nah…*
tonight.	**эти сутки.** *eh • tee soot • kee*
two nights.	**два дня.** *dvah dnyah*
one week.	**неделю.** *nee • dyeh • lyoo*
Does the hotel have…?	**В гостинице есть…?** *v gahs • tee • nee • tseh yest'…*
a computer	**компьютер** *kahm • pyoo • ter*
an elevator [lift]	**лифт** *leeft*
(wireless) internet service	**(беспроводной) интернет** *(bees • prah • vahd • noy) een • ter • net*
room service	**обслуживание номеров** *ahp • sloo • zhih • vah • nee • yeh nah • mee • rof*
a gym	**спортзал** *sport • zahl*
a pool	**бассейн** *bah • seyn*
I need…	**Мне нужно…** *mnyeh noozh • nah…*
an extra bed	**ещё одну кровать** *ee • shchoh ahd • noo krah • vaht'*
a cot	**раскладушку** *rahs • klah • doosh • koo*
a crib [child's cot]	**детскую кроватку** *dyets • koo • yoo krah • vaht • koo*

PRICE

How much per night/week?

Сколько в сутки/неделю?
skol' • kah f <u>soot</u> • kee/nee • <u>dyeh</u> • lyoo

Does the price include breakfast/ sales tax [VAT]?

Цена включает завтрак/НДС?
tsih • nah klyoo • <u>chah</u> • eet <u>zahf</u> • trahk/ en • deh • es

Are there any discounts?

Есть скидки?
yest' <u>skih</u> • dkih

PREFERENCES

Can I see the room?	**Могу я посмотреть номер?**	
	mah • goo yah pos • maht • ret' noh • mehr	
I'd like a...room.	**Мне нужен номер...**	
	mneh noo zhyen noh • mehr	
better	**лучше**	
	loo • chshye	
bigger	**больше**	
	bol' • shye	
cheaper	**дешевле**	
	deh • shyev • leh	
quieter	**тише**	
	tih • shye	
I'll take it.	**Я сниму его.**	
	yah snee • moo • eh • voh	
No, I won't take it.	**Я не буду его снимать.**	
	yah neh boo • doo ehvoh snih • maht'	

QUESTIONS

Where's...?	**Где...?**	
	gdyeh...	
the bar	**бар**	
	bahr	
the toilets	**туалет**	
	too • ah • lyet	
the elevator [lift]	**лифт**	
	leeft	
Can I have...?	**Можно мне...?**	
	mozh • nah mnyeh...	
a blanket	**одеяло**	
	ah • dee • yah • lah	

an iron	**утюг**
	oo • _tyook_
the room key/ key card	**ключ/ключ-карта от номера**
	klyooch/klyooch _kahr_ • tah ot _noh_ • meh • rah
a pillow	**подушку**
	pah • _doosh_ • koo
soap	**мыло**
	mih • lah
toilet paper	**туалетную бумагу**
	too • ah • _lyet_ • noo • yoo boo • _mah_ • goo
a towel	**банное полотенце**
	bahn • nah • yeh pah • lah • _tyen_ • tseh
Do you have an adapter for this?	**У вас есть адаптер для этого?**
	oo vahs yest' ah • _dahp_ • ter dlyah _eh_ • tah • vah
How do I turn on the lights?	**Как мне включить свет?**
	kahk mnyeh fklyoo • _cheet'_ svyet
Wake me at…	**Разбудите меня в…**
	rahz • boo • _dee_ • tee mee • _nyah_ v…
Could I have my things from the safe?	**Можно взять вещи из сейфа?**
	mozh • nah vzyaht' _vyeh_ • shchee ees _sey_ • fah

Is there mail/ a message for me?	**Есть почта/сообщение для меня?** *yest'poch • tah/sah • ahp • shchyeh • nee • yeh dlyah mee • nyah*
Do you have a laundry service?	**У Вас есть прачечная?** *oo vahs yest'prah • cheech • nah • yah*

YOU MAY SEE...

ОТ СЕБЯ/НА СЕБЯ *aht see • byah/nah see • byah*	push/pull
ТУАЛЕТ *too • ah • lyet*	restroom [toilet]
ДУШ *doosh*	shower
ЛИФТ *leeft*	elevator [lift]
ЛЕСТНИЦА *lyes • nee • tsah*	stairs
ПРАЧЕЧНАЯ *prah • cheech • nah • yah*	laundry
НЕ БЕСПОКОИТЬ *nyeh bees • pah • koh • eet'*	do not disturb
АВАРИЙНЫЙ ВЫХОД *ah • vah • reey • niy vih • khaht*	emergency exit
ВЫХОД *vih • khaht*	exit
БУДИЛЬНИК *boo • deel' • neek*	wake-up call

PROBLEMS

There's a problem.	**Есть проблема.**
	yest' prah • blyeh • mah
I've lost my key/key card.	**Я потерял m /потеряла f ключ/ электронный ключ.**
	yah pah • tee • ryahl/pah • tee • ryah • lah klyooch/ee • leek • tron • niy klyooch
I've locked myself out of my room.	**Я случайно захлопнул m / захлопнула f дверь.**
	yah sloo • chie • nah zah • khlop • nool/ zah • khlop • noo • lah dvyer'
There's no hot water/toilet paper.	**Нет горячей воды/туалетной бумаги.**
	nyet gah • ryah • chey vah • dih/ too • ah • lyet • nie boo • mah • gee
The room is dirty.	**В комнате грязно.**
	f kom • nah • tyeh gryahz • nah
There are bugs in. our room.	**У нас в комнате насекомые.**
	oo nahs f kom • nah • tyeh nah • see • koh • mih • yeh
The...has broken down.	**...не работает.**
	...nee rah • boh • tah • yet
Can you fix...?	**Можно починить...?**
	mozh • nah pah • chee • neet'...
the air- -conditioning	**кондиционер**
	kahn • dee • tsih • ah • nyer
the fan	**вентилятор**
	veen • tee • lyah • tahr
the heat [heating]	**отопление**
	ah • tahp • lyeh • nee • yeh
the light	**свет**
	svyet
the TV	**телевизор**
	tee • lee • vee • zahr

the toilet	**туалет** *too • ah • lyet*
I'd like to move to another room.	**Я хотел** *m* /**хотела** *f* **бы другую комнату.** *yah khah • tyel/khah • tyeh • lah bih droo • goo • yoo kom • nah • too*

(i)

While 220 volt AC tends to be standard in Russia, you'll still find 110-120 volt AC in some places. Russian outlets differ from Western ones, but large hotels often have outlets that will take Western plugs. Since suitable adapters are sometimes hard to find in Russia, especially outside major cities, it is prudent to travel with one. If you are traveling with electronics built to support multiple voltages, you may want to bring a surge protector suitable for Russian outlets. If your electronics do not support 220 volt current, you will need both an adapter and a step-down transformer.

CHECKING OUT

When's check-out?	**Во сколько надо освободить комнату?** *vah skol' • kah nah • dah ah • svah • bah • deet' kom • nah • too*
Could I leave my bags here until…?	**Можно мне оставить вещи здесь до…?** *mozh • nah mnyeh ah • stah • veet' vyeh • shchee zdyes' dah…*
Can I have an itemized bill/ a receipt?	**Можно детальный счёт/чек?** *mozh • nah dee • tahl' • niy shchot/chehk*
I think there's a mistake in this bill.	**Мне кажется, в счёте ошибка.** *mnyeh kah • zhee • tsah v shchoh • tee ah • shihp • kah*

I'll pay in cash/by credit card.	**Я заплачу наличными/по кредитной карточке.**

yah zah • plah • <u>choo</u> nah • <u>leech</u> • nih • mee/ pah kree • <u>deet</u> • nie <u>kahr</u> • tahch • kyeht

Tips of 10-20% are generally appropriate in restaurants and taxis, depending on the level of service. Porters and maids will certainly expect and appreciate a dollar or two (or the ruble equivalent) for each bag they carry or day that they clean.
As anywhere else, generous tippers will often get better service than those who tip poorly or not at all. Tour guides and their drivers, especially if they have gone 'above and beyond' to get you into restaurants and museums, will expect to be compensated somewhat above the agreed rate.

RENTING

I've reserved an apartment/a room.	**Я заказывал** *m* **/заказывала** *f* **квартиру/комнату.**

yah zah • <u>kah</u> • zih • vahl/ zah • <u>kah</u> • zih • vah • lah kvahr • <u>tee</u> • roo/ <u>kom</u> • nah • too

My name is…	**Меня зовут…**

mee • <u>nyah</u> zah • <u>voot</u>…

Can I have the key/key card?	**Можно получить ключ/электронный ключ?**

<u>mozh</u> • nah pah • <u>loo</u> • <u>cheet'</u> klyooch/ ee • leek • <u>tron</u> • niy klyooch

Are there…?	**Есть…?**

yest'…

dishes and utensils	**посуда**
	pah • <u>soo</u> • dah
pillows	**подушки**
	pah • <u>doosh</u> • kee
sheets	**простыни**
	<u>proh</u> • stih • nee
towels	**полотенца**
	pah • lah • <u>tyen</u> • tsah
When/Where do I put out the bins?	**Когда/Куда выносить мусор?**
	kahg • <u>dah</u>/koo • <u>dah</u> vih • nah • <u>seet'</u> <u>moo</u> • sahr
...is broken.	**...не работает.**
	...nee rah • <u>boh</u> • tah • yet
How does...work?	**Как работает...?**
	kahk rah • <u>boh</u> • tah • yet...
the air-conditioner	**кондиционер**
	kahn • dee • tsih • ah • <u>nyer</u>
the dishwasher	**посудомоечная машина**
	pah • soo • dah • <u>moh</u> • eech • nah • yah mah • <u>shih</u> • nah
the freezer	**морозильная камера**
	mah • rah • <u>zeel'</u> • nah • yah kah <u>kah</u> • mee • rah
the heater	**обогреватель**
	ah • bah • gree • <u>vah</u> • teel'
the microwave	**микроволновка**
	meek • rah • vahl • <u>nof</u> • kah
the refrigerator	**холодильник**
	khah • lah • <u>deel'</u> • neek
the stove	**плита**
	plee • <u>tah</u>
the washing machine	**стиральная машина**
	stee • <u>rahl'</u> • nah • yah mah • <u>shih</u> • nah

DOMESTIC ITEMS

I need...	**Мне нужно...**
	mnyeh <u>noozh</u> • nah...
an adapter	**адаптер**
	ah • <u>dahp</u> • ter
aluminum	**фольга**
[kitchen] foil	*fahl' • <u>gah</u>*
a bottle opener	**открывалка**
	aht • krih • <u>vahl</u> • kah
a broom	**веник**
	<u>vyeh</u> • neek
a can opener	**консервный нож**
	kahn • <u>syerv</u> • niy nosh
cleaning supplies	**моющие средства**
	moh • yoo • shchee • yeh <u>sryet</u> • stvah
a corkscrew	**штопор**
	<u>shtoh</u> • pahr
detergent	**стиральный порошок**
	stee • <u>rahl'</u> • niy pah • rah • <u>shok</u>
dishwashing	**жидкость для мытья посуды**
liquid	*zhiht • kahst' dlyah mih • <u>tyah</u>*
	pah • <u>soo</u> • dih

bin bags	**мешки для мусора**
	meesh • <u>kee</u> dlyah <u>moo</u> • sah • rah
a light bulb	**лампочка**
	<u>lahm</u> • pahch • kah
matches	**спички**
	<u>speech</u> • kee
a mop	**швабра**
	<u>shvahb</u> • rah
napkins	**салфетки**
	sahl • <u>fyet</u> • kee
paper towels	**бумажные полотенца**
	boo • <u>mahzh</u> • nih • ee pah • lah • <u>tyen</u> • tsah
I need…	**Мне нужно…**
	mnyeh noozh • nah…
plastic wrap [cling film]	**продуктовая плёнка**
	prah • dook • <u>toh</u> • vah • yah <u>plyon</u> • kah
a plunger	**вантуз**
	<u>vahn</u> • toos
scissors	**ножницы**
	<u>nozh</u> • nee • tsih
a vacuum cleaner	**пылесос**
	pih • lee • <u>sor</u>

For In the Kitchen, see page 193.

AT THE HOSTEL

Do you have any places left for tonight?	**Есть свободные места на сегодня?** *yest' svah • bod • nih • yeh mee • stah nah see • vod • nyah*
Can I have...?	**Можно мне...?** *mozh • nah mnyeh...*
a single/double room	**одноместный/двухместный номер** *ahd • nah • myes • niy/dvookh • myes • niy noh • meer*
a blanket	**одеяло** *ah • dee • yah • lah*
a pillow	**подушку** *pah • doosh • koo*
sheets	**простыни** *proh • stih • nee*
a towel	**полотенце** *pah • lah • tyen • tseh*
Do you have lockers?	**У Вас есть запирающиеся шкафчики?** *oo vahs yest' zah • pee • rah • yoo • shcheeyeh • sya shkaf • chee • kee*

What time do you lock up?	**Во сколько закрывается вход?** _vah skol' • kahzah • krih • vah • ee • tsah fkhot_
Do I need a membership card?	**Нужна ли мне членская карта?** _noozh • nah lee mneh chlehn • skaya kahr • tah_
Here's my international student card.	**Вот мой международный студенческий билет.** _vot moy meezh • doo • nah • rod • niy stoo • dehn • chyes • keey bee • lyet_

Спутник _spoot • neek_ (Sputnik), the Russian youth travel association, organizes group tours for students with accommodation in **молодёжная турбаза** _mah • lah • dyozh • nah • yah toor • bah • zah_ (youth hostels).

GOING CAMPING

Can I camp here?	**Здесь можно разбить лагерь?** _zdyes' mozh • nah rahz • beet' lah • geer'_
Is there a campsite near here?	**Здесь есть кемпинг поблизости?** _zdyes' yest' kehm • peenk pah • blee • zahs • tee_
What is the charge per day/week?	**Сколько стоит в день/неделю?** _skol' • kah stoh • eet v dyen'/ nee • dyeh • lyoo_
Are there…?	**Есть…?** _yest'…_
cooking facilities	**кухня** _kookh • nyah_
electrical outlets	**электроточки** _ee • lyek • trah • toch • kee_
laundry facilities	**прачечная** _prah • cheech • nah • yah_

showers	**душ**
	doosh
tents for hire	**палатки напрокат**
	pah • laht • kee nah • prah • kaht
Where can I empty the chemical toilet?	**Куда мне выбросить содержимое химического туалета?**
	koo • dah mnyeh vih • brah • seet'
	sah • deer • zhih • mah • yeh
	khee • mee • chees • kah • vah
	too • ah • lyeh • tah

For In the Kitchen, see page 193.

YOU MAY SEE...   👁

ПИТЬЕВАЯ ВОДА	drinking
peet' • ee • vah • yah vah • dah	water
СТОЯНКА ЗАПРЕЩЕНА	no camping
stah • yahn • kah zah • pree • shchee • nah	
КОСТРЫ ЗАПРЕЩЕНЫ	no fires
kahst • rih zah • pree • shchee • nih	

COMMUNICATIONS

NEED TO KNOW

Where's an internet cafe?	**Где находится интернет-кафе?**
	gdyeh nah • khoh • dee • tsah
	een • ter • net kah • feh
Can I access the internet here/ check e-mail?	**Здесь можно войти в Интернет/ проверить электронную почту?**
	zdyes'mozh • nah vie • tee v
	een • ter • net/prah • vyeh • reet'
	ee • leek • tron • noo • yoo poch • too
How much per half hour/hour?	**Сколько за полчаса/час?**
	skol' • kah zah pol • chee • sah/chahs
How do I connect/ log on?	**Как мне подключиться/ зарегистрироваться?**
	kahk mnyeh paht • klyoo • chee • tsah/
	zah • ree • gee • stree • rah • vah • tsah
I'd like a phone card, please.	**Телефонную карточку, пожалуйста.**
	tee • lee • fon • noo • yoo
	kahr • tahch • koo pah • zhahl • stah
Can I have your phone number?	**Можно Ваш номер телефона?**
	mozh • nah vahsh noh • meer
	tee • lee • foh • nah
Here's my number/ e-mail address.	**Вот мой номер/адрес электронной почты.**
	vot moy noh • meer/ahd • rees
	ee • leek • tron • nie poch • tih
Call me.	**Звоните.**
	zvah • nee • tee
E-mail me.	**Напишите мне по электронной почте.**
	nah • pee • shih • tee mnyeh pah
	ee • leek • tron • nie poch • tyeh

Hello. This is…	**Алло. Это…**
	ah • <u>loh</u> <u>eh</u> • tah…
I'd like to speak to…	**Я хотел m /хотела f бы поговорить с…**
	yah khah • <u>tyel</u>/khah • <u>tyeh</u> • lah bih
	pah • gah • vah • <u>reet'</u> s…
Repeat that, please.	**Повторите, пожалуйста.**
	pahf • tah • <u>ree</u> • tee
	pah • <u>zhahl</u> • stah
I'll call back later.	**Я перезвоню попозже.**
	yah pee • ree • zvah • <u>nyoo</u>
	pah • <u>pozh</u> • zheh
Bye.	**До свидания.**
	dah svee • <u>dah</u> • nee • yah
Where is the nearest/main post office?	**Где здесь ближайшая почта/ главпочтамт?**
	gdyeh zdyes' blee • <u>zhie</u> • shah • yah
	<u>poch</u> • tah/glahf • pahch • <u>tamt</u>
I'd like to send this to…	**Я хотел m /хотела f бы отправить это в…**
	yah khah • <u>tyel</u>/khah • <u>tyeh</u> • lah bih
	aht • <u>prah</u> • veet' <u>eh</u> • tah v…

ONLINE

Where's an internet cafe?	**Где находится интернет-кафе?**
	gdyeh nah • <u>khoh</u> • dee • tsah een • ter • <u>net</u> kah • <u>feh</u>
Does it have wireless internet?	**Есть беспроводной Интернет?**
	yest' bees • prah • vahd • <u>noy</u> een • ter • <u>net</u>
What is the WiFi password?	**Какой пароль от WiFi?**
	kah • <u>koy</u> pah • rol' ot WiFi
Is the WiFi free?	**WiFi бесплатный?**
	WiFi behs • <u>plaht</u> • niy

Do you have bluetooth?	**У Вас есть bluetooth?** *oo vas yest' bluetooth*
How do I turn the computer on/off?	**Как мне включить/выключить компьютер?** *kahk mnyeh fklyoo • cheet'/ vih • klyoo • cheet' kahm • pyoo • ter*
Can I...?	**Я смогу...?** *yah smah • goo...*
access the internet here	**войти в Интернет здесь** *vie • tee v een • ter • net zdyes'*
check e-mail	**проверить электронную почту** *prah • vyeh • reet' ee • leek • tron • noo • yoo poch • too*
print	**распечатать** *rahs • pee • chah • taht'*
plug in/charge my laptop/iPhone/ iPad/BlackBerry	**подключить/зарядить ноутбук/ iPhone/iPad/BlackBerry** *pod • klyoo • cheet'/zah • rya • deet' notebook /iPhone/iPad/BlackBerry*
access Skype	**войти в Skype** *voy • tee v Skype*
How much per hour/half hour?	**Сколько за час/полчаса?** *skol' • kah zah chahs/pol • chah • sah*

YOU MAY SEE...

ЗАКРОЙТЕ *zah • kroy • tee*	close
УДАЛИТЕ *oo • dah • lee • tee*	delete

ЭЛЕКТРОННАЯ ПОЧТА	e-mail
ee • leek • tron • nah • yah poch • tah	
ВЫХОД	exit
vih • khaht	
СПРАВКА	help
sprahf • kah	
МГНОВЕННЫЙ ОБМЕН	instant
СООБЩЕНИЯМИ	messenger
mgnah • vyen • niy ahb • myen	
sah • ahp • shchyeh • nee • yah • mee	
ИНТЕРНЕТ	internet
een • ter • net	
ВХОД В СИСТЕМУ	login
fhot f sees • tyeh • moo	
НОВОЕ (СООБЩЕНИЕ)	new (message)
noh • vah • yeh	
(sah • ahp • shchyeh • nee • yeh)	
ВКЛ/ВЫКЛ	on/off
fkl/vihkl	
ОТКРЫТЬ	open
aht • kriht'	
РАСПЕЧАТАТЬ	print
rahs • pee • chah • taht'	
СОХРАНИТЬ	save
sah • khrah • neet'	
ОТПРАВИТЬ	send
aht • prah • veet'	
ИМЯ ПОЛЬЗОВАТЕЛЯ/ПАРОЛЬ	username/
ee • myah	password
pol' • zah • vah • tee • lyah/pah • rol'	
БЕСПРОВОДНОЙ ИНТЕРНЕТ	wireless internet
bees • prah • vahd • noy een • ter • net	

How do I...?	**Как мне...?**
	kahk mnyeh...
connect/	**подключиться/отключиться**
disconnect	*paht • klyoo • chee • tsah/*
	aht • klyoo • chee • tsah
log on/off	**войти/выйти**
	vie • tee/viy • tee
type this symbol	**напечатать этот символ**
	nah • pee • chah • taht' eh • taht
	seem • vahl
What's your e-mail?	**Какой у вас адрес электронной почты?**
	kah • koy oo vahs ahd • rees
	ee • leek • tron • nie poch • tih
My e-mail is...	**Мой адрес электронной почты...**
	moy ahd • rees ee • leek • tron • nie
	poch • tih...
Do you have	**У Вас есть сканер?**
a scanner?	*oo vas est' skah • nehr*

SOCIAL MEDIA

Are you on Facebook/	**Вы есть в Facebook/Twitter?**
Twitter?	*vih est' v Facebook/Twitter*
What's your user	**Какое у Вас имя пользователя?**
name?	*kah • koh • eh oo vas ee • mya*
	pol' • zo • vah • tyeh • lya
I'll add you as	**Я добавлю Вас в друзья.**
a friend.	*yah doh • bahv • lyoo vas v drooz' • ya*
I'll follow you on	**Я присоединюсь к Вам в Twitter.**
Twitter.	*yah pree • soh • eh • dee • nyus' k vam v*
	Twitter
Are you following...?	**Вы присоединились...?**
	vih pree • soh • eh • dee • nee • lees'...

I'll put the pictures on Facebook/Twitter.	**Я выложу фотографии на Facebook/Twitter.**
	yah_vih • lah • zhoo fo • to • grah • fee • ee na Facebook/Twitter
I'll tag you in the pictures.	**Я отмечу Вас на фотографиях.**
	yah ot • meh • choo vas na foh • to • grah • fee • yakh

PHONE

A phone card/ prepaid phone, please.	**Телефонную карточку/ оплаченный телефон, пожалуйста.**
	tee • lee • fon • noo • yoo kahr • tahch • koo/ ah • plah • cheen • niy tee • lee • fon pah • zhahl • stah
How much?	**Сколько?**
	skol' • kah
Where's the pay phone?	**Где есть таксофон?**
	gdeh est' tah • xo • fohn
What's the area/ country code for…?	**Какой код города/страны для…?**
	kah • koy kot goh • rah • dah/strah • nih dlyah…
What's the number for Information?	**Какой номер справочной службы?**
	kah • koy noh • meer sprah • vahch • nie sloozh • bih

I'd like the number for...

Мне нужен номер...
mnyeh <u>noo</u> • zhihn <u>noh</u> • meer...

I'd like to call collect [reverse the charges].

Я хочу позвонить за счет абонента [удержать оплату].
yah kho • <u>choo</u> poz • voh • <u>neet'</u> zah shchot ah • boh • <u>nehn</u> • tah [oo • dehr • <u>zhat'</u> op • <u>lah</u> • too]

YOU MAY HEAR...

Кто говорит?
ktoh gah • vah • <u>reet</u>
Who's calling?

Подождите, пожалуйста.
pah • dah • <u>zhdee</u> • tee pah • <u>zhahl</u> • stah
Hold on, please.

Соединяю.
sah • ee • dee • <u>nyah</u> • yoo
I'll put you through.

Боюсь, что его/её нет.
bah • <u>yoos'</u> shtoh yee • <u>voh</u>/yee • <u>yoh</u> nyet
I'm afraid he's/she's not in.

Он/Она не может подойти к телефону.
on/ah • <u>nah</u> nee moh • zhiht pah • die • <u>tee</u> k tee • lee • <u>foh</u> • noo
He/She can't come to the phone.

Хотите оставить сообщение?
khah • <u>tee</u> • tee ah • <u>stah</u> • veet' sah • ahp • <u>shcheh</u> • nee • yeh
Would you like to leave a message?

Перезвоните позже/через десять минут.
pee • ree • zvah • <u>nee</u> • tee pozh • zheh/<u>cheh</u> • reez dyeh • seet' mee • <u>noot</u>
Call back later/in 10 minutes.

Он/Она может перезвонить Вам?
on/ah • <u>nah</u> moh • zhiht pee • ree • zvah • <u>neet'</u> vahm
Can he/she call you back?

Можно Ваш номер телефона?
<u>mozh</u> • nah vahsh <u>noh</u> • meer tee • lee • <u>foh</u> • nah
What's your number?

My phone doesn't work here.	**Мой телефон здесь не работает.**
	moy tee • lee • fon zdyes' nee
	rah • boh • tah • eet
What network are you on?	**К какой сети Вы подключены?**
	k kah • koy sye • tee vih pod • klyoo • cheh • nih
Is it 3G?	**Это 3G?**
	eh • tah 3G
I have run out of credit/minutes.	**У меня закончились единицы/ минуты.**
	oo meh • nya zah • kohn • chee • lees'
	eh • dee • nee • tsih/mee • noo • tih
Can I buy some credit?	**Могу я приобрести единицы?**
	moh • goo yah pree • obrye • stee
	ye • dee • nee • tsih
Do you have a phone charger?	**У Вас есть зарядное устройство для телефона?**
	u vas est' zah • ryad • no • he
	oost • roy • stvoh dlya teh • leh • foh • nah
Can I have your number?	**Можно Ваш номер телефона?**
	mozh • nah vahsh noh • meer
	tee • lee • foh • nah
Here's my number.	**Вот мой телефон.**
	vot moy tee • lee • fon
Call me.	**Звоните.**
	zvah • nee • tee
Text me.	**Пришлите СМС.**
	pree • shlee • tee es • em • es
I'll call you.	**Я позвоню Вам.**
	yah pah • zvah • nyoo vahm
I'll text you.	**Я пришлю Вам СМС.**
	yah pree • shlyoo vahm es • em • es

TELEPHONE ETIQUETTE

Hello. This is…	**Алло. Это…**
	ah • loh eh • tah…
I'd like to speak to…	**Я хотел m /хотела f бы поговорить с…**
	yah khah • tyel/khah • tyeh • lah bih
	pah • gah • vah • reet' s…

Extension…	**Добавочный номер…**
	dah • <u>bah</u> • vahch • niy <u>noh</u> • meer…
Speak louder/more slowly, please.	**Говорите громче/медленнее, пожалуйста.**
	gah • vah • <u>ree</u> • tee <u>grom</u> • cheh/ <u>myed</u> • leen • nee • yeh pah • <u>zhahl</u> • stah
Repeat that, please.	**Повторите, пожалуйста.**
	pahf • tah • <u>ree</u> • tee pah • <u>zhahl</u> • stah
I'll call back later.	**Я перезвоню попозже.**
	yah pee • ree • zvah • <u>nyoo</u> pah • <u>pozh</u> • zheh
Bye.	**До свидания.**
	dah svee • <u>dah</u> • nee • yah

FAX

Can I send/receive a fax here?	**Я могу здесь получить/отправить факс?**
	yah mah • <u>goo</u> zdyes' pah • loo • <u>cheet'</u>/ aht • <u>prah</u> • veet' fahks
What's the fax number?	**Какой номер факса?**
	kah • <u>koy</u> <u>noh</u> • meer fahk • sah

Fax this to…	**Отправьте это по факсу, номер…** *aht • prahf' • tee eh • tah pah fahk • soo* *noh • meer…*

POST

Where's the post office/mailbox?	**Где почта/почтовый ящик?** *gdyeh poch • tah/pahch • toh • viy* *yah • shcheek*
A stamp for this postcard/letter, please.	**Дайте марку на эту открытку/это письмо, пожалуйста.** *die • tee mahr • koo nah eh • too* *aht • kriht • koo/eh • tah pees' • moh* *pah • zhahl • stah*
How much?	**Сколько?** *skol' • kah*
I want to send this package by airmail/express.	**Я хочу послать эту посылку авиа/экспресс почтой.** *yah khah • choo pah • slaht' eh • too* *pah • sihl • koo ah • vee • ah/eeks • press* *poch • toy*
A receipt, please.	**Дайте чек, пожалуйста.** *die • tee chek pah • zhahl • stah*

(i)

The main post offices in Moscow and St. Petersburg offer round-the-clock service. Other post offices are generally open Monday through Saturday from 8:00 a.m. to 7:00 p.m. and Sunday from 9:00 a.m. to 7:00 p.m. Major hotels have their own postal and telephone services. Both incoming and outgoing international mail is slow, so allow plenty of time. While DHL has the greatest presence in Russia among Western express shipping companies, FedEx, UPS and other companies also provide service to and from Russia.

YOU MAY HEAR...

Пожалуйста, заполните таможенную декларацию.
pah • zhahl • stah zah • pol • nee • tee
tah • moh • zhihn • noo • yoo
dee • klah • rah • tsih • yoo

Please fill out the customs declaration form.

Какая стоимость?
kah • kah • yah
stoh • ee • mahst'

What's the value?

Что там?
shtoh tahm

What's inside?

SIGHTSEEING

TOURIST INFORMATION

Do you have any information on...?

У Вас есть информация по...?
oo vahs yest'
een • fahr • mah • tsih • yah pah...

Can you recommend...?

Вы можете порекомендовать...?
vih moh • zhih • tee
pah • ree • kah • meen • dah • vaht'...

  a boat trip

водную экскурсию
vod • noo • yoo eks • koor • see • yoo

  an excursion

экскурсию
eks • koor • see • yoo

  a sightseeing tour

обзорную экскурсию
ahb • zor • noo • yoo eks • koor • see • yoo

For Asking Directions, see page 65.

NEED TO KNOW

Where's the tourist information office?	**Где турбюро?**
	gdyeh <u>toor</u> • byoo • <u>roh</u>
What are the main points of interest?	**Какие главные достопримечательности?**
	kah • <u>kee</u> • yeh <u>glahv</u> • nih • yeh dah • stah • pree • mee • <u>chah</u> • teel' • nahs • tee
Do you have tours in English?	**У вас есть экскурсии на английском?**
	oo vahs yehst' ehks • <u>koor</u> • see • ee nah ahn • <u>gleey</u> • skahm
Can I have a map/ guide?	**Можно мне карту/путеводитель?**
	<u>mozh</u> • nah mnyeh <u>kahr</u> • too/ poo • tee • vah • <u>dee</u> • teel

Intourist hotels have **бюро обслуживания** *byoo • <u>roh</u> ahp • <u>sloo</u> • zhih • vah • nee • yah* (service bureaus) manned by multilingual staff who provide information, arrange outings and excursions, make reservations and give general assistance. Other useful sources of information are the tourist information offices, English-language newspapers, *The Moscow Times* and *Where in St. Petersburg?*, found in many hotels and available from kiosks.

ON TOUR

I'd like to go on the tour to…	**Я хотел m /хотела f бы поехать на экскурсию в…**
	yah khah • tyel/khah • tyeh • lah bih pah • yeh • khaht' nah eks • koor • see • yoo v…
When's the next tour?	**Когда будет следующая поездка?**
	kahg • dah boo • deht sleh • doo • yu • shchah • ya poh • yehzd • kah
Are there tours in English?	**Есть экскурсии на английском?**
	yest' eks • koor • see • ee nah ahn • gleey • skahm
Is there an English guide book/audio guide?	**Есть путеводитель/аудиокнига на английском языке?**
	est' poo • teh • voh • dee • tehl'/ ah • oo • dee • oh • knee • gah nah ahng • leey • skohm yaz • ihkeh
What time do we leave/return?	**Во сколько отправляемся/ возвращаемся?**
	vah skol' • kah aht • prahv • lyah • eem • syah/ vahz • vrah • shchah • eem • syah
We'd like to have a look at the…	**Нам хотелось бы посмотреть…**
	nahm khah • tyeh • las' bih pah • smah • tryet'…
Can we stop here…?	**Можно здесь остановиться, чтобы…?**
	mozh • nah zdyes' ah • stah • nah • vee • tsah shtoh • bih…
to take photographs	**пофотографировать**
	pah • fah • tah • grah • fee • rah • vaht'
to buy souvenirs	**купить сувениры**
	koo • peet' soo • vee • nee • rih

to use the restroom [toilet]	**сходить в туалет** *skhah • deet' f too • ah • lyet*
Is there access for the disabled?	**Есть условия для инвалидов?** *yest' oos • loh • vee • yah dlyah* *een • vah • lee • dahf*

For Tickets, see page 43.

SEEING THE SIGHTS

Where is…?	**Где…?** *gdye…*
the battleground	**место сражения** *myes • tah srah • zheh • nee • yah*
the botanical garden	**ботанический сад** *bah • tah • nee • chees • keey saht*
the castle	**замок** *zah • mahk*
the downtown area	**центр города** *tsentr goh • rah • dah*
the fountain	**фонтан** *fahn • tahn*
the library	**библиотека** *bee • blee • ah • tyeh • kah*
the market	**рынок** *rih • nahk*
the museum	**музей** *moo • zey*
the old town	**старый город** *stah • riy goh • raht*
the opera house	**опера** *oh • peh • rah*
the palace	**дворец** *dvah • ryets*

the park	**парк** *pahrk*
the ruins	**руины** *roo•<u>een</u>•y*
the shopping area	**торговый район** *tahr•<u>goh</u>•viy rah•<u>yon</u>*
the town square	**центральная площадь** *tsihn•<u>trahl'</u>•nah•yah ploh•shchaht'*
Show me on the map.	**Покажите мне на карте.** *pah•kah•<u>zhih</u>•tee mnyeh nah <u>kahr</u>•tye*
It's…	**Это…** *<u>eh</u>•tah…*
amazing	**удивительно** *oo•dee•<u>vee</u>•tehl'•noh*
beautiful	**прекрасно** *pree•<u>krahs</u>•nah*
boring	**скучно** *<u>skoosh</u>•nah*
It's…	**Это…** *<u>eh</u>•tah…*
interesting	**интересно** *een•tee•<u>ryes</u>•nah*
magnificent	**великолепно** *vee•lee•kah•<u>lyep</u>•nah*
romantic	**романтично** *rah•mahn•<u>teech</u>•nah*
strange	**странно** *<u>strah</u>•noh*
terrible	**ужасно** *oo•<u>zhahs</u>•nah*
ugly	**безобразно** *bee•zah•<u>brahz</u>•nah*
I (don't) like it.	**Мне это (не) нравится.** *mnyeh <u>eh</u>•tah (nee) <u>nrah</u>•vee•tsah*

RELIGIOUS SITES

Where's…?	**Где…?**
	gdyeh…
the Catholic/	**церковь католическая/**
Protestant church	**протестантская**
	tser • kahf' kah • toh • lee • che • ska • ya/
	pro • tye • stahn • ska • ya
the mosque	**мечеть**
	mee • <u>chet'</u>
the shrine	**обитель**
	ah • <u>bee</u> • teel'
the synagogue	**синагога**
	see • nah • <u>goh</u> • gah
the temple	**храм**
	khrahm
What time is mass/	**Когда будет месса/служба?**
the service?	*kahg • <u>dah boo</u> • deet*
	<u>myes</u> • sah/<u>sloozh</u> • bah

ACTIVITIES

SHOPPING

NEED TO KNOW

Where is the shop/ mall?	**Где магазин/торговый центр?** *gdyeh mah • gah • zeen/tahr • goh • viy tsehntr*
I'm just looking.	**Я просто смотрю.** *yah proh • stah smath • ryoo*
Can you help me?	**Можете мне помочь?** *moh • zhih • tee mnyeh pah • mohch*
I'm being helped.	**Меня уже обслуживают.** *mee • nyah oo • zheh ahp • sloo • zhih • vah • yoot*
How much?	**Сколько?** *skol' • kah*
That one.	**Вон то.** *vohn toh*
That's all, thanks.	**Это всё, спасибо.** *eh • tah fsyoh spah • see • bah*
Where do I pay?	**Куда платить?** *koo • dah plah • teet'*
I'll pay in cash/ by credit card.	**Я заплачу наличными/по кредитной карточке.** *yah zah • plah • choo nah • leech • nih • mee/pah kree • deet • noy kahr • tahch • kee*
A receipt, please.	**Чек, пожалуйста.** *chehk pah • zhahl • stah*

AT THE SHOPS

Shopping in Moscow and St. Petersburg now looks
very much like shopping in New York and London, at
least in the city centers and malls. Moscow does its serious
shopping in the mega-stores along the outer ring-road,
where names like Ikea and Marks & Spencer can be found.
The Tyoply Stan mega mall claims to be Europe's busiest
shopping center.

Both cities also offer thriving and rich open-air markets, for
example, Moscow's Izmailovsky Market, near Partizanskaya
metro station, or St. Petersburg's market, near the Nevsky
Prospect metro station. These are great places to pick up
souvenirs.

Where is…?	**Где…?** *gdyeh…*
the antiques store	**антикварный магазин** *ahn • tee • <u>kvahr</u> • niy mah • gah • <u>zeen</u>*
the bakery	**булочная** *<u>boo</u> • lahch • nah • yah*
the bank	**банк** *bahnk*
the bookstore	**книжный магазин** *<u>kneezh</u> • niy mah • gah • <u>zeen</u>*
Where is…?	**Где…?** *gdyeh…*
the clothing store	**магазин одежды** *mah • gah • <u>zeen</u> ah • dyezh • dih*
the delicatessen	**гастроном** *gah • stroh • <u>nohm</u>*

the department store	**универмаг** oo • nee • veer • <u>mahk</u>
the gift shop	**магазин подарков** mah • gah • <u>zeen</u> poh • <u>dahr</u> • kohv
the jeweler	**ювелирный магазин** yoo • vee • <u>leer</u> • niy mah • gah • <u>zeen</u>
the liquor store [off-license]	**винный магазин** <u>veen</u> • niy mah • gah • <u>zeen</u>
the market	**рынок** <u>rih</u> • nahk
the music store	**музыкальный магазин** moo • zih • <u>kahl'</u> • niy mah • gah • <u>zeen</u>
the pastry store	**кондитерская** kahn • <u>dee</u> • teer • skah • yah
the pharmacy	**аптека** ahp • <u>tyeh</u> • kah
the shoe store	**обувной магазин** ah • boov • <u>noy</u> mah • gah • <u>zeen</u>
Where is…?	**Где…?** gdyeh…
the shopping mall	**торговый центр** tahr • <u>goh</u> • viy tsehntr
the souvenir store	**магазин сувениров** mah • gah • <u>zeen</u> soo • vee • <u>nee</u> • rahf

the supermarket	**универсам**
	oo • nee • veer • <u>sahm</u>
the tobacconist	**табачный киоск**
	tah • <u>bahch</u> • niy kee • <u>osk</u>
the toy store	**магазин игрушкек**
	mah • gah • <u>zeen</u> ee • <u>groo</u> • shek

ASK AN ASSISTANT

What are the hours of operation?	**В какие часы работает?**
	f kah • <u>kee</u> • yeh chah • <u>sih</u>
	rah • <u>boh</u> • tah • yet
Where is…?	**Где…?**
	gdyeh…
the cashier [cash desk]	**касса**
	<u>kahs</u> • sah
the escalator	**эскалатор**
	es • kah • <u>lah</u> • tahr
the elevator [lift]	**лифт**
	leeft
the fitting room	**примерочная**
	pree • <u>myeh</u> • rahch • nah • yah
the store directory	**перечень отделов**
	pyeh • ree • cheen' ahd • <u>dyeh</u> • lahf
Help me, please.	**Помогите мне, пожалуйста.**
	pah • mah • <u>gee</u> • tee mnyeh
	pah • <u>zhahl</u> • stah
I'm just looking.	**Я просто смотрю.**
	yah <u>proh</u> • stah smah • <u>tryoo</u>
I'm being helped.	**Меня уже обслуживают.**
	mee • <u>nyah</u> oo • <u>zheh</u>
	ahp • <u>sloo</u> • zhih • vah • yoot
Do you have…?	**У Вас есть…?**
	oo vahs yest'…

YOU MAY SEE...

ОТКРЫТО/ЗАКРЫТО	open/
aht • _krih_ • tah/zah • _krih_ • toh	closed
ЗАКРЫТО НА ОБЕД	closed for lunch
zah • _krih_ • toh nah ah • _byed_	
ПРИМЕРОЧНАЯ	fitting room
pree • _meh_ • rah • chnah • ya	
КАССА	cashier
kah • sah	
ТОЛЬКО НАЛИЧНЕ	cash only
tohl' • koh nah • _lich_ • nih • ee	
ПРИНИМАЮТСЯ КРЕДИТНЫЕ КАРТЫ	credit cards
pree • nee • _mah_ • yoot • sah	accepted
kreh • _deet_ • nihye _kahr_ • tih	
ЧАСЫ РАБОТЫ	business hours
chah • _sih_ rah • bohty	
ВЫХОД	exit
vih • khaht	

Where is...?	**Где...?**
	gdyeh...
Could you show me...?	**Можете мне показать...?**
	moh • zhih • tee mnyeh pah • kah • _zaht'_...
Can you ship/ wrap it?	**Вы можете доставить/завернуть это?**
	vih _moh_ • zhih • tee dah • _stah_ • veet'/
	zah • veer • _noot'_ eh • tah
How much?	**Сколько?**
	skol' • kah
That's all, thanks.	**Это всё, спасибо.**
	_eh_ • tah fsyoh spah • _see_ • bah

YOU MAY HEAR...

Я вас слушаю.
yah vahs <u>sloo</u> • shah • yoo

Can I help you?

Одну минуту.
ahd • <u>noo</u> mee • <u>noo</u> • too

One moment.

Что вы хотите?
shtoh vih khah • <u>tee</u> • tee

What would you like?

Что ещё?
shtoh ee • <u>shchoh</u>

Anything else?

For Souvenirs, see page 125.

PERSONAL PREFERENCES

I'd like something...	**Я хочу что-нибудь...** *yah khah • <u>choo</u> <u>shtoh</u> • nee • boot'...*
cheap/expensive	**дешёвое/дорогое** *dee • <u>shoh</u> • vah • yeh/dah • rah • <u>goh</u> • yeh*
larger/smaller	**побольше/поменьше** *pah • <u>bol'</u> • sheh/pah • <u>myen'</u> • sheh*
from this region	**из этого региона** *eez eh • tah • vah reh • gih • <u>oh</u> • nah*
around... rubles	**примерно... рублей** *pree • <u>mehr</u> • noh ... roob • <u>lyey</u>*
Is it real?	**Это настоящее?** *eh • tah nahs • tah • <u>yah</u> • shchee • yeh*
Could you show me this/that?	**Можете показать мне это/вон то?** *<u>moh</u> • zhih • tee pah • kah • <u>zaht'</u> mnyeh eh • tah/von toh*
That's not quite what I want.	**Это не совсем то, что я хочу.** *eh • tah nee sahf • <u>syem</u> toh shtoh yah khah • <u>choo</u>*

I don't like it.	**Это мне не нравится.**
	_eh_ • _tah mnyeh nee <u>nrah</u>_ • _vee_ • _tsah_
That's too	**Это слишком дорого.**
expensive.	_eh_ • _tah <u>sleesh</u>_ • _kahm <u>doh</u>_ • _rah_ • _gah_
I'd like to think	**Надо подумать.**
about it.	_<u>nah</u>_ • _dah pah_ • _<u>doo</u>_ • _maht'_
I'll take it.	**Я возьму это.**
	yah vahz' • _moo eh_ • _tah_

PAYING & BARGAINING

How much?	**Сколько?**
	<u>skol'</u> • _kah_
I'll pay…	**Я заплачу…**
	yah zah • _plah_ • _<u>choo</u>_…
in cash	**наличными**
	nah • _<u>leech</u>_ • _nih_ • _mee_
by credit card	**по кредитной карточке**
	pah kree • _<u>deet</u>_ • _noy <u>kar</u>_ • _tach_ • _kee_
by traveler's	**дорожным чеком**
cheque	_dah_ • _<u>rozh</u>_ • _nihm cheh_ • _kahm_
A receipt, please.	**Можно чек, пожалуйста.**
	<u>mozh</u> • _nah chehk pah_ • _<u>zhahl</u>_ • _stah_

YOU MAY HEAR...

Как будете платить?
kahk boo•dee•tee plah•teet'

How are you paying?

Кредитная карта не принята.
kreh•deet•nah•ya kahr•tah neh pree•nya•tah

Your credit card has been declined.

Только наличные, пожалуйста.
tol'•kah nah•leech•nih•yeh pah•zhahl•stah

Cash only, please.

Удостоверение личности пожалуйста.
oo•dahs•ta•veer•en•ye leech•nus•tee pah•zhahl•stah

ID, please.

У Вас есть деньги мельче?
oo vahs yest' dyen'•gee myel'•cheh

Do you have any smaller change?

That's too much.	**Это слишком дорого.**	
	eh•tah sleesh•kahm doh•rah•gah	
I'll give you...	**Я дам вам...**	
	yah dahm vahm...	
I only have...rubles.	**У меня только...рублей.**	
	oo mee•nyah tol'•kah...roob•lyey	
Is that your best price?	**Это ваша последняя цена?**	
	eh•tah vah•shah pahs•lyed•nee•yah tsih•nah	
Can you give me a discount?	**Вы можете дать мне скидку?**	
	vih moh•zhih•tee daht' mnyeh skeet•koo	

While credit cards are increasingly common in Russia and fairly safe to use, especially in large and mid-sized cities, you should avoid using them in places that do not inspire complete confidence.

MAKING A COMPLAINT

I'd like…	**Я хотел m /хотела f бы…**
	yah khah • <u>tyel</u>/khah • <u>tyeh</u> • lah bih…
to exchange this	**обменять это**
	ahb • mee • <u>nyaht'</u> <u>eh</u> • tah
to return this	**возвратить это**
	vahz • vrah • <u>teet'</u> <u>eh</u> • tah
a refund	**возврат денег**
	vahz • <u>vraht</u> <u>dye</u> • neek
to see the manager	**увидеть менеджера**
	oo • <u>vee</u> • deet' <u>myeh</u> • ned • zhih • rah

SERVICES

Can you recommend…?	**Вы можете порекомендовать…?**
	vih <u>moh</u> • zhih • tee
	pah • ree • kah • meen • dah • <u>vaht'</u>…
a barber	**парикмахерскую**
	pah • reek • <u>mah</u> • kheer • skoo • yoo
a dry cleaner	**химчистку**
	kheem • <u>cheest</u> • koo
a hairdresser	**парикмахерскую**
	pah • reek • <u>mah</u> • kheer • skoo • yoo
a laundromat [launderette]	**прачечную**
	<u>prah</u> • cheech • noo • yoo
a nail salon	**маникюрный салон**
	mah • nee • <u>kyoor</u> • niy sah • <u>lon</u>
a spa	**спа**
	spah
a travel agency	**бюро путешествий**
	byoo • <u>roh</u> poo • tee • <u>shest</u> • veey
Can you…this?	**Вы можете это…?**
	vih <u>moh</u> • zhih • tee <u>eh</u> • tah…

alter	**переделать**
	pee • ree • dyeh • lat'
clean	**почистить**
	pah • chees • teet'
mend	**заштопать**
	zah • shtoh • paht'
press	**погладить**
	pah • glah • deet'
When will it be ready?	**Когда будет готово?**
	kahg • dah boo • deet gah • toh • vah

HAIR & BEAUTY

I'd like…	**Я хотел** *m* **/хотела** *f* **бы…**
	yah khah • tyel/khah • tyeh • lah bih…
an appointment for today/tomorrow	**записаться на сегодня/завтра**
	zah • pee • sah • tsah nah see • vod • nyah/ zahf • trah
some colour/ highlights	**покрасить волосы/сделать мелирование**
	pah • kra • seet' voh • loh • sih/sdeh • laht' meh • lee • roh • vah • nee • yeh
my hair styled/ blow-dried	**модельную стрижку/укладку феном**
	mah • del' • noo • yoo streesh • koo/ ook • lahd • koo • feh • nohm
a haircut	**постричься**
	pah • streech • syah
an eyebrow/ bikini wax	**восковую эпиляцию бровей/зоны бикини**
	vos • kah • voo • yoo eh • pee • lyah • tsih • yoo brah • vyey/zoh • nih bee • kee • nee
a facial	**чистку лица**
	cheest • koo lee • tsah
a manicure/ pedicure	**маникюр/педикюр**
	mah • nee • kyoor/pee • dee • kyoor

a (sports) massage	**(спортивный) массаж**
	(spahr • teev • niy) mahs • sahsh
a trim	**подравнивание**
	pahd • rahv • nee • vah • nee • yeh
Don't cut it too short.	**Не слишком коротко.**
	nee sleesh • kahm koh • raht • kah
Shorter here.	**Здесь покороче.**
	zdyes' pah • kah • roh • cheh
Do you do…?	**Вы делаете…?**
	vih dyeh • lah • ee • tee…
acupuncture	**иглотерапию**
	eeg • lah • tee • rah • pee • yoo
aromatherapy	**ароматерапию**
	ah • roh • mah • tee • rah • pee • yoo
oxygen treatment	**кислородотерапию**
	kees • lah • roh • dah • tee • rah • pee • yoo
Is there a sauna?	**Есть сауна?**
	yest' sah • oo • nah

Natural approaches to health and beauty include
herb remedies and **баня** *bah • nyah* (Russian steam
bath); these are deeply ingrained in Russian traditional folk
medicine. Today these approaches have been combined
with modern spa and wellness resources. Even outside of
Moscow and St. Petersburg you will find a variety of day
and overnight spas. Most hotels offer facials, massage and
a number of other day spa services right on the premises.
It is customary to tip from 10-20% depending on your
satisfaction with services provided.

ANTIQUES

How old is this?	**Какой возраст этой вещи?** *kah • koy voz • rahst eh • tie vyeh • shchee*
Do you have anything from the…period?	**У Вас есть что-нибудь на период с …?** *oo vahs yest' shtoh•nee•boot' nah peh•ree•ot s*
Do I have to fill out any forms?	**Нужно заполнить формы?** *noozh • nah zah • pohl • neet' fohr • mih*
Will I have problems with customs?	**Могут быть проблемы на таможне?** *moh • goot biht' prah • blyeh • mih nah tah • mozh • nee*
Is there a certificate of authenticity?	**Есть сертификат подлинности?** *yest' seer • tee • fee • kaht pod • lyeen • nahs • tee*
Can you ship/ wrap it?	**Вы можете доставить/упаковать?** *vih moh • zhih • tye dah • stah • veet'/ oo • pah • kah • vaht'*

CLOTHING

I'd like…	**Я хотел *m* /хотела *f* бы…** *yah khah • tyel/khah • tyeh • lah bih…*
Can I try this on?	**Можно это примерить?** *mozh • nah eh • tah pree • myeh • reet'*
It doesn't fit.	**Не подходит.** *nee paht • khoh • deet*
It's too big/small.	**Слишком велико/мало.** *sleesh • kahm vee • lee • koh/mah • loh*
It's too short/long.	**Слишком коротко/длинно.** *sleesh • kahm koh • raht • kah/dleen • nah*
It's too tight/loose.	**Слишком туго/слабо.** *slee•shkohm too•goh/slah•boh*

Do you have this in size…?	**У Вас есть размер…?** *oo vahs yest' rahz • myer…*
Do you have this in a bigger/smaller size?	**У Вас есть это большего/меньшего размера?** *oo vahs yest' eh • tah bol' • shee • vah/ myen' • shee • vah rahz • myeh • rah*

For Numbers, see page 18.

YOU MAY HEAR…

That looks great on you.	**Вам очень идет.** *vahm oh • chen' eed • yoht*
How does it fit?	**Как Вам нравится?** *kahk vahm nrah • vee • tsya*
We don't have your size.	**У нас нет Вашего размера.** *oo nahs neht vah • sheh • vah rahz • meh • rah*

YOU MAY SEE…

МУЖСКАЯ ОДЕЖДА *moosh • skah • yah ah • dyezh • dah*	men's clothing
ЖЕНСКАЯ ОДЕЖДА *zhen • skah • yah ah • dyezh • dah*	women's clothing
ДЕТСКАЯ ОДЕЖДА *dyets • kah • yah ah • dyezh • dah*	children's clothing

---

COLORS

I'm looking for something in…	**Я ищу что-нибудь…** *yah ee • shchoo shtoh • nee • boot'…*

beige	**бежевое** _byeh_ • zhih • vah • yeh
black	**чёрное** _chor_ • nah • yeh
blue	**синее** _see_ • nee • yeh
brown	**коричневое** kah • _reech_ • nee • vah • yeh
green	**зелёное** zee • _lyoh_ • nah • yeh
gray	**серое** _syeh_ • rah • yeh
orange	**оранжевое** ah • _rahn_ • zhih • vah • yeh
pink	**розовое** _roh_ • zah • vah • yeh
purple	**фиолетовое** fee • ah • _lyeh_ • tah • vah • yeh
red	**красное** _krahs_ • nah • yeh
white	**белое** _byeh_ • lah • yeh
yellow	**жёлтое** _zhol_ • tah • yeh

CLOTHES & ACCESSORIES

a backpack	**рюкзак** ryook • _zahk_
a belt	**ремень** ree • _myen'_
a bikini	**бикини** bee • _kee_ • nee
a blouse	**блузка** _bloos_ • kah

a bra	**бюстгальтер**
	byoost • gahl • teer
briefs [underpants]	**трусы**
	troo • sih
a coat	**пальто**
	pahl' • toh
a dress	**платье**
	plaht' • yeh
a hat	**шапка**
	shahp • kah
a jacket	**пиджак**
	peed • zhahk
jeans	**джинсы**
	dzhihn • sih
pajamas	**пижама**
	pee • zhah • mah
pants [trousers]	**брюки**
	bryoo • kee
pantyhose [tights]	**колготки**
	kahl • got • kee
a purse [handbag]	**сумка**
	soom • kah
a raincoat	**плащ**
	plahshch

a scarf	**шарф**
	shahrf
a shirt	**рубашка**
	roo • bahsh • kah
shorts	**шорты**
	shor • tih
a skirt	**юбка**
	yoop • kah
socks	**носки**
	nahs • kee
a suit	**костюм**
	kahs • tyoom
sunglasses	**солнечные очки**
	sol • neech • nih • yeh ahch • kee
a sweater	**пуловер**
	poo • loh • veer
a sweatshirt	**свитер**
	svee • tehr
swimming trunks	**плавки**
	plahf • kee
a swimsuit	**купальник**
	koo • pahl' • neek
a T-shirt	**майка**
	mie • kah
a tie	**галстук**
	gahls • took
underwear	**нижнее бельё**
	neezh • nee • yeh bee • lyoh

FABRIC

I'd like…	**Я хотел *m*/хотела *f* бы…**
	yah khah • tyel/khah • tyeh • lah bih…
cotton	**хлопок**
	khloh • pahk

denim	**джинс**
	dzhihns
lace	**кружева**
	kroo • zhih • <u>vah</u>
leather	**кожа**
	<u>koh</u> • zhah
linen	**лен**
	lyon
silk	**шёлк**
	sholk
wool	**шерсть**
	sherst'
Is it machine washable?	**Это можно стирать в машине?**
	<u>eh</u> • tah <u>mozh</u> • nah stee • <u>raht'</u> v mah • <u>shih</u> • nyeh

SHOES

I'd like…	**Я хотел m /хотела f бы…**
	yah khah • <u>tyel</u>/khah • <u>tyeh</u> • lah bih…
high-heeled shoes/flat shoes	**туфли на высоком/низком каблуке**
	<u>toof</u> • lee nah vih • <u>soh</u> • kahm/nees • kahm kahb • loo • <u>kyeh</u>
boots	**сапоги**
	sah • pah • <u>gee</u>
loafers	**мокасины**
	mah • kah • <u>see</u> • nih
sandals	**сандалии**
	sahn • <u>dah</u> • lee • ee
shoes	**туфли**
	<u>toof</u> • lee
slippers	**тапочки**
	<u>tah</u> • pahch • kee
sneakers	**кроссовки**
	krah • <u>sof</u> • kee

In size…	**Размер…**
	rahz • <u>myer</u>…

For Numbers, see page 18.

SIZES

small (S)	**малый**
	<u>mah</u> • liy
medium (M)	**средний**
	<u>sryed</u> • neey
large (L)	**большой**
	bahl' • <u>shoy</u>
extra large (XL)	**очень большой**
	<u>oh</u> • cheen' bahl' • <u>shoy</u>
petite	**маленький**
	<u>mah</u> • leen' • keey
plus size	**для полных**
	dlyah <u>pol</u> • nihkh

NEWSAGENT & TOBACCONIST

Do you sell English-language books/newspapers?	**Есть в продаже английские книги/газеты?**
	yest' f prah • <u>dah</u> • zheh
	ahn • <u>gleey</u> • skee • yeh <u>knee</u> • gee/
	gah • <u>zyeh</u> • tih
I'd like…	**Дайте…**
	<u>die</u> • tee…
candy	**конфеты**
	kohn • <u>feh</u> • tih
chewing gum	**жевательную резинку**
	zhih • <u>vah</u> • teel • 'noo • yoo ree • <u>zeen</u> • koo
a chocolate bar	**плитку шоколада**
	<u>pleet</u> • koo shoh • koh • <u>lah</u> • dah

cigars	**сигары**
	see • gah • rih
a pack/carton of cigarettes	**пачку/блок сигарет**
	pahch • koo/blok see • gah • ryet
a lighter	**зажигалку**
	zah • zhih • gahl • koo
a magazine	**журнал**
	zhoor • nahl
matches	**спички**
	speech • kee
a newspaper	**газету**
	gah • zyeh • too
a pen	**ручку**
	rooch • koo
a road/town map of...	**карту автомобильных дорог/города...**
	kahr • too ahf • tah • mah • beel' • nihkh dah • rok/goh • rah • dah...
stamps	**марки**
	mahr • kee

PHOTOGRAPHY

I'm looking for...camera.	**Я ищу...фотоаппарат.**
	yah ee • shchoo... fah • tah • ah • pah • raht
an automatic	**автоматический**
	ahf • tah • mah • tee • chees • keey
a digital	**цифровой**
	tsihf • rah • voy
a disposable	**одноразовый**
	ahd • nah • rah • zah • viy
I'd like...	**Я хотел m /хотела f бы...**
	yah khah • tyel/khah • tyeh • lah bih...
a battery	**батарейку**
	bah • tah • ryey • koo

digital prints	**цифровые фотографии**
	tsihf • rah • <u>vih</u> • yeh fah • tah • <u>grah</u> • fee • ee
a memory card	**карту памяти**
	<u>kahr</u> • too <u>pah</u> • myah • tee
Can I print digital photos here?	**Здесь можно напечатать цифровые фотографии?**
	zdyes' <u>mozh</u> • nah nah • pee • <u>chah</u> • taht' tsihf • rah • <u>vih</u> • yeh fah • tah • <u>grah</u> • fee • ee

SOUVENIRS

amber	**янтарь**
	yeen • <u>tahr'</u>
balalaika (traditional musical instrument)	**балалайка**
	bah • lah • <u>lie</u> • ka
caviar	**икра**
	eek • <u>rah</u>
chess set	**шахматы**
	<u>shahkh</u> • mah • tih
fur hat	**меховая шапка**
	mee • khah • <u>vah</u> • yah <u>shahp</u> • kah
key ring	**брелок**
	bree • <u>lok</u>

nesting doll	**матрёшка**
	maht • ryosh • kah
Palekh box	**палехская шкатулка**
	pah • leekh • skah • yah shkah • tool • kah
postcard	**открытка**
	aht • kriht • kah
poster	**плакат**
	plah • kaht
rug from Tekin	**текинский ковер**
	tee • keen • skeey kah • vyor
samovar	**самовар**
	sah • mah • vahr
shawl	**шаль**
	shahl'
souvenir guide	**альбом**
	ahl' • bom
tea towel	**кухонное полотенце**
	koo • khahn • nah • yeh pah • lah • tyen • tseh
T-shirt	**майка**
	mie • kah
wood carving	**резьба по дереву**
	reez' • bah pah dyeh • ree • voo

wooden spoons	**деревянные ложки**
	dee • ree • vyan • nih • yeh losh • kee
Can I see this/ that?	**Можно посмотреть это/вон то?**
	mozh • nah pah • smah • tryet' eh • tah/ von toh
It's the one in the window/display case.	**Это то, что на витрине/стеллаже.**
	eh • tah toh shtoh nah vee • tree • nyeh/ stee • lah • zheh
I'd like…	**Я хотел m /хотела f бы…**
	yah khah • tyel/khah • tyeh • lah bih…
a battery	**батарейку**
	bah • tah • ryey • koo
a bracelet	**браслет**
	brahs • lyet
a brooch	**брошь**
	brosh
earrings	**серьги**
	syer' • gee
a necklace	**ожерелье**
	ah • zhih • ryel' • yeh
a ring	**кольцо**
	kal' • tsoh
a watch	**часы**
	chah • sih
copper	**медь**
	myet'
crystal (quartz)	**хрусталь**
	khroo • stahl'
diamond	**брильянт**
	breel' • yahnt
white/yellow gold	**белое/желтое золото**
	byeh • lah • yhe/zhol • tah • yeh zoh • lah • tah
pearl	**жемчуг**
	zhem • chook

pewter	**олово**
	oh • lah • vah
platinum	**платину**
	plah • tee • noo
sterling silver	**чистое серебро**
	chees • tah • yeh see • reeb • roh
Is this real?	**Это настоящее?**
	eh • tah nah • stah • yah • shchee • yeh
Can you engrave it?	**Вы можете сделать на нем гравировку?**
	vih moh • zhih • tee zdyeh • laht' nah nyom grah • vee • rof • koo

---

In the past shops called **Подарки** *pah • dahr • kee*
(gifts) were the traditional places for Russians to buy
souvenirs. There are similar departments in almost every
department store nowadays. Worth a visit, these stores
carry everything from crystal & jewelry to toiletries. Favorite
gifts for Russians are flowers, chocolate, wine, cognac
and crystal. Visitors take home matreshkas (nesting dolls),
lacquered wood boxes, scarves, jewelry, etc.

SPORT & LEISURE

NEED TO KNOW

When's the game?	**Во сколько игра?**
	vah skohl' • kah eeg • rah
Where's...?	**Где...?**
	gdyeh...
the beach	**пляж**
	plyahsh
the park	**парк**
	pahrk
the pool	**бассейн**
	bah • syehyn
Is it safe to swim/ dive here?	**Здесь не опасно плавать/нырять?**
	zdyehs' nee ah • pahs • nah plah • vaht'/ nih • ryaht'
Can I hire golf clubs?	**Я могу взять напрокат клюшки для гольфа?**
	yah mah • goo vzyaht' nah • prah • kaht klyoosh • kee dlyah gohl' • fah
How much per hour?	**Сколько стоит в час?**
	skohl' • kah stoh • eet f chahs
How far is it to...?	**Далеко до...отсюда?**
	dah • lee • koh dah... aht • syoo • dah
Can you show me on the map?	**Можете показать мне на карте?**
	moh • zhih • tyeh pah • kah • zaht' mnyeh nah kahr • tyeh

WATCHING SPORT

When's…?	**Когда…?** *kahg • dah…*
the baseball game	**бейсбольный матч** *beys • bohl' • niy mahtch*
the basketball game	**баскетбольный матч** *bahs • keed • bol' • niy mahtch*
the boxing match	**боксёрский матч** *bahk • syor • skeey mahtch*
the cricket game	**игра в крикет** *eeg • rah v kree • kyet*
the cycling race	**велогонка** *vyeh • lah • gon • kah*
the golf tournament	**турнир по гольфу** *toor • neer pah gol' • foo*
the soccer [football] game	**футбольный матч** *foot • bol' • niy mahtch*
the tennis match	**теннисный матч** *teh • nees • niy mahtch*
the volleyball game	**волейбольный матч** *vah • leey • bol' • niy mahtch*

Which teams are playing?	**Какие команды играют?**
	kah • kee • yeh kah • mahn • dih ee • grah • yoot
Where's…?	**Где…?**
	gdyeh…
the horse track	**ипподром**
	eep • pah • drom
the racetrack	**автодром**
	ahf • tah • drom
the stadium	**стадион**
	stah • dee • on
Where can I place a bet?	**Где я могу сделать ставку?**
	gdyeh yah mah • goo zdyeh • laht' stahf • koo

The most popular sports in Russia are ice hockey, skiing and skating in winter, and soccer, volleyball and horseback riding in summer. Water sports, especially swimming, are very popular all year round, as are hunting and fishing.
A turkish-style public bath (**баня** *bah • nyah*) is a very popular form of relaxation and a fun way to meet people.

PLAYING SPORT

Where's…?	**Где…?**
	gdyeh…
the golf course	**поле для гольфа**
	poh • lyeh dlyah gol' • fah
the gym	**спортзал**
	sport • zahl
the park	**парк**
	pahrk

the tennis courts	**теннисные корты**
	teh • nees • nih • yeh kor • tih
How much…?	**Сколько стоит…?**
	skohl' • kah stoh • eet…
per day	**в день**
	v dyen'
per hour	**в час**
	f chahs
per game	**за игру**
	zah eeg • roo
per round	**за круг**
	zah krook
Can I hire…?	**Я могу взять напрокат…?**
	yah mah • goo vzyaht' nah • prah • kaht…
golf clubs	**клюшки для гольфа**
	klyoosh • kee dlyah gohl' • fah
equipment	**снаряжение**
	snah • ree • zheh • nee • yeh
a racket	**ракетку**
	rah • kyet • koo

AT THE BEACH/POOL

Where's the beach/pool?	**Где пляж/бассейн?**
	gdyeh plyahsh/bah • seyn
Is there…?	**Здесь есть…?**
	zdyes' yest'…
a kiddie pool	**детский бассейн**
	dyets • keey bah • seyn
an indoor/outdoor pool	**закрытый/открытый бассейн**
	zah • krih • tiy/aht • krih • tiy bah • seyn
a lifeguard	**спасатель**
	spah • sah • teel'
Is it safe…?	**Здесь не опасно…?**
	zdyes' nee ah • pahs • nah…

to swim	**плавать**
	plah • vaht'
to dive	**нырять**
	nih • _ryat'_
for children	**для детей**
	dlyah dee • _tyey_
I want to hire…	**Я хочу взять напрокат…**
	yah khah • _choo_ vzyaht' nah • prah • _kaht_…
a deck chair	**шезлонг**
	shez • _lonk_
diving equipment	**водолазное снаряжение**
	voh•doh•_lahz_•noh•ye
	snah•rya•_zheh_•nee•ye
a jet-ski	**водный мотоцикл**
	vod • niy mah • tah • _tsihkl_
a motorboat	**моторную лодку**
	mah • _tor_ • noo • yoo lot • koo
a rowboat	**лодку**
	lot • koo
snorkeling equipment	**сняряжение для подводного плавания**
	snah•rya•_zheh_•nee•ye dlya
	pohd•_vohd_•navah plah•_vahn'ya_
I want to hire…	**Я хочу взять напрокат…**
	yah khah choo vzyaht' nah prah kaht…
a surfboard	**доску для серфинга**
	dahs • _koo_ dlyah _ser_ • feen • gah
a towel	**полотенце**
	pah • lah • _tyen_ • tseh
an umbrella	**зонт**
	zont
water skis	**водные лыжи**
	vod • nih • yeh lih • zhih
a windsurfer	**виндсерфер**
	vind • _syer_ • fehr

(i)

Although the Russian summer is short, it can be hot. During the warmer months, Russians head to local lakes and rivers to swim or to a number of popular resorts on the Black Sea. The tourist infrastructure that went into decline after the fall of the Soviet Union is gradually being updated and the Black Sea coast is becoming an appealing international vacation destination, especially the town of Sochi, host of the 2014 Winter Olympics.

WINTER SPORTS

A lift pass for a day/five days, please.	**Абонемент на подъемник на день/пять дней, пожалуйста.** ah • bah • nee • _ment_ nah pahd' • _yom_ • neek nah dyen'/pyaht' dnyey pah • _zhahl_ • stah
I want to hire…	**Я хотел m/хотела f бы взять напрокат…** yah khah • _tyel_/khah • tyeh • _lah_ bih vzyaht' nah • prah • _kaht_…
boots	**лыжные ботинки** _lihzh_ • nih • ee bah • _teen_ • kee
a helmet	**шлем** shlyem
poles	**лыжные палки** _lihzh_ • nih • ee _pahl_ • kee
skis	**лыжи** _lih_ • zhih
a snowboard	**сноуборд** _snoh_ • oo • bort
snowshoes	**снегоступы** snee • gah • _stoo_ • pih

These are too big/small.	**Это слишком велико/мало.**
	eh • tah <u>sleesh</u> • kahm vee • lee • <u>koh</u>/ mah • loh
Are there lessons?	**Есть уроки?**
	yest' oo • <u>roh</u> • kee
I'm a beginner.	**Я новичок.**
	ya noh • vee • <u>chohck</u>
I'm experienced.	**Я опытный лыжник.**
	yah <u>oh</u> • piht • niy <u>lizh</u> • neek
A trail [piste] map, please.	**Схему трассы, пожалуйста.**
	<u>skhyeh</u> • moo<u>trah</u> • sih pah • <u>zhahl</u> • stah

Skiing, particularly cross-country, is a popular sport
in Russia. Moscow even has two downhill ski slopes,
one in Krylatskoye and one in Bitsevsky Park. Adventurous
tourists can find guided skiing adventures in remote areas
of the taiga, while others can rent skis in city parks, such
as Moscow's Sokolniki and Bitsevsky. Skating is also very
popular. There are ice rinks in large parks and squares.
Russians also enjoy traditional horse-drawn sleighs.

YOU MAY SEE...

ПОДЪЁМНИК	drag lift
phad • *yom* • neek	
ВАГОН ПОДВЕСНОЙ ДОРОГИ	cable car
vah • *gon* pahd • vees • *noy* dah • *roh* • gee	
ПОДВЕСНОЙ ПОДЪЁМНИК	chair lift
pahd • vees • *noy* phad • *yom* • neek	
ДЛЯ НАЧИНАЮЩИХ	novice
dlyah nah • chee • *nah* • yoo • shcheekh	
ДЛЯ ОПЫТНЫХ	intermediate
dlyah *oh* • piht • nihkh	
ДЛЯ МАСТЕРОВ	expert
dlyah mahs • tee • *rof*	
ТРАССА ЗАКРЫТА	trail [piste]
trah • sah zah • *krih* • tah	closed

OUT IN THE COUNTRY

I'd like a map of…	**Я хотел m /хотела f бы карту...**
	yah khah • *tyel*/khah • *tyeh* • lah bih
	kahr • too…
this region	**этого района**
	eh • tah • vah rah • *yoh* • nah
the walking routes	**пешеходных маршрутов**
	pee • shee • *khod* • nihkh
	mahrsh • *roo* • tahf
the bike routes	**велосипедных маршрутов**
	vee • lah • see • *pyed* • nihkh
	mahrsh • *roo* • tahf
the trails	**трасс**
	trahs

Is it easy/difficult?	**Он легкий/сложный?**
	on lyokh • keey/slozh • niy
Is it far/steep?	**Он длинный/крутой?**
	on dleen • niy/kroo • toy
How far is it to…?	**Какое расстояние до…?**
	kah • koh • yeh rah • stah • yah • nee • yeh dah…
Can you show me on the map?	**Можете показать мне на карте?**
	moh • zhih • tee pah • kah • zaht' mnyeh nah kahr • tyeh
I'm lost.	**Я заблудился** *m/***заблудилась** *f* .
	yah zah • bloo • deel • syah/ zah • bloo • dee • lahs'
Where's…?	**Где…?**
	gdyeh…
the bridge	**мост**
	most
the cave	**пещера**
	pee • shchyeh • rah
the cliff	**обрыв**
	ah • brihf
the farm	**ферма**
	fyer • mah
the field	**поле**
	poh • leh
the forest	**лес**
	lyes
the hill	**холм**
	khohlm
the lake	**озеро**
	oh • zee • rah
the mountain	**гора**
	gah • rah
the nature preserve	**заповедник**
	zah • pah • vyed • neek

the overlook	**смотровая площадка**
	smah • trah • <u>vah</u> • yah plah • <u>shchaht</u> • kah
the park	**парк**
	pahrk
the path	**тропинка**
	trah • <u>peen</u> • kah
the peak	**пик**
	peek
the picnic area	**площадка для пикника**
	plah • <u>shchaht</u> • kah dlyah peek • nee • <u>kah</u>
the pond	**пруд**
	prood
the river	**река**
	ree • <u>kah</u>
the sea	**море**
	<u>moh</u> • ryeh
the thermal spring	**минеральный источник**
	mee • nee • <u>rahl'</u> • nihy ees • <u>toch</u> • neek
the stream	**течение**
	tye • <u>chye</u> • nyeh
the valley	**долина**
	dah • <u>lee</u> • nah
the vineyard	**виноградник**
	vee • noh • <u>grahd</u> • nik
the waterfall	**водопад**
	vah • dah • <u>paht</u>

For Asking Directions, see page 65.

TRAVELING WITH CHILDREN

NEED TO KNOW

Is there a discount for children?	**Есть скидка для детей?** *yest' skeet • kah dlyah dee • tyey*
Can you recommend a babysitter?	**Вы можете порекомендовать няню?** *vih moh • zhih • tee pah • ree • kah • men • dah • vaht' nyah • nyoo*
Could we have a child's seat/ highchair?	**Можно детский/высокий стульчик?** *mozh • nah dyets • keey/ vih • soh • keey stool' • cheek*
Where can I change the baby?	**Где можно переодеть ребёнка?** *gdyeh mozh • nah pee • ree • ah • dyet' ree • byon • kah*

OUT & ABOUT

Can you recommend something for the kids?	**Можете порекомендовать что-нибудь для детей?** *moh • zhih • tee pah • ree • kah • meen • dah • vaht' shtoh • nee • boot' dlyah dee • tyey*
Where's...?	**Где...?** *gdyeh...*
the amusement park	**парк с аттракционононами** *pahrk s aht • rahk • tsih • oh • nah • mee*

the arcade	**зал аттракционов**
	zahl aht • rahk • tsih • oh • nahf
the kiddie pool	**детский бассейн**
	dyets • keey bah • seyn
the park	**парк**
	pahrk
the playground	**детская площадка**
	dyets • kah • yah plah • shchaht • kah
the zoo	**зоопарк**
	zah • ah • pahrk
Are kids allowed?	**Детям можно?**
	dyeh • tyam mozh • nah
Is it safe for kids?	**Здесь неопасно для детей?**
	zdyes' nee • ah • pahs • nah dlyah dee • tyey
Is it suitable for…year olds?	**Это подходит для…летних?**
	eh • tah paht • khoh • deet dlyah… let • neekh

For Numbers, see page 18.

BABY ESSENTIALS

Do you have…?	**У Вас есть…?**
	oo vahs yest'…
a baby bottle	**детская бутылочка**
	dyets • kah • yah boo • tih • lahch • kah
baby food	**детское питание**
	deht • skoh • ye pee • tah • nee • yeh
baby wipes	**гигиенические салфетки**
	gee • gee • ee • nee • chees • kee • yeh
	sahl • fyet • kee
a car seat	**детское сиденье**
	dyets • kah • yeh see • dyen' • yeh
a children's	**меню/порции для детей**
menu/portion	*mee • nyoo/por • tsih • ee dlyah dee • tyey*
a child's seat/	**детский/высокий стульчик**
highchair	*dyets • keey/vih • soh • keey stool' • cheek*
a crib/cot	**колыбель/детская кроватка**
	kah • lih • byel'/dyets • kah • yah
	krah • vaht • kah
diapers [nappies]	**подгузники**
	pahd • gooz • nee • kee
formula	**молочная смесь**
	mah • loch • nah • yah smyes'

a pacifier [dummy]	**соска**
	sos • kah
a playpen	**манеж**
	mah • _nyesh_
a stroller	**прогулочная коляска**
[pushchair]	prah • _goo_ • lahch • nah • yah
	kah • _lyas_ • kah
Can I breastfeed	**Я могу здесь покормить грудью**
the baby here?	**ребёнка?**
	yah mah • _goo_ zdyes' pah • kahr • _meet'_
	grood' • yoo ree • _byon_ • kah
Where can	**Где можно покормить/переодеть**
I breastfeed/	**ребёнка?**
change the baby?	gdyeh _mozh_ • nah pah • kahr • _meet'_/
	pee • ree • ah • _dyet'_ ree • _byon_ • kah

For Dining with Children, see page 176.

YOU MAY HEAR…

Какой хорошенький! *m* /**Какая хорошенькая** *f* !	How cute!
kah • koy khah • roh • shen' • keey/ kah • kah • yah	
khah • roh • shihn' • kah • yah	
Как его/её зовут?	What's his/her name?
kak yee • voh/yee • yoh zah • voot	
Сколько ему/ей лет?	How old is he/ she?
skol' • kah ee • moo/yey lyet	

BABYSITTING

Can you recommend a babysitter?	**Вы можете порекомендовать няню?**
	vih moh • zhih • tee pah • ree • kah • meen • dah • vaht' nyah • nyoo
What's the charge?	**Сколько стоит?**
	skol' • kah stoh • eet
We'll be back by…	**Мы вернёмся к…**
	mih veer • nyom • syah k…
I can be reached at…	**Со мной можно связаться…**
	sah mnoy mozh • nah svee • zah • tsah…

HEALTH & SAFETY

EMERGENCIES

Help!	**Помогите!**
	pah • mah • <u>gee</u> • tee
Go away!	**Идите отсюда!**
	ee • <u>dee</u> • tee aht • <u>syoo</u> • dah
Stop, thief!	**Держите вора!**
	deer • <u>zhih</u> • tee <u>voh</u> • rah
Get a doctor!	**Вызовите врача!**
	<u>vih</u> • zah • vee • tee vrah • <u>chah</u>
Fire!	**Пожар!**
	pah • <u>zhahr</u>
I'm lost.	**Я заблудился** *m* /**заблудилась** *f.*
	yah zah • bloo • <u>deel</u> • syah/ zah • bloo • <u>dee</u> • lahs'
Help me, please.	**Помогите мне, пожалуйста.**
	pah • mah • <u>gee</u> • tee mnyeh pah • <u>zhahl</u> • stah

In an emergency, dial:
02 for the police
01 for the fire brigade
03 for the ambulance

POLICE

NEED TO KNOW

Call the police!	**Вызовите милицию!** _vih_ • zah • vee • tee mee • _lee_ • tsih • yoo
Where's the police station?	**Где отделение милиции?** gdyeh aht • dee • _lyeh_ • nee • yeh mee • _lee_ • tsih • ee
There has been an accident.	**Произошла авария.** prah • ee • zah • _shlah_ ah • _vah_ • ree • yah
My child is missing.	**У меня пропал ребёнок.** oo mee • _nyah_ prah • _pahl_ ree • _byoh_ • nahk
I need an interpreter.	**Мне нужен переводчик.** mnyeh _noo_ • zhehn pee • ree • _vot_ • cheek
I need to contact my lawyer.	**Мне нужно связаться с моим адвокатом.** mnyeh _noozh_ • nah svyah • _zah_ • tsah s mah • _eem_ ahd • vah • _kah_ • tahm
I need to make a phone call.	**Мне нужно позвонить.** mnyeh _noozh_ • nah pah • zvah • _neet'_
I'm innocent.	**Я невиновен.** yah nee • vee • _noh_ • veen

CRIME & LOST PROPERTY

YOU MAY HEAR...

Заполните бланк. zah • *pol* • nee • tyeh blahnk	Please fill out this form.
Ваши документы, пожалуйста. *vah* • shih dah • koo • *myen* • tih pah • *zhahl* • stah	Your identification, please.
Где/Когда это произошло? gdyeh/kahg • *dah eh* • tah prah • ee • zah • *shloh*	When/Where did it happen?
Как он/она выглядит? kahk on/ah • *nah vih* • glyah • deet	What does he/she look like?

I want to report...	**Я хочу заявить о...** yah khah • *chyoo* zah • ee • *veet'* ah...
a mugging	**ограблении** ah • grahb • *lyeh* • nee • ee
a rape	**изнасиловании** eez • nah • *see* • lah • vah • nee • ee
a theft	**краже** *krah* • zheh
I've been mugged.	**Меня ограбили.** meh • *nya* oh • *grah* • bee • lee
I've been robbed.	**Меня ограбили.** mee • *nyah* ah • *grah* • bee • lee
I've lost my...	**Я потерял m /потеряла f...** yah pah • tee • *ryahl*/pah • tee • *ryah* • lah...
My...has been stolen.	**У меня украли...** oo mee • *nyah* oo • *krah* • lee...
backpack	**рюкзак** ryoog • *zahk*

bicycle	**велосипед**
	vee • lah • see • pyet
camera	**фотоаппарат**
	fah • tah • ah • pah • raht
car	**машину**
	mah • shih • noo
computer	**компьютер**
	kahm • pyoo • ter
credit card	**кредитную карточку**
	kree • deet • noo • yoo kahr • tahch • koo
jewelry	**драгоценности**
	drah • gah • tseh • nahs • tee
money	**деньги**
	dyen' • gee
passport	**паспорт**
	pahs • pahrt
purse [handbag]	**сумочку**
	soo • mach • koo
traveler's cheques	**дорожные чеки**
	dah • rozh • nih • ee cheh • kee
wallet	**бумажник**
	boo • mahzh • neek
I need a police report.	**Мне нужно обратиться в полицию.**
	mneh nuzh • noh oh • brah • tee t' • sya v poh • lee • tsih • yoo
Where is the British/ American/Irish embassy?	**Где находится британское/ американское/ирландское консульство?**
	gdyeh nah • khoh • deet • sya bree • tahn • sko • ye/ ah • meh • ree • kahn • sko • ye/ eer • lahnd • sko • ye kon • sool' • stvoh

HEALTH

NEED TO KNOW

I'm sick [ill].	**Я заболел** m **/заболела** f.
	yah zah • bah • lyel/zah • bah • lyeh • lah
I need an English-speaking doctor.	**Мне нужен англоговорящий врач.**
	mnyeh noo • zhen
	ahn • glah • gah • vah • ryah • shcheey vrahch
It hurts here.	**Мне больно вот здесь.**
	mnyeh bohl' • nah voht zdyehs'
I have a stomachache.	**У меня болит живот.**
	oo mee • nyah bah • leet zhih • voht

FINDING A DOCTOR

Can you recommend a doctor/dentist?	**Можете порекомендовать врача/дантиста?**
	moh • zhih • tee
	pah • ree • kah • meen • dah • vaht' vrah • chah/dahn • tees • tah
Could the doctor come to see me here?	**Не мог бы врач прийти осмотреть меня здесь?**
	nee mog bih vrahch pree • tee ah • smah • tryet' mee • nyah zdyes'
I need an English-speaking doctor.	**Мне нужен англоговорящий врач.**
	mnyeh noo • zhihn ahn • glah • gah • vah • ryah • shcheey vrahch
What are the office hours?	**Какие часы работы?**
	kah • kee • yeh chah • sih rah • boh • tih

Can I make an appointment...?	**Можно записаться к врачу на прием...?**
	mozh • nah zah • pee • _sah_ • tsah k vrah • _choo_ nah pree • _yom_...
for today	**на сегодня**
	nah see • _vod_ • nyah
for tomorrow	**на завтра**
	nah _zahf_ • trah
as soon as possible	**как можно скорее**
	kahk _mozh_ • nah skah • _ryeh_ • yeh
It's urgent.	**Это срочно.**
	_eh_ • tah _sroch_ • nah

SYMPTOMS

I'm...	**У меня...**
	oo mee • _nyah_...
bleeding	**кровотечение**
	krah • vah • tee • _cheh_ • nee • yeh
constipated	**запор**
	zah • _por_
dizzy	**кружится голова**
	kroo • zhih • tsah gah • lah • _vah_
I'm nauseous/ vomiting.	**Меня подташнивает/тошнит.**
	mee • _nyah_ paht • _tahsh_ • nee • vah • eet/ tahsh • _neet_
It hurts here.	**Мне больно вот здесь.**
	mnyeh _bohl'_ • nah vaht zdyes'
I have...	**У меня...**
	oo mee • _nyah_...
an allergic reaction	**аллергическая реакция**
	ah • leer • _gee_ • chees • kah • yah ree • _ahk_ • tsih • yah
a chest pain	**боли в груди**
	boh • lee v groo • _dee_
cramps	**спазмы**
	spah • zmih

diarrhea	**понос** *pah•nohs*
an earache	**болит ухо** *bah•leet oo•khah*
a fever	**жар** *zhahr*
pain	**боли** *boh•lee*
a rash	**сыпь** *sihp'*
a sprain	**растяжение** *rahs•tee•zheh•nee•yeh*
some swelling	**опухоль** *oh•poo•khahl'*
a sore throat	**болит горло** *boh•leet gohr•loh*
a stomachache	**болит живот** *bah•leet zhih•voht*
sunstroke	**солнечный удар** *sol•neech•niy oo•dahr*
I've been sick [ill] for...days.	**Я болею...дней.** *yah bah•lyeh•yoo...dnyey*

For Numbers, see page 18.

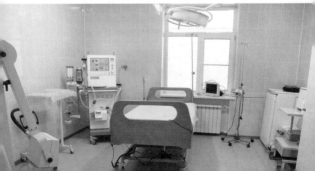

CONDITIONS

I'm...	**У меня...**
	oo mee • nyah...
anemic	**анемия**
	ah • nee • mee • yah
asthmatic	**астма**
	ahst • mah
diabetic	**диабет**
	dee • ah • byet
epileptic	**эпилепсия**
	ehpee • lehp • see • ya
I'm allergic to antibiotics/ penicillin.	**У меня аллергия на антибиотики/ пенициллин.**
	oo mee • nyah ah • leer • gee • yah nah ahn • tee • bee • oh • tee • kee/ pee • nee • tsih • leen
I have arthritis/ high/low blood pressure.	**У меня артрит/высокое/низкое давление.**
	oo mee • nyah ahrt • reet/ vih • soh • kah • ye/nees • kah • yeh dahv • lyeh • nee • yeh
I have a heart condition.	**У меня больное сердце.**
	oo mee • nyah bahl' • noh • yeh ser • tseh
I'm on...	**Я принимаю...**
	yah pree • nee • mah • yoo...

For Dietary Requirements, see page 175.

YOU MAY HEAR...

Что случилось?
shtoh sloo•chee•lahs'

What's wrong?

Где болит?
gdyeh bah•leet

Where does it hurt?

Вы принимаете другое лекарство?
*vih pree•nee•mah•ee•tee
droo•goh•yeh lee•kahr•stvah*

Are you taking any other medication?

Аллергия на что-нибудь?
*ah•leer•gee•yah
nah shtoh•nee•boot'*

Are you allergic to anything?

Откройте рот.
aht•kroy•tee rot

Open your mouth.

Дышите глубоко.
dih•shih•tee gloo•bah•koh

Breathe deeply.

Покашляйте.
poh•kahsch•lyai•tye

Cough, please.

Обратитесь в больницу.
obh•rah•tee•tehs' v bohl'•nee•tsoo

Go to the hospital.

TREATMENT

Do I need a prescription/ medicine?
Can you prescribe a generic drug [unbranded medication]?

У меня нет рецепта/лекарства?
oo meh•nya neht reh•tsehp•tah/ leh•kahr•stvah

Вы можете прописать непатентованный препарат [без марочного названия]?
vih moh•zheh•teh proh•pee•saht' neh•pah•tehn•toh•vah•niy preh•pah•raht [bez naz•vah•neeya]

Where can I get it?	**Где можно его приобрести?**
	gdyeh mozh • noh ye • voh
	pree • ohb • rehs • tee

For Pharmacy, see page 158.

HOSPITAL

Please notify my family.	**Пожалуйста, сообщите моей семье.**
	pah • zhahl • stah sah • ahb • shchee • tee
	mah • yey seem' • yeh
I'm in pain.	**У меня боли.**
	oo mee • nyah boh • lee
I need a doctor/ nurse.	**Мне нужен врач/нужна медсестра.**
	mnyeh noo • zhin vrahch/noozh • nah
	myet • sees • trah
When are visiting hours?	**Когда часы посещений?**
	kahg • dah chah • sih
	pah • see • shcheh • neey
I'm visiting…	**Я навещаю…**
	yah nah • vee • shchah • yoo…

DENTIST

I've broken a tooth/ lost a filling.	**У меня сломался зуб/выпала пломба.**
	oo mee • nyah slah • mahl • syah zoop/
	vih • pah • lah plom • bah
I have a toothache.	**У меня болит зуб.**
	oo mee • nyah bah • leet zoop
Can you fix this denture?	**Вы можете починить этот протез?**
	vih moh • zhih • tee pah • chee • neet'
	eh • taht prah • tes

GYNECOLOGIST

I have menstrual cramps/a vaginal infection.	**У меня менструальные колики/ вагинальная инфекция.** *oo mee • nyah meen • stroo • ahl' • nih • ee koh • lee • kee/vah • gee • nahl' • nah • yah een • fyek • tsih • yah*
I missed my period.	**У меня не было менструации.** *oo mee • nyah nyeh • bih • lah meen • stroo • ah • tsih • ee*
I'm on the Pill.	**Я принимаю противозачаточные таблетки.** *yah pree • nee • mah • yoo prah • tee • vah • zah • chah • tahch • nih • ee tahb • lyet • kee*
I'm (...months) pregnant.	**Я беременна (на...месяце).** *ya beh • reh • meh • nah (nah ... meh • sya • tse)*
I'm (not) pregnant.	**Я (не) беременна.** *yah (nee) bee • ryeh • mee • nah*
I haven't had my period for...months.	**У меня нет менструации уже... месяца.** *oo mee • nyah nyet meen • stroo • ah • tsih • ee oo • zheh...myeh • see • tsah*

OPTICIAN

I've lost…	**Я потерял m /потеряла f…** *yah pah • tee • ryahl/pah • tee • ryah • lah…*
a contact lens	**контактную линзу** *kahn • tahkt • noo • yoo leen • zoo*
my glasses	**мои очки** *mah • ee ahch • kee*
a lens	**линзу** *leen • zoo*

PAYMENT & INSURANCE

How much?	**Сколько?** *skol' • kah*
Can I pay by credit card?	**Можно платить кредитной карточкой?** *mozh • nah plah • teet' kree • deet • nie kahr • tahch • kie*
I have insurance.	**У меня есть страховка.** *oo mee • nyah yest' strah • khof • kah*
Can I have a receipt for my insurance?	**Можете дать мне квитанцию для моей страховки?** *moh • zhih • tee daht' mnyeh kvee • tahn • tsih • yoo dlyah mah • yey strah • khof • kee*

For Money, see page 28.

PHARMACY

NEED TO KNOW

Where's the nearest pharmacy?	**Где ближайшая аптека?** *gdyeh blee•zhie•shah•yah ahp•tyeh•kah*
What time does it open/close?	**Во сколько аптека открывается/ закрывается?** *vah skol'•kah ahp•tyeh•kah aht•krih•vah•ee•tsah/ zah•krih•vah•ee•tsah*
What would you recommend for...?	**Что порекомендуете от...?** *shtoh pah•ree•kah•meen•doo•ee•tee aht...*
How much should I take?	**Сколько нужно принимать?** *skol'•kah noozh•nah pree•nee•maht'*
Can you fill [make up] this prescription for me?	**Вы можете приготовить это лекарство?** *vih moh•zhih•tee pree•gah•toh•veet'•eh•tah lee•kahr•stvah*
I'm allergic to...	**У меня аллергия на...** *oo mee•nyah ah•leer•gee•yah nah...*

(i)

In Russia, a wide range of medication is available without a prescription. **Аптека** *ahp • tyeh • kah* (a pharmacy) in Russia's larger cities is likely to carry many brand-name medications. Drugs are also available from kiosks, but it is best to obtain them from a pharmacy or private clinics and hospitals, such as the American Clinic in Moscow or the American Medical Center in St. Petersburg. As a foreigner, you will have to pay for treatment in state-run hospitals. Russian doctors in these facilities are not well paid, and it is customary to give them something to express your gratitude for their care, a box of chocolates or a bottle of wine, for example. Before leaving home, be sure that your insurance coverage is valid for treatment in Russia.

WHAT TO TAKE

How much do I take?	**Какая дозировка?** *kah • kah • ya doh • zee • rohv • kah*
How often?	**Как часто?** *kahk chahs • tah*
Is it suitable for children?	**Это можно детям?** *eh • tah mozh • nah dyeh • tyahm*
I'm taking…	**Я принимаю…** *yah pree • nee • mah • yoo…*
Are there side effects?	**Есть побочные эффекты?** *yest' pah • boch • nih • ee ee • fyek • tih*
I'd like some medicine for…	**Мне нужно лекарство от…** *mnyeh noozh • nah lee • kahrs • tvah aht…*
a cold	**простуды** *prah • stoo • dih*
a cough	**кашля** *kahsh • lyah*

YOU MAY SEE...

ОДИН/ТРИ РАЗА В ДЕНЬ	once/three
ah • deen/tree rah • zah v dyen'	times a day
ТАБЛЕТКИ	tablets
tahb • lyet • kee	
КАПЛИ	drops
kahp • lee	
ДО/ПОСЛЕ/ВО ВРЕМЯ ЕДЫ	before/after/with
doh/pos • lee/vah vryeh • myah yeh • dih	meals
НА ПУСТОЙ ЖЕЛУДОК (НАТОЩАК)	on an empty
nah poos • toy zhih • loo • dahk (nah • tah • shchahk)	stomach
ТОЛЬКО ДЛЯ НАРУЖНОГО ПРИМЕНЕНИЯ	for external use only
tol' • kah dlyah nah • roozh • nah • vah pree • mee • nyeh • nee • yah	

diarrhea	**поноса**
	pah • noh • sah
a headache	**головной боли**
	goh • lohv • noi boh • lee

insect bites	**укусов насекомых**
	oo • koo • sahf nah • see • koh • mihkh
motion [travel] sickness	**морской болезни**
	mahr • skoy bah • lyez • nee
a sore throat	**воспаления горла**
	vahs • pah • lyeh • nee • yah gor • lah
sunburn	**солнечного ожёга**
	sol • neech • nah • vah ah • zhoh • gah
a toothache	**зубной боли**
	zoob • noi boh • lee
an upset stomach	**расстройства желудка**
	rahs • troy • stvah zhih • loot • kah

BASIC SUPPLIES

I'd like…	**Я хотел m/хотела f бы…**
	yah khah • tyel/khah • tyeh • lah bih…
acetaminophen [paracetamol]	**парацетамол**
	pah • rah • tsih • tah • mol
antiseptic cream	**антисептическую мазь**
	ahn • tee • sep • tee • chees • koo • yoo mahz'
aspirin	**аспирин**
	ahs • pee • reen

bandages [plasters]	пластырь
	plahs • _tihr'_
a comb	расчёску
	rah • _shchos_ • _koo_
I'd like…	Я хотел m /хотела f бы…
	yah khah • _tyel_/_khah_ • _tyeh_ • _lah bih…_
condoms	презервативы
	pree • _zeer_ • _vah_ • _tee_ • _vih_
contact lens solution	раствор для контактных линз
	rahst • _vor dlyah kahn_ • _tahkt_ • _nihkh leens_
deodorant	дезодорант
	dee • _zah_ • _dah_ • _rahnt_
a hairbrush	щётку для волос
	shchot • _koo dlyah vah_ • _los_
hair spray	лак для волос
	lahk dlyah vah • _los_
ibuprofen	ибупрофен
	_ee_ • _boo_ • _prah_ • _fyen_
insect repellent	репеллент
	ree • _pee_ • _lyent_
lotion	лосьон
	lohs' _yohn_
a nail file	пилочку для ногтей
	pee • _lahch_ • _koo dlyah nahk_ • _tyey_

a (disposable) razor	**(одноразовую) бритву**
	(ahd • nah • rah • zah • voo • yoo) <u>breet</u> • voo
razor blades	**лезвия**
	lyez • vee • yah
sanitary napkins [towels]	**гигиенические салфетки**
	gee • gee • ee • <u>nee</u> • chees • kee • yeh sahl • <u>fyet</u> • kee
shampoo/ conditioner	**шампунь/кондиционер**
	shahm • <u>poon'</u>/kahn • dee • tsih • ah • <u>nyer</u>
soap	**мыло**
	<u>mih</u> • lah
sunscreen	**крем для загара**
	kryem dlyah zah • <u>gah</u> • rah
tampons	**тампоны**
	tahm • <u>poh</u> • nih
tissues	**бумажные салфетки**
	boo • <u>mahzh</u> • nih • ee sahl • <u>fet</u> • kee
toilet paper	**туалетную бумагу**
	too • ah • <u>lyet</u> • noo • yoo boo • <u>mah</u> • goo
a toothbrush	**зубную щетку**
	zoob • <u>noo</u> • yoo <u>shchot</u> • koo
toothpaste	**зубную пасту**
	zoob • <u>noo</u> • yoo <u>pahs</u> • too

For Baby Essentials, see page 141.

CHILD HEALTH & EMERGENCY

Can you recommend a pediatrician?	**Можете порекомендовать педиатра?**
	<u>moh</u> • zhih • tee pah • ree • kah • meen • dah • <u>vaht'</u> pee • <u>dee</u> • aht • rah
My child is allergic to…	**У моего ребёнка аллергия на…**
	oo mah • ee • <u>voh</u> ree • <u>byon</u> • kah ah • leer • <u>gee</u> • yah nah…

My child is missing.	**У меня пропал ребёнок.**
	oo mee • nyah prah • pahl ree • byoh • nahk
Have you seen a boy/girl?	**Вы видели мальчика/девочку?**
	vih vee • dee • lee mahl' • chee • kah/ dyeh • vahch • koo

For Police, see page 147.

DISABLED TRAVELERS

NEED TO KNOW

Is there...?	**Есть...?**
	yest'...
access for the disabled	**условия для инвалидов**
	oos • loh • vee • yah dlyah een • vah • lee • dahf
a wheelchair ramp	**пандус для инвалидного кресла**
	pahn • doos dlyah een • vah • leed • nah • vah kryes • lah
a disabled-accessible toilet	**туалет с условиями для инвалидов**
	too • ah • lyet s oos • loh • vee • yah • mee dlyah een • vah • lee • dahf
I need assistance.	**Мне нужна помощь.**
	mnyeh noozh • nah poh • mahshch
I need an elevator [lift].	**Мне нужен лифт.**
	mnyeh noo • zhehn left
I need a ground-floor room.	**Мне нужен номер на первом этаже.**
	mnyeh noo • zhehn noh • meer nah pyer • vahm eh • tah • zheh

ASKING FOR ASSISTANCE

I'm disabled.	**Я инвалид.** yah een • vah • _leet_
I'm deaf.	**Я глухой** m /**глухая** f. yah gloo • _khoy_/gloo • _khah_ • yah
I'm visually/ hearing impaired.	**У меня плохое зрение/слух.** oo mee • _nyah_ plah • _khoh_ • yeh _zryeh_ • nee • yeh/slookh
I'm unable to walk far/use the stairs.	**Я не могу ходить далеко/ пользоваться лестницей.** yah nee mah • _goo_ khah • _deet'_ dah • _lee_ • koh/_pol'_ • zah • tsah _lyes_ • nee • tsey
Can I bring my wheelchair?	**Я могу привезти своё инвалидное кресло?** yah mah • _goo_ pree • vees • tee _svah_ • yoh een • vah • _leed_ nah • yeh kres • lah
Are guide dogs permitted?	**Сюда допускаются собаки-поводыри?** syoo • _dah_ dah • poos • _kah_ • yoo • tsah sah • _bah_ • kee pah • vah • dih • _ree_
Help me, please.	**Помогите мне, пожалуйста.** pah • mah • _gee_ • tee mnyeh pah • _zhahl_ • stah
Please open/hold the door.	**Пожалуйста, откройте/придержите дверь.** pah • _zhahl_ • stah aht • _kroy_ • tee/ pree • deer • _zhih_ • tee dvyer'

For Emergencies, see page 146.

FOOD & DRINK

EATING OUT

NEED TO KNOW

Can you recommend a good restaurant/bar?	**Можете посоветовать хороший ресторан/бар?**
	moh • zhih • tee pah • sah • vyeh • tah • vaht' khah • roh • shiy ree • stah • rahn/bahr
Is there a traditional Russian/an inexpensive restaurant near here?	**Здесь есть традиционный русский/недорогой ресторан поблизости?**
	zdyes' yest' trah • dee • tsih • on • niy roos • keey/nee • dah • rah • goy ree • stah • rahn pah • blee • zahs • tee
A table for…, please.	**Столик на…, пожалуйста.**
	stoh • leek nah…pah • zhahl • stah
Could we sit…?	**Можно нам сесть…?**
	mozh • nah nahm syehst'…
here/there	**здесь/там**
	zdyehs'/tahm
outside	**на улице**
	nah oo • lee • tseh
in a non-smoking area	**где не курят**
	gdyeh nee koo • ryaht
I'm waiting for someone.	**Я кое-кого жду.**
	yah koh • ee kah • voh zhdoo
Where are the toilets?	**Где туалет?**
	gdyeh too • ah • lyeht
A menu, please.	**Меню, пожалуйста.**
	mee • nyoo pah • zhahl • stah
What do you recommend?	**Что вы посоветуете?**
	shtoh vih pah • sah • vyeh • too • ee • tee

I'd like...	**Я хотел m /хотела f бы...**
	yah khah • _tyel_/khah • _tyeh_ • lah bih...
Some more..., please.	**Можно ещё..., пожалуйста.**
	mozh • nah ee • _shchoh_...
	pah • _zhahl_ • stah
Enjoy your meal!	**Приятного аппетита!**
	pree • _yaht_ • nah • vah
	ah • pee • _tee_ • tah
The check [bill], please.	**Счёт, пожалуйста.**
	shchoht pah • _zhahl_ • stah
Is service included?	**Счёт включает обслуживание?**
	shchot fklyoo • _chah_ • eet
	ahp • _sloo_ • zhih • vah • nee • yeh
Can I pay by credit card?	**Можно платить кредитной карточкой?**
	mozh • nah plah • _teet'_ kree • _deet_ • noy
	kahr • tahch • kie
Can I have a receipt?	**Можно чек?**
	mozh • nah chek
Thank you!	**Спасибо!**
	spah • _see_ • bah

WHERE TO EAT

Can you recommend...?	**Вы можете порекомендовать...?**
	vih _moh_ • zhih • tee
	pah • _ree_ • kah • meen • dah • _vaht'_...
a restaurant	**ресторан**
	ree • stah • _rahn_
a bar	**бар**
	bahr
a cafe	**кафе**
	kah • _feh_

a fast-food place	**кафе быстрого обслуживания**
	kah • feh bihs • trah • vah
	ahp • sloo • zhih • vah • nee • yah
a cheap restaurant	**недорогой ресторан**
	neh • doh • roh • goy rehs • toh • rahn
an expensive restaurant	**дорогой ресторан**
	doh • roh • goy rehs • toh • rahn
a restaurant with a good view	**ресторан с хорошим видом из окна**
	rehs • toh • rahn s kho • roh • sheem
	vee • dohm eez ohk • nah
an authentic/ a non-touristy restaurant	**национальный/не туристический ресторан**
	nah • tsee • oh • nahl' niy/neh
	too • rees • tee • chehs • kiy
	reh • stoh • rahn
a blini bar	**блинную**
	bleen • noo • yoo

RESERVATIONS & PREFERENCES

I'd like to reserve a table…	**Я хотел** *m* **/хотела** *f* **бы заказать столик…**
	yah khah • tyel/khah • tyeh • lah bih
	zah • kah • zaht' stoh • leek…
for two	**на двоих**
	nah dvah • eekh
I'd like to reserve a table…	**Я хотел** *m* **/хотела** *f* **бы заказать столик…**
	yah khah • tyel/khah • tyeh • lah bih
	zah • kah • zaht' stoh • leek…
for this evening	**на сегодня на вечер**
	nah see • vod • nyah nah vyeh • cheer
for tomorrow at…	**на завтра на…**
	nah zahf • trah nah…

YOU MAY HEAR...

У вас заказан столик?
oo vahs zah • _kah_ • zahn <u>stoh</u> • leek

Do you have
a reservation?

Сколько?
skol' • kah

How many?

Для курящих или некурящих?
dlyah koo • _ryah_ • shcheekh ee • lee
nee • koo • _ryah_ • shcheekh

Smoking or non-
smoking?

Будете заказывать?
<u>boo</u> • dee • tee zah • _kah_ • zih • vaht''

Are you ready to
order?

Что вы желаете?
shtoh vih zhih • _lah_ • ee • tee

What would you
like?

**Я бы рекомендовал m /
рекомендовала f...**
yah bih ree • _kah_ • meen • dah • <u>vahl</u>/
ree • _kah_ • meen • dah • <u>vah</u> • lah

I recommend...

Приятного аппетита!
pree • <u>yaht</u> • nah • vah ah • pee • <u>tee</u> • tah

Enjoy your meal!

A table for two, please.	**Столик на двоих, пожалуйста.** <u>stoh</u> • leek nah dvah • <u>eekh</u> pah • <u>zhahl</u> • stah
We have a reservation.	**У нас заказ.** oo nahs zah • <u>kahs</u>
My name is...	**Меня зовут...** mee • <u>nyah</u> zah • <u>voot</u>...
Can we sit...?	**Можем мы сесть ...?** <u>moh</u> • zhehm mih sehst'
here/there	**здесь/там** zdyes'/tahm
outside	**снаружи** snah • <u>roo</u> • zhih

in a non-smoking area	**в некурящем зале** *v nye • koo • rya • shcheem zah • leh*
by the window	**возле окна** *voz • leh okh • nah*
in the shade	**в тени** *v teh • nee*
in the sun	**на солнце** *nah sohln • tseh*
Where is the restroom [toilet]?	**Где туалет?** *gdyeh too • ah • lyet*

HOW TO ORDER

Waiter!/Waitress!	**Официант!/Девушка!** *ah • fee • tsih • ahnt/dyeh • voosh • kah*
We're ready to order.	**Мы готовы сделать заказ.** *mih gah • toh • vih zdyeh • laht' zah • kahs*
May I see the wine list?	**Можно посмотреть карту вин?** *mozh • nah pah • smah • tryet' kahr • too veen*
I'd like…	**Я хотел m /хотела f бы…** *yah khah • tyel/khah • tyeh • lah bih…*
a bottle of…	**бутылку…** *boo • tihl • koo…*
a carafe of…	**графин…** *grah • feen…*
a glass of…	**бокал…** *bah • kahl…*
The menu, please.	**Меню, пожалуйста.** *mee • nyoo pah • zhahl • stah*
Do you have…?	**У вас есть…?** *oo vahs yest'…*
a menu in English	**меню на английском** *mee • nyoo nah ahn • gleeys • kahm*

YOU MAY SEE...

НАЦЕНКА	cover
nah • <u>tsen</u> • kah	charge
КОМПЛЕКСНЫЙ МЕНЮ	fixed-price menu
<u>kom</u> • plyeks • niy меню	
МЕНЮ ДНЯ	menu of the day
mee • <u>nyoo</u> dnyah	
ОБСЛУЖИВАНИЕ (НЕ) ВКЛЮЧЕНО	service (not)
ahp • <u>sloo</u> • zhih • vah • nee • yeh (nee)	included
fklyoo • chee • <u>noh</u>	
БЛЮДО ДНЯ	specials
<u>blyoo</u> • dah dnyah	

a fixed-price menu	**комплексное меню**	
	<u>kom</u> • pleeks • nah • yeh mee • <u>nyoo</u>	
a children's menu	**детское меню**	
	<u>dyets</u> • kah • yeh mee • <u>nyoo</u>	
What do you	**Что вы посоветуете?**	
recommend?	shtoh vih pah • sah • <u>vyeh</u> • too • ee • tee	
What's this?	**Что это?**	
	shtoh <u>eh</u> • tah	
What's in it?	**Что туда входит?**	
	shtoh too • <u>dah</u> fkhoh • deet	
Is it spicy?	**Это острое?**	
	<u>eh</u> • tah <u>os</u> • trah • yeh	
I'd like...	**Я хотел m /хотела f бы...**	
	yah khah • <u>tyel</u>/khah • <u>tyeh</u> • lah bih...	
More...please.	**Можно ещё...пожалуйста.**	
	<u>mozh</u> • nah yee • <u>shchoh</u>...pah • <u>zhahl</u> • stah	
With/Without...	**С/Без...**	
	s/byes...	

I can't have…	**Мне нельзя есть…**
	mnyeh neel' • zyah yest'…
rare	**с кровью**
	s krov' • yoo
medium	**средне прожаренный**
	sryed • nee prah • zhah • ree • niy
well-done	**хорошо прожаренный**
	khah • rah • shoh prah • zhah • ree • niy
It's to go [take away].	**Это с собой.**
	eh • tah s sah • boy

COOKING METHODS

baked	**печеный**
	pee • choh • niy
boiled	**варёный**
	vah • ryoh • niy
braised	**тушёный**
	too • shoh • niy
breaded	**панированный**
	pah • nee • roh • vah • niy
creamed	**со сливками**
	soh sleev • kah • mee
diced	**нарезанный мелкими кубиками**
	nah • ryeh • zah • niy myel • kee • mee
	koo • bee • kah • mee
filleted	**филе**
	fee • lyeh
fried	**жареный**
	zhah • ree • niy
grilled	**жареный на гриле**
	zhah • ree • niy nah gree • lee
poached	**отварной**
	aht • vahr • noy

roasted	**запечёный**
	zah • pee • <u>choh</u> • nih
sautéed	**соте**
	sah • <u>teh</u>
smoked	**копчёный**
	kahp • <u>choh</u> • niy
steamed	**паровой**
	pah • rah • <u>voy</u>
stewed	**тушёный**
	too • <u>shoh</u> • niy
stuffed	**фаршированный**
	fahr • shih • <u>roh</u> • vah • niy

DIETARY REQUIREMENTS

I'm diabetic.	**Я диабетик.**
	yah dee • ah • <u>byeh</u> • teek
I'm lactose intolerant.	**У меня непереносимость лактозы.**
	oo mee • <u>nyah</u>
	nee • pee • ree • nah • <u>see</u> • mahst'
	lahk • <u>toh</u> • zih
I'm vegetarian.	**Я вегетарианец.**
	yah vee • gee • tah • ree • <u>ah</u> • neets
I'm vegan.	**Я вегетарианец.**
	yah vee • gee • tah • ree • <u>ah</u> • neets
I'm allergic to…	**У меня аллергия на…**
	oo mee • <u>nyah</u> ah • leer • gee • <u>yah</u> nah…
I can't eat…	**Мне нельзя есть…**
	mnyeh neel' • <u>zyah</u> yest'…
dairy	**молочные продукты**
	mah • <u>loch</u> • nih • yeh prah • <u>dook</u> • tih
gluten	**растительный белок**
	rahs • <u>tee</u> • tyel' • niy bee • <u>lok</u>
nuts	**орехи**
	ah • <u>ryeh</u> • khee

pork	**свинину**
	svee • _nee_ • noo
shellfish	**раков**
	rah • kahf
spicy foods	**острую пищу**
	_os_ • troo • yoo _pee_ • shchoo
wheat	**пшеничную муку**
	pshih • _neech_ • noo • yoo moo • _koo_
Is it halal/kosher?	**Это халяль/кошерное?**
	_eh_ • tah khah • _lyahl'_/kah • _sher_ • nah • yeh
Do you have...?	**У Вас есть...?**
	oo vas est'
skimmed milk	**обезжиренное молоко**
	oh • bez • _zhee_ • reh • noh • ye
	moh • loh • _koh_
whole milk	**цельное молоко**
	tsehl' • noye moh • loh • _koh_
soya milk	**соевое молоко**
	soh • yeh • voh • ye moh • loh • _koh_

DINING WITH CHILDREN

Do you have children's portions?	**У вас есть детские порции?**
	oo vahs yest' _dyets_ • kee • yeh _por_ • tsih • ee
A highchair/child's seat, please.	**Высокий детский стульчик/Детское сидение, пожалуйста.**
	vih • _soh_ • keey dyets • keey _stool'_ • cheek/ dyets • kah • yeh see • _dyeh_ • nee • yeh pah • _zhahl_ • stah
Where can I feed/ change the baby?	**Где мне покормить/переодеть ребёнка?**
	gdyeh mnyeh pah • kahr • _meet'_/ pee • ree • ah • _dyet'_ree • _byon_ • kah
Can you warm this?	**Вы можете подогреть это?**
	vih _moh_ • zhih • tee pah • dah • _gryet'_ _eh_ • tah

For Traveling with Children, see page 139.

HOW TO COMPLAIN

How much longer will our food be?	**Сколько ещё ждать?** *skol' • kah ee • shchoh zhdaht'*
We can't wait any longer.	**Мы не можем больше ждать.** *mih nee moh • zhem bol' • sheh zhdaht'*
We're leaving.	**Мы уходим.** *mih oo • khoh • deem*
I didn't order this.	**Это не то, что я заказывал** *m* / **заказывала** *f*. *eh • tah nee toh shtoh yah* *zah • kah • zih • vahl/zah • kah • zih • vah • lah*
I ordered…	**Я просил** *m* /**просила** *f*… *yah prah • seel/prah • see • lah…*
I can't eat this.	**Это невозможно есть.** *eh • tah nee • vahz • mozh • nah yest'*
This is too…	**Это слишком…** *eh • tah slee • shkam…*
cold/hot	**холодное/горячее** *khah • lod • nah • yeh/gah • ryah • chee • yeh*
salty/spicy	**солёное/острое** *sah • lyoh • nah • yeh/os • trah • yeh*
tough/bland	**жёсткое/мягкое** *zhost • kah • yeh/myahkh • kah • yeh*
This isn't clean/ fresh.	**Это грязное/несвежее.** *eh • tah gryahz • nah • yeh/ nee • svyeh • zhih • yeh*

PAYING

The check [bill], please.	**Счёт, пожалуйста.** *shchot pah • zhahl • stah*
We'd like to pay separately.	**Мы будем платить отдельно.** *mih boo • deem plah • teet' ahd • dyel' • nah*

It's all together.	**Всё вместе.**
	fsyoh <u>vmyes</u> • tee
Is service included?	**Счёт включает обслуживание?**
	shchot fklyoo • <u>chah</u> • eet
	ahp • <u>sloo</u> • zhih • vah • nee • yeh
What's this amount for?	**А это за что?**
	ah eh • tah zah shtoh
I didn't have that.	**Я это не заказывал** *m* **/заказывала** *f*.
	yah <u>eh</u> • tah nee zah • <u>kah</u> • zih • vahl/
	zah • <u>kah</u> • zih • vah • lah
I had…	**У меня было…**
	oo mee • <u>nyah</u> bih • lah…
Can I pay by credit card?	**Можно платить кредитной карточкой?**
	<u>mozh</u> • nah plah • <u>teet'</u> kree • <u>deet</u> • nie
	<u>kahr</u> • tahch • kie
Can I have an itemized bill/ a receipt?	**Можно детальный счёт/чек?**
	<u>mozh</u> • nah dee • <u>tahl'</u> • niy shchot/chek
That was a very good meal.	**Всё было очень вкусно.**
	fsyoh bih • lah oh • cheen' <u>fkoos</u> • nah
I've already paid.	**Я уже оплатил.**
	yah oo • <u>zheh</u> oplah • teel

MEALS & COOKING

The country's geographic, climatic and ethnic variety is reflected in a rich and varied cuisine. Russians have a sweet tooth and are very fond of desserts and pastries, as well as their excellent ice cream.
Eating plays an important part in Russian social life, and it is while dining that you'll find Russians at their most hospitable. Don't forget to wish your table companions a hearty appetite: **Приятного аппетита!** pree • yaht • nah • vah ah • pee • tee • tah. At the end of a meal Russians will often thank those who dined with them. The proper response is **На здоровье!** nah zdah • rov' • yeh.

BREAKFAST

boiled egg	**вареное яйцо**
	vah • ryoh • nah • yeh yie • tsoh
bread	**хлеб**
	khlyep
fried eggs	**яичница**
	yah • eesh • nee • tsah
fruit juice	**фруктовый сок**
	frook • toh • viy sok
grapefruit juice	**грейпфрутовый сок**
	greyp • froo • tah • viy sok
ham and eggs	**яичница с ветчиной**
	yah • eesh • nee • tsah s veet • chee • noy
honey	**мёд**
	myot
jam	**джем**
	dzhem

oatmeal	**овсянка**
	ahf • syahn • kah
orange juice	**апельсиновый сок**
	ah • peel' • see • nah • viy sok
scrambled eggs	**яичница-болтунья**
	yah • eesh • nee • tsah bahl • toon' • yah
toast	**тост**
	tost
yogurt	**йогурт**
	yoh • goort

APPETIZERS

assorted meat	**ассорти мясное**
	ah • sahr • tee myahs • noh • yeh
assorted fish	**ассорти рыбное**
	ah • sahr • tee rihb • nah • yeh
caviar	**икра**
	eek • rah
ham	**ветчина**
	veet • chee • nah
herring	**сельдь**
	syel't'

(i)

Appetizers are often divided into hot and cold. If you want to indicate that a particular item will be an appetizer, just indicate that it is **На закуску** nah zah • <u>koos</u> • koo. **Блины** blee • <u>nih</u> (pancakes) are often made with yeast and stuffed with different fillings. Smaller and thicker than western pancakes, they are usually served with sour cream (**сметана** smee • <u>tah</u> • nah) and/or butter (**масло** <u>mahs</u> • lah).

mushrooms	**грибы**
	gree • <u>bih</u>
hot pancake filled with cheese (Georgian dish)	**хачапури**
	khah • chah • <u>poo</u> • ree
pancakes…	**блины…**
	blee • <u>nih</u>…
with caviar	**с икрой**
	s eek • <u>roy</u>
with jam	**с вареньем**
	s vah • <u>ryen'</u> • yem
with salmon	**с сёмгой**
	s <u>syom</u> • gie
with sheep's cheese	**с брынзой**
	s <u>brihn</u> • zie
with sour cream	**со сметаной**
	sah smee • <u>tah</u> • nie
paté (mostly liver)	**паштет**
	pahsh • <u>tyet</u>
pie	**пирог**
	pee • <u>rok</u>

sausage	**колбаса**
	kahl • bah • sah
shrimp [prawns]	**креветки**
	kree • vyet • kee
spiced herring	**кильки**
	keel' • kee
sturgeon	**осетрина**
	ah • seet • ree • nah

SOUP

beet soup (borsch)	**борщ**
	borshch
beet soup with extra bacon	**московский**
	mahs • kof • skeey
chicken soup	**суп из курицы**
	soop ees koo • ree • tsih
cold beet soup	**холодник**
	khah • lahd • neek
cold soup made from kvass, cucumbers, eggs, onions and sour cream	**окрошка**
	ah • krosh • kah
fish soup	**уха**
	oo • khah
spicy Georgian soup made with mutton and rice	**харчо**
	khahr • choh
mushroom soup	**грибной суп**
	greeb • noy soop
pea soup	**гороховый суп**
	gah • roh • khah • viy soop
potato soup	**картофельный**
	kahr • toh • feel' • niy soop

soup made with salted cucumbers and olives	**солянка** *sah • lyahn • kah*
thick soup made with cabbage or sauerkraut	**щи** *shchee*
Uzbek mutton soup with bacon and tomatoes	**шурпа** *shoor • pah*
Ukrainian beet soup with garlic	**украинский борщ** *oo • krah • een • skeey borshch*

FISH & SEAFOOD

carp	**карп** *kahrp*
crab	**краб** *krahp*
halibut	**палтус** *pahl • toos*
herring	**сельдь** *syel't'*
lobster	**омар** *ah • mahr*
mackerel	**макрель** *mahk • ryel'*
oysters	**устрицы** *oos • tree • tsih*
pike perch fried in butter/poached	**судак жареный в тесте/отварной** *soo • dahk zhah • ree • niy f tyes • tee/ aht • vahr • noy*
shrimp [prawns]	**креветки** *kree • vyet • kee*

salmon	**сёмга**
	syom • gah
sprats	**шпроты**
	shproh • tih
trout	**форель**
	fah • _ryel'_
tuna	**тунец**
	too • _nyets_
sturgeon...	**осетрина...**
	ah • seet • _ree_ • nah...
served with	**под белым соусом**
a white sauce	pahd byeh • lihm _soh_ • oo • sahm
poached	**по-русски**
	pah _roos_ • kee
steamed	**паровая**
	pah • rah • _vah_ • yah

MEAT & POULTRY

beef	**говядина**
	gah • _vyah_ • dee • nah
beef stroganoff	**бефстроганов**
	beef • _stroh_ • gah • nahf
braised beef with	**говядина тушёная**
aromatic vegetables	gah • _vyah_ • dee • nah too • _shoh_ • nah • yah
cabbage stuffed	**голубцы**
with meat and rice	gah • loop • _tsih_
chicken	**курица**
	koo • ree • tsah
chopped meat in	**азу**
a savory sauce	ah • _zoo_
duck	**утка**
	oot • kah

duck roasted with apples	утка тушёная с яблоками
	oot • kah too • shoh • nah • yah s yahb • lah • kah • mee
goose	гусь
	goos'
lamb	молодая баранина
	mah • lah • dah • yah bah • rah • nee • nah
lamb kebabs	шашлык
	shahsh • lihk
liver	печёнка
	pee • chon • kah
pork	свинина
	svee • nee • nah
rabbit	кролик
	kroh • leek
stuffed breast of chicken	котлеты по-киевски
	kaht • lyeh • tih pah kee • eef • skee
stuffed pasta	пельмени
	peel' • myeh • nee
turkey	индейка
	een • dyey • kah

veal	**телятина**	
	tee • lyah • tee • na	

VEGETABLES & STAPLES

beans	**фасоль**	
	fah • sol'	
beet	**свёкла**	
	svyok • lah	
bread	**хлеб**	
	khlyep	
cabbage	**капуста**	
	kah • poos • tah	
carrots	**морковь**	
	mahr • kof'	
cauliflower	**цветная капуста**	
	tsveet • nah • yah kah • poos • tah	
cucumber	**огурец**	
	ah • goo • ryets	
eggplant [aubergine]	**баклажан**	
	bahk • lah • zhahn	
mushrooms	**грибы**	
	greeb • ih	
noodles	**лапша**	
	lahp • shah	
onion	**лук**	
	look	
pasta	**макароны**	
	mah • kah • roh • nih	
stuffed pasta	**пельмени**	
	peel' • myeh • nee	
small pastries with various sweet or savoury fillings	**пирожки**	
	pee • rahsh • kee	

peas	**горох** _gah_ • _rokh_
pepper	**перец** _pyeh_ • _reets_
porridge	**каша** _kah_ • _shah_
potato	**картофель** _kahr_ • _toh_ • _feel'_
rice	**рис** _rees_
spaghetti	**спагетти** _spah_ • _gyeh_ • _tee_
sweet corn	**сладкая кукуруза** _slaht_ • _kah_ • _yah koo_ • _koo_ • _roo_ • _zah_
tomato	**помидор** _pah_ • _mee_ • _dor_
zucchini [courgette]	**молодой кабачок** _mah_ • _lah_ • _doy kah_ • _bah_ • _chok_

FRUIT

apple	**яблоко** _yahb_ • _lah_ • _kah_
apricot	**абрикос** _ab_ • _ree_ • _kos_
banana	**банан** _bah_ • _nahn_
cherry	**черешня** _chee_ • _ryesh_ • _nyah_
currants	**смородина** _smah_ • _roh_ • _dee_ • _nah_
gooseberry	**крыжовник** _krih_ • _zhov_ • _neek_
grapes	**виноград** _vee_ • _nah_ • _graht_

lemon	**лимон** _lee_ • _mon_
melon	**дыня** _dih_ • nyah
orange	**апельсин** ah • peel' • _seen_
peach	**персик** _pyer_ • seek
pear	**груша** _groo_ • shah
pineapple	**ананас** ah • nah • _nahs_
plum	**слива** _slee_ • vah
strawberry	**клубника** kloob • _nee_ • kah
watermelon	**арбуз** ahr • _boos_

CHEESE

baked sour milk, often served chilled	**ряженка** _ryah_ • zhihn • kah
...cheese	**сыр...** sihr...
Latvian	**латвийский** laht • _veey_ • skeey
Poshekhonsky	**пошехонский** pah • shih • _khon_ • skeey
Russian	**российский** rah • _seey_ • skeey
sharp ewe's milk cheese	**брынза** _brihn_ • zah
fresh white cheese or spread	**сырок** sih • _rok_

white unsalted cheese similar to cottage cheese	**творог** tvah • _rok_

DESSERT

apple baked in pastry	**яблоко в тесте** _yahb_ • lah • kah f _tyes_ • tee
cottage cheese pastry	**ватрушка** vah • _troosh_ • kah
Ukrainian dumplings filled with white cheese	**вареники** vah • _ryeh_ • nee • kee
fruit compote	**компот** kahm • _pot_
fruit jelly-like drink	**кисель** kee • _syel'_
...ice cream	**...мороженое** ...mah • _roh_ • zhih • nah • yeh
chocolate	**шоколадное** shah • kah • _lad_ • nah • yeh
fruit	**фруктовое** frook • _toh_ • vah • yeh

vanilla	**ванильное**
	vah • neel' • nah • yeh
pie…	**пирог…**
	pee • rok…
with cottage cheese	**с творогом**
	s tvah • rah • gom
with fruit	**с фруктами**
	s frook • tah • mee
with lemon	**с лимоном**
	s lee • moh • nahm
rice pudding	**рисовый пудинг**
	ree • sah • viy poo • deenk
small apple pancakes	**оладьи с яблоками**
	ah • lahd' • yee s yahb • lah • kah • mee
small pancakes served with jam	**блинчики с вареньем**
	bleen • chee • kee s vah • ryen' • yem
sponge roll	**рулет**
	roo • lyet
whipped cream	**взбитые сливки**
	vzbee • tih • yeh sleef • kee
yeast cake saturated in liquor	**ромовая баба**
	roh • mah • vah • yah bah • bah
white cheese fritters served with sour cream	**сырники со сметаной**
	sihr • nee • kee sah smee • tah • nie

SAUCES & CONDIMENTS

mustard	**горчица**
	gahr • chee • tsah
pepper	**перец**
	pyeh • reets
salt	**соль**
	sol'

sugar	**сахар** _sah_ • khahr
ketchup	**кетчуп** _Keht_ • choop

AT THE MARKET

Where are the trolleys/baskets?	**Где здесь тележки/корзинки?** gdyeh zdyes' tee • _lyesh_ • kee/ kahr • _zeen_ • kee
Where is…?	**Где…?** gdyeh…

Measurements in Russia are metric — and that applies to the weight of food too. If you tend to think in pounds and ounces, it's worth brushing up on what the metric equivalent is before you go shopping for fruit and veg in markets and supermarkets. Five hundred grams, or half a kilo, is a common quantity to order, and that converts to just over a pound (17.65 ounces, to be precise).

YOU MAY HEAR…

Я вас слушаю.
yah vahs _sloo_ • shah • yoo

Can I help you?

Что вы хотите?
shtoh vih khah • _tee_ • tee

What would you like?

Что ещё?
shtoh ee • _shchoh_

Anything else?

Это…рублей.
eh • tah…roob • _lyey_

That's…rubles.

192 • FOOD & DRINK

Today, Russia's cities feature supermarkets very much like those in western Europe and the United States. The business and tourism districts of Moscow and St. Petersburg now feature small stores very much like the American convenience store, where you can buy a drink and snack.

I'd like some of that/those.	**Дайте, пожалуйста, вон то/те.** _die_ • tee pah • _zhahl_ • stah von toh/tyeh
Can I taste it?	**Можно это попробовать?** _mozh_ • nah eh • tah pah • _proh_ • bah • vaht'
I'd like…	**Дайте, пожалуйста,…** _die_ • tee pah • _zhahl_ • stah…
a kilo/half-kilo of…	**кило/полкило…** kee • _loh/pol_ • kee • _loh_…
a liter/half-liter of…	**литр/пол-литра…** leetr/pol • _leet_ • rah…
a piece of…	**кусочек…** koo • _soh_ • cheek…
a slice of…	**ломтик…** _lom_ • teek…
More./Less.	**Побольше./Поменьше.** pah • _bol'_ • sheh/pah • _myen'_ • sheh
How much?	**Сколько?** _skol_ • kah
Where do I pay?	**Куда платить?** koo • _dah_ plah • _teet'_
A bag, please.	**Пакет, пожалуйста.** pah • _kyet_ pah • _zhahl_ • stah
I'm being helped.	**Меня уже обслуживают.** mee • _nyah_ oo • _zheh_ ahp • _sloo_ • zhih • vah • yoot

YOU MAY SEE...

ГОДЕН ДО...	best if
goh • deen dah...	used by...
КАЛОРИЙ	calories
kah • loh • reey	
ОБЕЗЖИРЕННЫЙ	fat free
ah • beezh • zhih • ree • niy	
ХРАНИТЬ В ХОЛОДИЛЬНИКЕ	keep refrigerated
khrah • neet' f khah • lah • deel' • nee • kee	
МОЖЕТ СОДЕРЖАТЬ СЛЕДЫ...	may contain
moh • zhiht sah • deer • zhaht' slee • dih...	traces of...
РЕАЛИЗОВАТЬ ДО... '	sell by...
ree • ah • lee • zah • vaht dah...	
ВЕГЕТАРИАНСКОЕ ПИТАНИЕ	suitable for
vee • gee • tah • ree • ahn • skah • yeh	vegetarians
pee • tah • nee • yeh	

IN THE KITCHEN

bottle opener	**открывалка**
	aht • krih • vahl • kah
bowl	**миска**
	mees • kah
can opener	**консервный нож**
	kahn • syerv • niy nosh
corkscrew	**штопор**
	shtoh • pahr
cup	**чашка**
	chahsh • kah
fork	**вилка**
	veel • kah

frying pan	**сковорода**
	skah • vah • rah • <u>dah</u>
glass	**стакан**
	stah • <u>kahn</u>
knives	**ножи**
	nah • <u>zhih</u>
measuring cup/	**мерная чашка/ложка**
spoon	*<u>myer</u> • nah • yah <u>chahsh</u> • kah/losh • kah*
napkin	**бумажные салфетки**
	boo • <u>mahzh</u> • nih • yeh sahl • <u>fyet</u> • kee
plate	**тарелка**
	tah • <u>ryel</u> • kah
pot	**высокая кастрюля**
	vih • <u>soh</u> • kah • yah kahs • <u>tryoo</u> • lyah
saucepan	**кастрюля**
	kahs • <u>tryoo</u> • lyah
spatula	**лопаточка**
	lah • <u>pah</u> • tahch • kah
spoons	**ложки**
	<u>losh</u> • kee

DRINKS

NEED TO KNOW

May I see the wine list/drink menu?	**Можно посмотреть карту вин/ меню напитков?** _mozh • nah pah • smah • tryet' kahr • too veen/mee • nyoo nah • peet • kahf_
What do you recommend?	**Что вы порекомендуете?** _shtoh vih pah • ree • kah • meen • doo • ee • tee_
I'd like a bottle/ glass of red/white wine.	**Я хотел m /хотела f бы бутылку/ бокал красного/белого вина.** _yah khah • tyel/khah • tyeh • lah bih boo • tihl • koo/bah • kahl krahs • nah • vah/byeh • lah • vah vee • nah_
The house wine, please.	**Вино ресторана, пожалуйста.** _vee • noh ree • stah • rah • nah pah • zhahl • stah_
Another bottle/ glass, please.	**Ещё одну бутылку/один бокал, пожалуйста.** _yee • shchoh ahd • noo boo • tihl • koo/ah • deen bah • kahl pah • zhahl • stah_
I'd like a local beer.	**Я хотел m /хотела f бы местного пива.** _yah khah • tyel/khah • tyeh • lah bih myes • nah • vah pee • vah_

Let me buy you a drink.	**Позвольте вам предложить что-нибудь выпить.**
	pahz • vol' • tee vahm preed • lah • zhiht' shtoh • nee boot' vih • peet'
Cheers!	**За ваше здоровье!**
	za vah • sheh zdah • rov' • yeh
A coffee/tea, please.	**Кофе/Чай, пожалуйста.**
	koh • fye/chie pah • zhahl • stah
Black.	**Чёрный.**
	chor • niy
With...	**С...**
	s...
milk	**молоком**
	mah • lah • kom
sugar	**сахаром**
	sah • khah • rahm
artificial sweetener	**заменителем сахара**
	zah • mee • nee • tee • lyem sah • khah • rah
..., please.	**..., пожалуйста.**
	...pah • zhahl • stah
Juice	**Сок**
	sok
Soda	**Содовую**
	soh • dah • voo • yoo
Sparkling/Still water	**Воду с газом/без газа**
	voh • doo z gah • zahm/beez gah • zah
Is the tap water safe to drink?	**Безопасно ли пить воду из крана?**
	bee • zah • pahs • nah lee peet' voh • doo ees krah • nah

NON-ALCOHOLIC DRINKS

apple/orange juice **яблочный/апельсиновый сок**
yahb • lahch • niy/ah • peel' • see • nah • viy sok

coffee... **кофе...**
koh • fyeh...

  black **чёрный**
chor • niy

  decaffeinated **без кафеина**
bees kah • fee • ee • nah

  with milk **с молоком**
s mah • lah • kom

iced tea **чай со льдом**
chie sah l'dom

kvass, soft drink **квас**
made from yeast *kvahss*

lemonade **лимонад**
lee • mah • naht

milk **молоко**
mah • lah • koh

milk shake **молочный коктейль**
mah • loch • niy kahk • teyl'

mineral water **минеральная вода**
mee • nee • rahl' • nah • yah vah • dah

soda **содовая**
soh • dah • vah • yah

tea **чай**
chie

water **вода**
vah • dah

Stores and kiosks in large towns and cities are full of imported and locally produced soft drinks, fruit juice and mineral water. Ice cream cafes offer something called **коктейль** kahk • teyl' (cocktail), a non-alcoholic drink made from fruit juice or lemonade, to which ice cream and sometimes whipped cream is added.

Квас kvahs is a popular traditional Russian soft drink and a good thirst quencher in the summer. Kvass, which looks like beer, is made from black bread and yeast.

YOU MAY HEAR...

Вам принести что-нибудь попить?
vahm pree • nees • tee
shtoh • nee • boot' pah • peet'

Can I get you a drink?

С молоком/сахаром?
s mah • lah • kom/sah • khah • rahm

With milk/sugar?

Воду с газом или без газа?
voh • doo z gah • zahm ee • lee beez gah • zah

Sparkling or still water?

APERITIFS, COCKTAILS & LIQUEURS

brandy (cognac)	**коньяк**
	kahn' • yahk
gin	**джин**
	dzhihn
liqueur	**ликёр**
	lee • kyor
rum	**ром**
	rom

sherry	**херес**
	khyeh • rees
vodka	**водка**
	vot • kah
whisky	**виски**
	vees • kee

Russian vodka is world famous. Kremlevskaya,
Stolichnaya, Moskovskaya and some other brands
are well-known internationally. Make sure you buy alcohol
from a licensed seller, in order to avoid purchasing a low-
quality counterfeit.

BEER

Moscow beer	**московское**
	mahs • kof • skah • ye
Russian beer	**жигулёвское**
	zhih • goo • lyof • skah • ye
Riga beer	**рижское**
	reesh • skah • yeh
dark/light	**темное/светлое**
	tyom • noh • ye/sveht • loye

local/imported	**местное/импортное**
	mehst • noh • ye/eem • port • noye
bottled/draft	**в бутылках/разливное**
	v boo • tihl • kahkh/rahz • leev • noh • eh
non-alcoholic	**безалкогольное**
	behz • ahl • koh • gohl' noh • eh

WINE

International brands of wine are available throughout
Russia. It is sometimes easier to find French, Californian and
Italian wines than to find old favorites from Georgia.
Russian sparkling wine is a popular drink. Dry, it can
accompany almost any meal; sweet, it is usually enjoyed
after meals or with dessert. Quality and price vary for wine
with the same label. In general, it is better to buy alcohol
in a liquor store than from a kiosk or street vendor.

champagne	**шампанское**
	sham • pahn • sko • ye
dry	**сухое**
	soo • khoh • yeh
sparkling wine	**игристое**
	eeg • rees • tah • yeh
red wine	**красное вино**
	krahs • nah • yeh vee • noh
rosé wine	**розовое вино**
	roh • zah • vah • yeh vee • noh
sweet	**сладкое**
	slaht • kah • yeh
white wine	**белое вино**
	byeh • lah • yeh vee • noh

ON THE MENU

aperitif	**аперитив**
	ah • pee • ree • _teef_
apple	**яблоко**
	yahb • lah • kah
apple baked in pastry	**яблоко в тесте**
	yahb • lah • kah f _tyes_ • tee
apricot	**абрикос**
	ahb • ree • _kos_
artificial sweetener	**заменитель сахара**
	zah • mee • _nee_ • teel' _sah_ • khah • rah
chopped meat in a savory sauce	**азу**
	ah • _zoo_
bacon	**грудинка**
	groo • _deen_ • kah
banana	**банан**
	bah • _nahn_
beans	**фасоль**
	fah • _sol'_
beef stroganoff	**бефстроганов**
	beef • _stroh_ • gah • nahf
beef	**говядина**
	gah • _vyah_ • dee • nah
beer	**пиво**
	pee • vah
beet [beetroot]	**свёкла**
	svyok • lah
beet soup (borsch)	**борщ**
	borshch
braised beef with aromatic vegetables	**говядина тушёная с кореньями**
	gah • _vyah_ • dee • nah too • _shoh_ • nah • yah s kah • _ryen'_ • yah • mee

brandy	**бренди**	
	bren • dee	
bread	**хлеб**	
	khlyep	
butter	**масло**	
	mahs • lah	
cabbage	**капуста**	
	kah • _poos_ • tah	
cake (large)	**торт**	
	tort	
cake (small)	**пирожное**	
	pee • _rozh_ • nah • yeh	
carrots	**морковь**	
	mahr • _kof'_	
caviar	**икра**	
	eek • _rah_	
cereal	**каша**	
	kah • shah	
champagne	**шампанское**	
	shahm • _pahn_ • skah • yeh	
cheese	**сыр**	
	sihr	
cherry	**вишня**	
	veesh • nyah	

stuffed breast of chicken	**котлеты по-киевски** *kaht • lyeh • tih pah kee • eef • skee*
chicken soup	**суп из курицы** *soop ees koo • ree • tsih*
chicken	**курица** *koo • ree • tsah*
chocolate	**шоколад** *shah • kah • laht*
chop	**отбивная** *aht • beev • nah • yah*
chopped meat	**рубленое мясо** *roob • lee • nah • yeh myah • sah*
coffee	**кофе** *koh • fyeh*
cold cuts [charcuterie]	**мясная закуска** *myahs • nah • yah zah • koos • kah*
cold soup made from kvass, cucumbers, eggs, onions and sour cream	**окрошка** *ah • krosh • kah*
cornmeal	**кукурузная мука** *koo • koo • rooz • nah • yah moo • kah*
cottage cheese tart	**ватрушка** *vaht • roosh • kah*
cottage cheese	**творог** *tvah • rok*
crab	**краб** *krahp*
crabmeat	**мясо краба** *myah • sah krah • bah*
cracker	**крекер** *kryeh • kyer*
cream	**сливки** *sleef • kee*

cucumber	**огурец**
	ah • goo • ryets
cumin	**тмин римский**
	tmeen reem • skeey
currants	**смородина**
	smah • roh • dee • nah
duck	**утка**
	oot • kah
dumpling	**клёцка**
	klyots • kah
egg	**яйцо**
	yie • tsoh
eggplant [aubergine]	**баклажан**
	bahk • lah • zhahn
fish soup	**уха**
	oo • khah
fish	**рыба**
	rih • bah
fresh white cheese	**сырок**
	sih • rok
fritter	**оладья**
	ah • lahd' • yah
fruit compote	**компот**
	kahm • pot
fruit jelly	**кисель**
	kee • syel'
fruit	**фрукты**
	frook • tih
garlic sauce	**чесночный соус**
	chees • noch • niy soh • oos
garlic	**чеснок**
	chees • nok
gin	**джин**
	dzhihn

ginger	**имбирь**	
	eem • beer'	
goat cheese	**сыр из козьего молока**	
	sihr ees koz' • yeh • vah mah • lah • kah	
goat	**козлятина**	
	kahz • lyah • tee • nah	
cabbage stuffed with rice and meat	**голубцы**	
	gah • loop • tsih	
goose	**гусь**	
	goos'	
gooseberry	**крыжовник**	
	krih • zhov • neek	
grapefruit	**грейпфрут**	
	greyp • froot	
grapefruit juice	**сок из грейпфрута**	
	sok eez greyp • froo • tah	
grapes	**виноград**	
	vee • nahg • raht	
halibut	**палтус**	
	pahl • toos	
ham	**ветчина**	
	veet • chee • nah	
hamburger	**гамбургер**	
	gahm • boor • geer	

herbs	**травы**
	trah • vih
herring	**сельдь**
	syel't'
honey	**мёд**
	myot
ice (cube)	**кубик льда**
	koo • beek l'dah
ice cream	**мороженое**
	mah • _roh_ • zhih • nah • yeh
jam	**варенье**
	vah • _ryen'_ • yeh
jelly	**желе**
	zhih • _lyeh_
juice	**фруктовый сок**
	frook • _toh_ • viy sok
kidney	**почка**
	poch • kah
lamb	**молодая баранина**
	mah • lah • _dah_ • yah bah • _rah_ • nee • nah
lamb kebabs	**шашлык**
	shahsh • _lihk_
lemon	**лимон**
	lee • _mon_
lemonade	**лимонад**
	lee • mah • _naht_
liqueur	**ликёр**
	lee • _kyor_
liver	**печень**
	pyeh • cheen'
lobster	**омар**
	ah • _mahr_
mackerel	**макрель**
	mahk • _ryel'_
meat	**мясо**
	myah • sah

melon	**дыня**
	dih • nyah
milk shake	**молочный коктейль**
	mah • _loch_ • niy kahk • _teyl'_
milk	**молоко**
	mah • lah • _koh_
mineral water	**минеральная вода**
	mee • nee • _rahl'_ • nah • yah vah • _dah_
mushroom	**гриб**
	greep
mustard	**горчица**
	gahr • _chee_ • tsah
mutton	**баранина**
	bah • _rah_ • nee • nah
noodles	**лапша**
	lahp • _shah_
nuts	**орехи**
	ah • _ryeh_ • khee
olive	**оливка**
	ah • _leef_ • kah
onions	**лук**
	look
orange juice	**апельсиновый сок**
	ah • peel' • _see_ • nah • viy sok
orange liqueur	**апельсиновый ликёр**
	ah • peel' • _see_ • nah • viy lee • _kyor_
orange	**апельсин**
	ah • peel' • _seen_
oyster	**устрица**
	oost • ree • tsah
pancakes	**блины**
	blee • _nih_
pasta	**макароны**
	mah • kah • _roh_ • nih

pastry	**кондитерские изделия** *kahn • dee • teer • skee • yeh* *eez • dyeh • lee • yah*
pâté	**паштет** *pahsh • tyet*
peach	**персик** *pyer • seek*
peanut	**арахис** *ah • rah • khees*
pear	**груша** *groo • shah*
peas	**горошек** *gah • roh • shek*
pepper	**перец** *pyeh • reets*
pie or tart served with a variety of fruit or cheese fillings	**пирог** *pee • rok*
pike perch fried in batter	**судак жареный в тесте** *soo • dahk zhah • ree • niy f tyes • tee*
pike perch poached	**судак отварной** *soo • dahk aht • vahr • noy*

pineapple	**ананас**
	ah • nah • nahs
plum	**слива**
	slee • vah
pork	**свинина**
	svee • nee • nah
potato chips [crisps]	**чипсы**
	cheep • sih
potatoes	**картофель**
	kahr • toh • feel'
rabbit	**кролик**
	kroh • leek
red currant	**красная смородина**
	krahs • nah • yah smah • roh • dee • nah
rice pudding	**рисовый пудинг**
	ree • sah • viy poo • deenk
rice	**рис**
	rees
roast beef	**ростбиф**
	rost • beef
roast duck with apples	**утка тушёная с яблоками**
	oot • kah too • shoh • nah • yah s yahb • lah • kah • mee
roast pork with plums	**жаркое из свинины с черносливом**
	zhahr • koh • yeh ees svee • nee • nih s cheer • nah • slee • vahm
roast	**жаркое**
	zhahr • koh • yeh
roll	**булочка**
	boo • lahch • kah
rum	**ром**
	rom
Russian soft drink	**квас**
	kvahs

salmon	**лосось**
	lah • sos'
salt	**соль**
	sol'
sauce	**соус**
	soh • oos
sausage	**колбаса**
	kahl • bah • sah
shellfish	**моллюски**
	mah • lyoos • kee
sherry	**херес**
	kheh • rees
shrimp	**креветка**
	kree • vyet • kah
small apple pancakes	**оладьи с яблоками**
	ah • lahd' • yee s yahb • lah • kah • mee
small pancakes with jam	**блинчики с вареньем**
	bleen • chee • kee s vah • ryen' • yem
snack	**лёгкая закуска**
	lyokh • kah • yah zah • koos • kah
soup	**суп**
	soop
sour cream	**сметана**
	smee • tah • nah
spaghetti	**спагетти**
	spah • gyeh • tee
spices	**приправы**
	pree • prah • vih
spicy Georgian soup made with mutton and rice	**харчо**
	khahr • choh
spirits	**спиртные напитки**
	speert • nih • yeh nah • peet • kee
sponge roll	**рулет**
	roo • lyet

steak	**бифштекс** _beef • <u>shteks</u>_
strawberries	**клубника** _kloob • <u>nee</u> • kah_
stuffed pasta	**пельмени** _peel' • <u>myeh</u> • nee_
sturgeon poached	**осетрина по-русски** _ah • seet • <u>ree</u> • nah pah <u>roos</u> • kee_
sturgeon served with a white sauce	**осетрина под белым соусом** _ah • seet • <u>ree</u> • nah pahd <u>byeh</u> • lihm <u>soh</u> • oo • sahm_
sturgeon steamed	**осетрина паровая** _ah • seet • <u>ree</u> • nah pah • rah • <u>vah</u> • yah_
sugar	**сахар** _<u>sah</u> • khahr_
sweet corn	**сладкая кукуруза** _<u>slaht</u> • kah • yah koo • koo • <u>roo</u> • zah_
syrup	**сироп** _see • <u>rop</u>_
tea	**чай** _chie_
thick soup made with cabbage or sauerkraut	**щи** _shchee_

toast	**тост**
	tost
tomato	**помидор**
	pah • mee • dor
trout	**форель**
	fah • ryel'
tuna	**тунец**
	too • nyets
turkey	**индейка**
	een • dyey • kah
Uzbek soup made with mutton, bacon and tomato	**шурпа**
	shoor • pah
vanilla	**ваниль**
	vah • neel'
veal	**телятина**
	tee • lyah • tee • nah
vegetables	**овощи**
	oh • vah • shchee
vodka	**водка**
	vot • kah
water	**вода**
	vah • dah

watermelon	**арбуз**
	arh • boos
wheat	**пшеница**
	pshih • nee • tsah
whipped cream	**взбитые сливки**
	vzbee • tih • yeh sleef • kee
whisky	**виски**
	vees • kee
wine	**вино**
	vee • noh
yeast cake	**ромовая баба**
saturated in liquor	*roh • mah • vah • yah bah • bah*
yogurt	**йогурт**
	yoh • goort
zucchini [courgette]	**цуккини**
	tsoo • kee • nee

GOING OUT

GOING OUT

NEED TO KNOW

What is there to do in the evenings?	**Что здесь можно делать по вечерам?** shtoh zdyehs' mozh • nah dyeh • laht' pah vee • chee • rahm
Do you have a program of events?	**У Вас есть программа мероприятий?** oo vahs yehst' prah • grah • mah mee • rah • pree • yah • teey
What's playing at the movies [cinema] tonight?	**Что идёт в кинотеатре сегодня вечером?** shtoh ee • dyot f kee • nah • tee • aht • ree see • vohd • nyah vyeh • chee • rahm
Where's...?	**Где...?** gdyeh...
the downtown area	**центр города** tsehntr goh • rah • dah
the bar	**бар** bahr
the dance club	**дискотека** dees • kah • tyeh • kah
Is there a cover charge?	**Нужно платить за вход?** noozh • nah plah • teet' zah fkhot

ENTERTAINMENT

Can you recommend...?	**Вы можете порекомендовать...?** vih moh • zhih • tee pah • ree • kah • meen • dah • vaht'...
a concert	**концерт** kahn • tsert

Most Russian restaurants have traditionally featured music and dancing, and Russians are less shy than others about getting out of their chairs and letting loose. Women do not wait for an invitation; it is not uncommon to see women dancing together or friends dancing as a group.

Moscow and St. Petersburg are developing solid reputations among young jet-setters as first-class party cities with a number of exclusive nightclubs. Many nightclubs and dance clubs are located in popular hotels and casinos.

a movie	**фильм**
	feel'm
an opera	**оперу**
	<u>oh</u> • pee • roo
a play	**пьесу**
	<u>pyeh</u> • soo
When does it start/end?	**Когда начинается/заканчивается?**
	kahg • <u>dah</u> nah • chee • <u>nah</u> • ee • tsah/ zah • <u>kahn</u> • chee • vah • ee • tsah
What's the dress code?	**Какая форма одежды?**
	kah • <u>kah</u> • yah <u>for</u> • mah ah • <u>dyezh</u> • dih

I like...	Я люблю...
	yah lyoob • lyoo...
classical music	**классическую музыку**
	klah • see • chees • koo • yoo moo • zih • koo
folk music	**народную музыку**
	nah • rod • noo • yoo moo • zih • koo
jazz	**джаз**
	dzhahs
pop music	**поп-музыку**
	pop • moo • zih • koo
rap	**рэп**
	rep

For Tickets, see page 43.

YOU MAY HEAR...

Выключите Ваши мобильные телефоны, пожалуйста.
vih • klyoo • chee • tee vah • shee mah • beel' • nih • ee tee • lee • foh • nih pah • zhahl • stah

Turn off your cell [mobile] phones, please.

ⓘ

There is extensive English-language information
available on the internet about the schedules of performances
at the Bolshoi Theater in Moscow and the Mariinsky Theater in
St. Petersburg. Both theaters offer free courier service that can
deliver tickets to your hotel or apartment.

NIGHTLIFE

What is there to do in the evenings?	**Что здесь можно делать по вечерам?** shtoh zdyehs' _mozh_ • nah _dyeh_ • laht' pah vee • chee • _rahm_
Can you recommend...?	**Вы можете порекомендовать...?** vih _moh_ • zhih • tee pah • ree • kah • meen • dah • _vaht'_...
a bar	**бар** bahr
a cabaret	**ресторан с эстрадным выступлением** reh • stah • _rahn_ s ehst • _rahd_ • nihm vihs • toop • _lehn_ • yehm
a casino	**казино** kah • zee • _noh_
a dance club	**дискотеку** dees • kah • _tyeh_ • koo
a gay club	**гейклуб** gyey • kloop
a jazz club	**джазовый клуб** _dzhah_ • zoh • viy kloob
a club with Russian music	**клуб с русской музыкой** kloob s _roos_ • koy _moo_ • zih • koy
a nightclub	**ночной клуб** nahch • _noy_ kloop

Is there live music?	**Там есть живая музыка?**
	tahm yest' zhih • vah • yah moo • zih • kah
How do I get there?	**Как туда добраться?**
	kahk too • dah dah • brah • tsah
Is there a cover charge?	**Нужно платить за вход?**
	noozh • nah plah • teet' zah fkhot
Let's go dancing.	**Пойдём танцевать.**
	pie • dyom tahn • tsih • vaht'
Is this area safe at night?	**В этом районе ночью безопасно?**
	v etohm rah • yoh • neh nohch' • yu beh • zoh • pahs • noh

For The Dating Game, see page 220.

ROMANCE

THE DATING GAME

Would you like to...?	**Хотите...?**
	khah • tee • tee...
go out for coffee	**выпить кофе где-нибудь**
	vih • peet' koh • fyeh gdyeh • nee • boot'
go for a drink	**пойти выпить где-нибудь**
	pie • tee vih • peet' gdyeh • nee • boot'
go for a meal	**пойти поесть где-нибудь**
	pie • tee pah • yest' gdyeh • nee • boot'
What are your plans for...?	**Какие у вас планы на...?**
	kah • kee • yeh oo vahs plah • nih nah...
today	**сегодня**
	seh • vohd • nya
tonight	**сегодняшний вечер**
	see • vod • neesh • neey vyeh • cheer

NEED TO KNOW

Would you like to go out for a drink/ meal?	**Не хотите выпить/поесть где- нибудь?**
	nee khah • <u>tee</u> • tee <u>vih</u> • peet'/ pah • <u>yest'</u> gdyeh • nee • boot'
What are your plans for tonight/ tomorrow?	**Какие у вас планы на сегодняшний вечер/завтра?**
	kah • <u>kee</u> • yeh oo vahs <u>plah</u> • nih nah see • <u>vod</u> • neesh • neey <u>vyeh</u> • cheer/<u>zahf</u> • trah
Can I have your number?	**Можно Ваш номер телефона?**
	<u>mozh</u> • nah vahsh <u>noh</u> • meer tee • lee • <u>foh</u> • nah
Can I join you?	**Можно к Вам присоединиться?**
	<u>mozh</u> • nah k vahm pree • sah • ee • dee • <u>nee</u> • tsah
Let me buy you a drink.	**Позвольте вам предложить что- нибудь выпить.**
	pahz • <u>vol'</u> • tee vahm preed • lah • <u>zheet'</u> shtoh • nee • boot' <u>vih</u> • peet'
I like you.	**Вы мне нравитесь.**
	vih mnyeh <u>nrah</u> • vee • tees'
I love you.	**Я Вас люблю.**
	yah vahs lyoob • <u>lyoo</u>

tomorrow	**завтра**
	<u>zahf</u> • trah
this weekend	**эти выходные**
	<u>eh</u> • tee vih • khahd • <u>nih</u> • yeh

Where would you like to go?	**Куда вы хотите пойти?** _koo • dah vih khah • tee • tee pie • tee_
I'd like to go to…	**Я хотел m /хотела f бы пойти в…** _yah khah • tyel /khah • tyeh • lah bih pie • tee v…_
Do you like…?	**Вы любите…?** _vih lyoo • bee • tee…_
Can I have your number/e-mail?	**Можно Ваш номер телефона/ электронный адрес?** _mozh • nah vahsh noh • meer tee • lee • foh • nah/ee • leek • tron • niy ahd • rees_
Are you on facebook/ Twitter?	**Вы есть в Facebook/Twitter?** _vih est' v facebook/Twitter_
Can I join you?	**Можно к Вам присоединиться?** _mozh • nah k vahm pree • sah • ee • dee • nee • tsah_
You're very attractive.	**Вы прекрасно выглядите.** _vih pree • krahs • nah vih • glee • dee • tee_
Shall we go somewhere quieter?	**Пойдём куда-нибудь в тихое место?** _pie • dyom koo • dah • nee • boot' f tee • khah • yeh myes • tah_

For Communications, see page 88.

ACCEPTING & REJECTING

Thank you! I'd love to.	**Спасибо! Я с удовольствием.** *spah • <u>see</u> • bah yah s* *oo • dah • <u>vol'</u> • stvee • yem*
Where shall we meet?	**Где встретимся?** *gdyeh <u>fstryeh</u> • teem • syah*
I'll meet you at the bar/your hotel.	**Встретимся в баре/вашем отеле.** *<u>fstryeh</u> • teem • syah v <u>bah</u> • ryeh/ vah • shem ah • <u>teh</u> • lee*
I'll come by at…	**Я зайду в…** *yah zayh • <u>doo</u> v…*
Thank you, but I'm busy.	**Спасибо, но я занят** *m* **/занята** *f.* *spah • <u>see</u> • bah noh yah <u>zah</u> • nyaht/ zah • nyah • tah*
I'm not interested.	**Меня это не интересует.** *mee • <u>nyah</u> eh • tah nee een • tee • ree • <u>soo</u> • eet*
Leave me alone.	**Оставьте меня в покое.** *ah • <u>stahf'</u> • tee mee • <u>nyah</u> f pah • <u>koh</u> • yeh*
Stop bothering me!	**Перестаньте мне надоедать!** *pee • ree • <u>stahn'</u> • tee mnyeh nah • dah • ee • <u>daht'</u>*

GETTING INTIMATE

Can I hug/kiss you?	**Можно тебя обнять/поцеловать?** *<u>mozh</u> • nah tee • <u>byah</u> ahb • <u>nyaht'</u>/ pah • tsih • lah • <u>vaht'</u>*
Yes.	**Да.** *dah*
No.	**Нет.** *nyet*

Stop!	**Перестань!**
	pee • ree • <u>stahn'</u>
I love you.	**Я Вас люблю.**
	yah vahs lyoob • <u>lyoo</u>

SEXUAL PREFERENCES

Are you gay?	**Ты гей** *m* **/лесбиянка** *f* **?**
	tih gyey/lez • bee • <u>yahn</u> • kah
I'm…	**Я…**
	yah…
heterosexual	**гетеросексуал**
	gyeh • teh • rah • sek • soo • <u>ahl</u>
homosexual	**гомосексуал**
	goh • mah • sek • soo • <u>ahl</u>
bisexual	**бисексуал**
	bee • sek • soo • <u>ahl</u>
Do you like men/ women?	**Вам нравятся мужчины/женщины?**
	vam <u>nrah</u> • vyat • sya moo • <u>zhchee</u> • nih/ <u>zhehn</u> • shchee • nih

* Есть пра...
философс...
место или с...
* Логика отто...
* Надобно хран...
* Не мнения люде...
формула поиска...
* Нельзя уверовать...

DICTIONARY

ENGLISH–RUSSIAN

A

a few несколько
nyeh • skahl' • kah

a little немного *nee • mnoh • gah*

a lot много *mnoh • gah*

a.m. до полудня *dah pah • lood • nyah*

about (approximately) около
oh • kah • lah

abroad заграницей
zah • grah • nee • tsey

accept v принимать
pree • nee • maht'

access n допуск *doh • poosk*

accessories принадлежности
pree • nahd • lyezh • nah • stee

accident несчастный
случай *nee • shchas • niy
sloo • chie*; **(road)** авария
ah • vah • ree • yah

accompany провожать
prah • vah • zhaht'

accountant бухгалтер
boo • gahl • teer

acetaminophen парацетамол
pah • rah • tsih • tah • mol

acne прыщ *prihshch*

across через *cheh • rees*

adapter адаптер *ah • dahp • ter*

address адрес *ah • drees*

adhesive bandage пластырь
plahs • tihr'

admission charge входная плата
fkhahd • nah • yah plah • tah

adult взрослый *vzros • liy*

after после *pos • lee*

aftershave лосьон после бритья
las' • yon pos • lee breet' • yah

age n возраст *voz • rahst*

agree соглашаться
sah • glah • shah • tsa

air воздух *voz • dookh*

air conditioning кондиционер
kahn • dee • tsih • ah • nyer

air mail авиапочта
ah • vee • ah • poch • tah

air pump воздушный насос
vahz • doosh • niy nah • sos

air sickness bag гигиенический
пакет *gee • gee • ee • nee •
chees • keey pah • kyet*

airport аэропорт
ah • eh • rah • port

aisle seat место у прохода
myes • tah oo prah • khoh • dah

alarm clock будильник
boo • deel' • neek

allergy аллергия
ah • leer • gee • yah

almost почти *pahch • tee*

alone один *ah • deen*

already уже *oo • zheh*

also также *tahg • zheh*

alter переделывать
pee • ree • dyeh • lih • vaht'

---

adj adjective   **BE** British English   **prep** preposition
adv adverb   **n** noun   **v** verb

aluminum foil фольга fahl' • _gah_
always всегда fseeg • _dah_
amazing поразительный
pah • rah • _zee_ • teel' • niy
ambassador посол pah • _sol_
ambulance скорая помощь
skoh • rah • yah poh • mahshch
American adj американский
ah • mee • ree • _kahn_ • skeey
amount сумма _soo_ • mah
anesthetic обезболивающее
ah • beez • _boh_ • lee • vah •
yoo • shchee • yeh
animal животное
zhih • _vot_ • nah • yeh
another другой droo • _goy_
antibiotic n антибиотик
ahn • tee • bee • _oh_ • teek
antique антикварный
ahn • tee • _kvahr_
antiques store антикварный
магазин ahn • tee • _kvahr_ • niy
mah • gah • _zeen_
antiseptic n антисептик
ahn • tee • sep • teek
any какой-либо
kah • _koy_ • lee • bah
anyone кто-нибудь
ktoh • nee • boot'
anything что-нибудь
shtoh • nee • boot'
apartment квартира
kvahr • _tee_ • rah
apologize просить
прощения prah • _seet'_
prah • _shcheh_ • nee • yah
appendix аппендикс
ah • _pyen_ • deeks
appointment приём pree • _yom_
approximately приблизительно
pree • blee • _zee_ • teel' • nah
area code код kot

arm рука roo • _kah_
around (place) по pah; **(time)**
около _oh_ • kah • lah
arrive прибывать pree • bih • _vaht'_
art gallery картинная галерея
kahr • _teen_ • nah • yah
gah • lee • _ryeh_ • yah
ashtray пепельница
pyeh • peel' • nee • tsah
ask просить prah • _seet'_
aspirin аспирин ah • spee • _reen_
asthmatic n астматик
ahst • _mah_ • teek
at в v
ATM банкомат bahn • kah • _maht_
attack n нападение
nah • pah • _dyeh_ • nee • yeh
attractive привлекательный
pree • vlee • _kah_ • teel' • niy
authentic настоящий
nah • stah • _yah_ • shcheey
authenticity подлинность
pod • leen • nahst'
available (unoccupied)
свободный svah • _bod_ • niy

B

baby ребёнок ree • _byoh_ • nahk
babysitter няня _nyah_ • nyah
back спина spee • _nah_
backache боль в спине bol' f
spee • _nyeh_
backpack рюкзак ryoog • _zahk_
bad плохой plah • _khoy_
baggage [BE] багаж bah • _gahzh_
baggage check
багажная квитанция
bah • _gahzh_ • nah • yah
kvee • _tahn_ • tsih • yah
bakery булочная
boo • lahch • nah • yah
balcony балкон bahl • _kon_

ball мяч *myahch*

ballet балет *bah • lyet*

band (musical group) группа *groo • pah*

bank банк *bahnk*

bar бар *bahr*

barber парикмахер *pah • reekh • mah • kheer*

basement подвал *pahd • vahl*

basket корзина *kahr • zee • nah*

basketball баскетбол *bahs • keet • bol*

battery (car) аккумулятор *ah • kah • moo • lyah • tahr;*
(camera, etc.) батарея *bah • tah • ryeh • yah*

be быть *biht'*

beach пляж *plyahsh*

beautiful красивый *krah • see • viy*

because потому что *pah • tah • moo • shtah*

bed кровать *krah • vaht'*

bedding постельное бельё *pahs • tel' • nah • yeh beel' • yoh*

bedroom спальня *spahl' • nyah*

before (time) до *dah*

begin начинать *nah • chee • naht'*

belong принадлежать *pree • nahd • lee • zhaht'*

belt ремень *ree • myen'*

bicycle велосипед *vee • lah • see • pyet*

big большой *bahl' • shoy*

bikini бикини *bee • kee • nee*

bill счёт *shchot*

binoculars бинокль *bee • noh • kahl'*

bird птица *ptee • tsah*

birthday день рождения *dyen' rahzh • dyeh • nee • yah*

bite *n* укус *oo • koos;* *v* кусать *koo • saht'*

bizarre причудливый *pree • chood • lee • viy*

bladder мочевой пузырь *mah • chee • voy poo • zihr'*

blanket одеяло *ah • dee • yah • lah*

bleach отбеливатель *aht • byeh • lee • vah • teel'*

bleeding *n* кровотечение *krah • vah • tee • cheh • nee • yeh*

blister волдырь *vahl • dihr'*

blood кровь *krof*

blood pressure кровяное давление *krah • vee • noh • yeh dahv • lyeh • nee • yeh*

blouse блузка *bloos • kah*

blow-dry фен *fyen*

boarding card посадочный талон *pah • sah • dahch • niy tah • lon*

boat лодка *lot • kah*

boat trip водная экскурсия *vod • nah • yah ehks • koor • see • yah*

bone кость *kost'*

book *n* книга *knee • gah;* *v* заказывать *zah • kah • zih • vaht'*

bookstore книжный магазин *kneezh • niy mah • gah • zeen*

boots сапоги *sa • pah • gee*

borrow одолжить *ah • dahl • zhit'*

botanical garden ботанический сад *bah • tah • nee • chees • keey saht*

bottle opener открывалка *aht • krih • vahl • kah*

boy мальчик *mahl' • cheek*

boyfriend друг *drook*

bra бюстгальтер *byoost • gahl • tyer*

bracelet браслет *brahs • lyet*

break *v* сломать *slah • maht'*

break down v сломаться
  slah • mah • tsah
break-in n взлом _vzlom_
breast грудь _groot'_
breathe дышать _dih • shaht'_
breathtaking захватывающий
  _zah • khvah • tih • vah • yoo •
  shcheey_
bridge мост _most_
British adj британский
  bree • tahn • skeey
brochure брошюра
  brah • shoo • rah
brooch брошь _brosh_
browse v просматривать
  prah • smah • tree • vaht'
bruise n синяк _see • nyahk_
bucket ведро _veed • roh_
build строить _stroh • eet'_
building здание _zdah • nee • yeh_
burn n ожог _ah • zhok_
bus автобус _ahf • toh • boos_
bus route автобусный
  маршрут _ahf • toh • boos • niy
  mahrsh • root_
bus station автобусная станция
  _ahf • toh • boos • nah • yah
  stahn • tsih • yah_
bus stop автобусная остановка
  _ahf • toh • boos • nah • yah
  ahs • tah • nof • kah_
business бизнес _beez • nees_
business trip командировка
  kah • mahn • dee • rof • kah
busy adj (occupied) занятый
  zah • nyah • tiy
but но _noh_
butane gas газовый баллон
  gah • zah • viy bah • lon
button кнопка _knop • kah_
buy покупать _pah • koo • paht'_
by (time) к _k_

C

cabin каюта _kah • yoo • tah_
calendar календарь
  kah • leen • dahr'
call v звать _zvaht'_; (for someone)
  заходить за _zah • khah • deet'
  zah;_ (phone) звонить
  zvah • neet'
camera фотоаппарат
  foh • tah • ah • pah • raht
camera case футляр _foot • lyahr_
campbed раскладушка
  rahs • klah • doosh • kah
camping кемпинг _kyem • peenk_
camping equipment снаряжение
  snah • ree • zheh • nee • yeh
campsite палаточный лагерь
  pah • lah • tahch • niy lah • geer'
can n банка _bahn • kah;_ v мочь
  moch
can opener консервный нож
  kahn • syerv • niy nosh
cancel отменять
  aht • mee • nyaht'
candle свеча _svee • chah_
cap (dental) коронка
  kah • ron • kah
car машина _mah • shih • nah;_
  (train compartment) вагон
  vahh • gon
car hire [BE] прокат
  автомобилей _prah • kaht
  ahf • tah • mah • bee • leey_
car park [BE] автостоянка
  ahf • tah • stah • yahn • kah
carafe графин _grah • feen_
careful осторожный
  ahs • tah • rozh • niy
carpet (rug) ковер _kah • vyor_
cart тележка _tee • lyesh • kah_
carton пакет _pah • kyet_

cash наличные
nah • leech • nih • yeh

cash desk касса *kah • sah*

cashier кассир *kah • seer*

casino казино *kah • zee • noh*

castle замок *zah • mahk*

cathedral собор *sah • bor*

cave пещера *pee • shcheh • rah*

CD компакт-диск *kahm • pahkt • deesk*

CD player лазерный проигрыватель *lah • zeer • niy prah • eeg • rih • vah • teel'*

cell phone мобильный телефон
mah • beel' • niy tee • lee • fon

center центр *tsentr*

ceramics керамика
kee • rah • mee • kah

certificate свидетельство
svee • dyeh • teel' • stvah

chain цепочка *tsih • poch • kah*

change *n* сдача *zdah • chah*;
v (alter) поменять
pah • mee • nyaht'; (buses, etc.) делать пересадку
dyeh • laht' pee • ree • saht • koo;
(baby) перепеленать
pee • ree • pee • lee • naht';
(money) обменять
ahb • mee • nyaht'

charge *n* плата *plah • tah*

charter flight чартерный рейс
chahr • ter • niy reys

cheap дешёвый *dee • shoh • viy*

check *n* чек *chek*; *v* проверять
prah • veh • ryaht'

check in *v* регистрироваться
ree • gees • tree • rah • vah • tsah

check-in desk
регистрационная стойка
ree • gee • strah • tsih • on • nah • yah stoy • kah

check out *v* (hotel) выезжать
vih • eezh • zhaht'

chemist [BE] аптека
ahp • tyeh • kah

cheque [BE] чек *chek*

chess шахматы *shahkh • mah • tih*

chest (body part) грудная клетка
grood • nah • yah klyet • kah

child *adj* детский *dyets • keey*;
n ребёнок *ree • byoh • nahk*

child seat (in car) детское сиденье *dyets • kah • yeh see • dyen' • yeh*

children дети *dyeh • teeh*

church церковь *tser • kahf'*

cigarette сигарета
see • gah • ryeh • tah

cigar сигара *see • gah • rah*

cinema [BE] кинотеатр
kee • nah • tee • ahtr

class (type of seat, etc.) класс
klahs

clean *adj* чистый *chees • tiy*;
v чистить *chees • teet'*

cliff скала *skah • lah*

cling film [BE]
продуктовая плёнка
prah • dook • toh • vah • yah plyon • kah

clock часы *chah • sih*

close *v* (store, etc.) закрываться
zah • krih • vah • tsah

clothes одежда *ah • dyezh • dah*

cloudy облачный *ob • lahch • niy*

clubs (golf) клюшки *klyoosh • kee*

coach (long-distance bus)
междугородний автобус
meezh • doo • gah • rod • niy ahf • toh • boos

coast побережье
pah • bee • ryezh • yeh

coat пальто *pahl' • toh*

coatcheck гардероб
gahr • dee • rop

code (area, dialing) код *kot*

coin монета *mah • nyeh • tah*

cold *adj* холодный *khah • lod • niy;*
n **(flu)** простуда *prah • stoo • dah*

colleague коллега *kah • lyeh • gah*

collect *v* забирать *zah • bee • raht'*

color цвет *tsvyet*

comb расчёска *rah • shchos • kah*

come приходить
pree • khah • deet'

commission комиссионный сбор
kah • mee • see • oh • niy zbor

compact компактный
kahm • pahk • tniy

company (business)
предприятие
preet • pree • yah • tee • yeh;
(companionship) компания
kahm • pah • nee • yah

compartment (train) купе
koo • peh

complaint жалоба
zhah • lah • bah

concert концерт *kahn • tsert*

concert hall концертный зал
kahn • tsert • niy zahl

concussion сотрясение мозга
sah • tree • syeh • nee • yeh
moz • gah

conditioner кондиционер
kahn • dee • tsih • ah • nyer

condom презерватив
pree • zeer • vah • teev

conductor дирижёр
dee • ree • zhor

confirm (reservation)
подтвердить *paht • tveer • deet'*

consulate консульство
kon • sool' • stvah

consult *v* консультироваться
kahn • sool' • tee • rah • vah • tsah

contact *v* связаться
svyah • zah • tsah

contagious инфекционный
een • feek • tsih • oh • niy

contain *v* содержать
sah • deer • zhaht'

cook *n* повар *poh • vahr;*
v готовить *gah • toh • veet'*

cooker [BE] плита *plee • tah*

copper медь *myet*

copy *n* копия *koh • pee • yah*

corkscrew штопор *shtoh • pahr*

corner угол *oo • gahl*

correct *adv* правильно
prah • veel' • nah

cosmetics косметика
kahs • myeh • tee • kah

cottage дача *dah • chah*

cotton вата *vah • tah*

cough *n* кашель *kah • shihl';*
v кашлять *kahsh • lyaht'*

country (nation) страна
strah • nah

cramps судороги
soo • dah • rah • gee

credit card кредитная карточка
kree • deet • nah • yah
kahr • tahch • kah

crib детская кроватка
dets • kah • yah krah • vaht • kah

crossroad перекрёсток
pee • ree • kryos • tahk

cruise *n* круиз *kroo • eez*

crutches костыли *kahs • tih • lee*

crystal хрусталь *khroos • tal'*

cup чашка *chahsh • kah*

cupboard шкаф *shkahf*

currency валюта *vah • lyoo • tah*

currency exchange office
обмен валюты ahb • _myen_
vah • _lyoo_ • tih

curtains занавеси
zah • nah • vee • see

customs таможня
tah • _mozh_ • nyah

customs declaration
таможенная декларация
tah • _moh_ • zhih • nah • yah
deek • lah • _rah_ • tsih • yah

cut порез pah • _ryes_

cycle route
велосипедный маршрут
vee • lah • see • _pyed_ • niy
mahrsh • _root_

cycling велоспорт
vyeh • lah • _sport_

D

daily ежедневно
ee • zhee • _dnyev_ • nah

damage v повредить
pah • vree • _deet'_

damp adv сыро _sih_ • rah;
n сырость _sih_ • rahst

dance n танец _tah_ • neets

dangerous adj опасный
ah • _pahs_ • niy

dark тёмный _tyom_ • niy

dawn рассвет rahs • _vyet_

day день dyen'

deaf глухой gloo • _khoy_

deck chair шезлонг shez • _lonk_

declare предъявлять
preed • yahv • _lyaht'_

deep глубокий gloo • _boh_ • keey

degree (temperature) градус
grah • doos

delay задержка zah • _dyersh_ • kah

deliver доставлять
dah • stahv • _lyat'_

denim джинсовый
dzhihn • _soh_ • viy

dentist зубной врач zoob • _noy_
vrahch

dentures протез prah • _tes_

deodorant дезодорант
dee • zah • dah • _rahnt_

depart (train, bus) отправляться
aht • prahv • _lyah_ • tsah

department отдел aht • _dyel_

departure lounge зал вылета
zahl _vih_ • lee • tah

deposit аванс ah • _vahns_

describe описывать
ah • _pee_ • sih • vaht'

destination место
назначения _myes_ • tah
nahz • nah • _cheh_ • nee • yah

details подробности
pahd • _rob_ • nahs • tee

detergent моющее средство
moh • yoo • shchee • yeh
sryet • stvah

diabetes диабет dee • ah • _byet_

diabetic n диабетик
dee • ah • _byeh_ • teek

diagnosis диагноз
dee • _ahg_ • nahs

diamond брильянт breel' • _yahnt_

diaper пелёнка pee • _lyon_ • kah

diarrhea понос pah • _nos_

dice кости _kos_ • tee

dictionary словарь slah • _vahr'_

diesel дизельное топливо
dee • zeel' • nah • yeh
top • lee • vah

diet n диета dee • _yeh_ • tah

difficult трудный _trood_ • niy

dining car вагон-ресторан
vah • _gon_ rees • tah • _rahn_

dining room столовая
stah • _loh_ • vah • yah

dinner ужин <u>oo</u> • zhihn

direct adj (train) прямой
pryah • <u>moy</u>; v направлять
nah • prahv • <u>lyaht'</u>

direction направление
nah • prahv • <u>lyeh</u> • nee • yeh

director директор dee • <u>ryek</u> • tahr

directory (telephone)
телефонный справочник
tee • lee • <u>foh</u> • niy
<u>sprah</u> • vahch • neek

dirty грязный <u>gryahz</u> • niy

disabled инвалид een • vah • <u>leet</u>

discount скидка <u>skeet</u> • kah

dish (meal) блюдо <u>blyoo</u> • dah

dishcloth тряпка <u>tryahp</u> • kah

dishwasher
посудомоечная машина
pah • soo • dah • <u>moh</u> • eech •
nah • yah mah • <u>shih</u> • nah

dishwashing liquid средство для
мытья посуды <u>sryet</u> • stvah dlyah
miht' • <u>yah</u> pah • <u>soo</u> • dih

disturb беспокоить
bees • pah • <u>koh</u> • eet'

dive нырять nih • <u>ryaht'</u>

diving equipment
снаряжение для дайвинга
snah • ree • zheh • nee • <u>yeh</u>
dlyah <u>die</u> • veen • gah

divorce развод rahz • vod

doctor врач vrahch

doll кукла <u>kook</u> • lah

door дверь dvyer'

double bed двуспальная
кровать dvoo • <u>spahl'</u> • nah • yah
krah • <u>vaht'</u>

double room двухместный номер
dvookh • <u>myes</u> • niy <u>noh</u> • meer

downtown area центр города
tsentr <u>goh</u> • rah • dah

dozen дюжина <u>dyoo</u> • zhih • nah

dress платье <u>plaht'</u> • yeh

drink v пить peet'

drive v ехать <u>yeh</u> • khaht'

driver водитель vah • <u>dee</u> • teel'

driver's licence водительские
права vah • <u>dee</u> • teel' • skee • ye
<u>prah</u> • vah

drugstore аптека ahp • <u>tyeh</u> • kah

drunk adj пьяный <u>pyah</u> • niy

dry clean v отдавать в
химчистку aht • dah • <u>vaht'</u> f
kheem • <u>cheest</u> • koo

dry cleaner химчистка
kheem • <u>cheest</u> • kah

during во время vah <u>vrye</u> • myah

dustbin [BE] мусорный бак
<u>moo</u> • sahr • niy bahk

duty пошлина <u>posh</u> • lee • nah

E

ear ухо <u>oo</u> • khah

earache боль в ухе bol'
v <u>oo</u> • khee

early ранний <u>rahn</u> • neey

earrings серьги <u>syer'</u> • gee

easy лёгкий <u>lyokh</u> • keey

eat есть yest'

economy class пассажирский
класс pah • sah • <u>zhihr</u> • skeey
klahs

electric outlet розетка
rah • <u>zyet</u> • kah

electric shaver электробритва
eh • <u>lyek</u> • trah • <u>breet</u> • vah

electricity электричество
eh • leek • <u>tree</u> • cheest • vah

elevator лифт leeft

else ещё ee • <u>shchoh</u>

e-mail электронная почта
ee • leek • <u>troh</u> • nah • yah
<u>poch</u> • tah

e-mail address адрес
электронной почты _ah_ • drees
ee • leek • _tron_ • nie poch • tih

e-ticket электронный билет
ee • leek • _tron_ • niy bee • _lyet_

embassy посольство
pah • _sol'_ • stvah

emerald изумруд ee • _zoom_ • root

emergency крайний случай
krie • neey sloo • chie

emergency exit аварийный
выход ah • vah • _reey_ • niy
vih • khaht

empty adj пустой poos • _toy_

enamel эмаль ee • _mahl'_

end v кончаться
kahn • _chah_ • tsah

England Англия _ahn_ • glee • yah

English adj английский
ahn • _gleey_ • skeey

enjoy нравиться _nrah_ • vee • tsah

enough достаточно
dah • _stah_ • tahch • nah

entrance fee входная плата
fkhahd • _nah_ • yah plah • tah

entry visa въездная виза
vyezd • _nah_ • yah vee • zah

envelope конверт kahn • _vyert_

epileptic n эпилептик
ee • pee • _lyep_ • teek

equipment оборудование
ah • bah • _roo_ • dah • vah •
nee • yeh; **(sports)** снаряжение
snah • ryah • _zheh_ • nee • yeh

error ошибка ah • _shihp_ • kah

escalator эскалатор
ees • kah • _lah_ • tahr

essential основной
ahs • nahv • _noy_

European Union (EU)
Европейский союз
yev • rah • _pey_ • skeey sah • _yoos_

event событие sah • _bih_ • tee • yeh

every каждый _kahzh_ • diy

example пример pree • _myer_

except кроме _kroh_ • mee

excess luggage перевес багажа
pee • ree • _vyes_ bah • gah • _zhah_

exchange v обменивать
ahb • _myeh_ • nee • vaht'

exchange rate курс обмена
koors ahb • _myeh_ • nah

excursion экскурсия
eks • _koor_ • see • yah

exit n выход _vih_ • khaht

expensive дорогой dah • rah • _goy_

express экспресс eks • _pres_

extension добавочный
номер dah • _bah_ • vahch • niy
noh • meer

extra adv ещё ee • _shchoh_

extract v удалять oo • dah • _lyaht'_

eye глаз glahs

F

fabric (material) ткань tkahn'

face лицо lee • _tsoh_

facial чистка лица _cheest_ • kah
lee • _tsah_

facilities удобства
oo • _dops_ • tvah

family семья seem' • _yah_

fan (air) вентилятор
veen • tee • _lyah_ • tahr

far далеко dah • lee • _koh_

far-sighted дальнозоркий
dahl' • nah • _zor_ • keey'

fare плата _plah_ • tah

farm ферма _fyer_ • mah

fast adv быстро _bihst_ • rah

faucet кран krahn

favorite любимый lyoo • _bee_ • miy

fax факс faks

feed кормить kar • _meet'_

ferry паром *pah • rom*

fever жар *zhahr*

few мало *mah • lah*

filling (dental) пломба *plom • bah*

film [BE] **(movie)** фильм *feel'm;* **(camera)** плёнка *plyon • kah*

filter фильтр *feel' • tr*

finger палец *pah • leets*

fire *n* пожар *pah • zhahr*

fire alarm пожарная тревога *pah • zhahr • nah • yah tree • voh • gah*

fire escape пожарная лестница *pah • zhahr • nah • yah lyes • nee • tsah*

fire extinguisher огнетушитель *ahg • nee • too • shih • teel'*

firewood дрова *drah • vah*

first class первый класс *pyer • viy klahs*

fit *v* **(clothes)** подходить *paht • khah • deet'*

fitting room примерочная *pree • myeh • rahch • nah • yah*

fix *v* чинить *chee • neet'*

flashlight фонарь *fah • nahr'*

flight рейс *reys*

floor этаж *eh • tahsh*

florist цветочный магазин *tsvyeh • toch • niy mah • gah • zeen*

flower цветок *tsvee • tok*

flu грипп *greep*

fog туман *too • mahn*

folk народный *nah • rod • niy*

follow *v* **(pursue)** преследовать *pree • slyeh • dah • vaht'*

food *n* еда *yee • dah*

foot (body) нога *nah • gah*

football [BE] футбол *food • bol*

footpath тропинка *trah • peen • kah*

for на *nah*

foreign currency иностранная валюта *ee • nah • strah • nah • yah vah • lyoo • tah*

forest лес *lyes*

forget забывать *zah • bih • vaht'*

fork вилка *veel • kah*

form *n* бланк *blahnk*

fountain фонтан *fahn • tahn*

foyer (hotel, theater) фойе *fie • yeh*

fracture (a bone) перелом *pee • ree • lom*

frame *n* **(glasses)** оправа *ah • prah • vah*

free *adj* **(not busy/available)** свободный *svah • bod • niy*

freezer морозильная камера *mah • rah • zeel' • nah • yah kah • mee • rah*

frequently часто *chahs • tah*

fresh свежий *svyeh • zhiy*

friend друг *drook*

friendly *adj* дружеский *droo • zhees • keey*

from (place) из *eez;* **(time)** с *s*

frost мороз *mah • roz*

frying pan сковорода *skah • vah • rah • dah*

full *adj* полный *pol • niy*

fun веселье *vee • syel' • yeh*

furniture мебель *myeh • beel'*

G

game игра *eeg • rah*

garage гараж *gah • rash*

garbage bag мусорный мешок *moo • sahr • niy mee • shok*

garden сад *saht*

gas (fuel) бензин *been • zeen*

gas station
заправочная станция
zah • _prah_ • vahch • nah • yah
stahn • tsih • yah

gate (airport) выход _vih_ • khaht

gauze бинт beent

genuine настоящий
nah • stah • _yah_ • shcheey

get (receive) получать
pah • loo • _chaht';_ **(to
destination)** добираться до
dah • bee • _rah_ • tsah doh

gift подарок pah • _dah_ • rahk

gift store магазин
подарков mah • gah • _zeen_
pah • _dahr_ • kahf

girl девочка _dyeh_ • vahch • kah

girlfriend подруга pah • _droo_ • gah

give давать dah • _vaht'_

glass стакан stah • _kahn_

glasses (optical) очки ahch • _kee_

glove перчатка peer • _chaht_ • kah

go ходить khah • _deet'_

go away уходить oo • khah • _deet'_

gold золото _zoh_ • lah • tah

golf гольф gol'f

golf course поле для гольфа
poh • lyeh dlyah _gol'_ • fah

good хороший khah • _roh_ • shiy

gram грамм grahm

grass трава trah • _vah_

gray серый _syeh_ • riy

Great Britain Великобритания
vee • lee • kah • bree • _tah_ • nee • yah

group группа _groo_ • pah

guarantee гарантия
gah • _rahn_ • tee • yah

guide (tour) гид geet

guidebook путеводитель
poo • tee • vah • _dee_ • teel'

guided tour экскурсия
eks • _koor_ • see • yah

guitar гитара gee • _tah_ • rah

gum десна dees • _nah_

gym спортзал sport • _zahl_

gynecologist гинеколог
gee • nee • _koh_ • lahk

H

hair волосы _voh_ • lah • sih

hairbrush щётка для волос
shchot • kah dlyah vah • _los_

haircut стрижка _streesh_ • kah

hairdresser парикмахер
pah • reek • _mah_ • kheer

hairspray лак для волос lahk
dlyah vah • _los_

half половина pah • lah • _vee_ • nah

hand рука roo • _kah_

hand luggage ручная кладь
rooch • nah • yah klahd'

handbag [BE] сумка _soom_ • kah

handicapped инвалид
een • vah • _leet_

handicraft ремесло
ree • _mees_ • loh

handkerchief платок plah • _tok_

hanger вешалка
vyeh • shahl • kah

hangover похмелье
pahkh • _myel'_ • yeh

harbor гавань _gah_ • vahn'

hat шапка _shahp_ • kah

hay fever сенная лихорадка
see • _nah_ • yah lee • khah •
raht • kah

head голова gah • lah • _vah_

headache головная боль
gah • lahv • _nah_ • yah bol'

health insurance
медицинское страхование
mee • dee • _tsihn_ • skah • yah
strah • _khof_ • kah

hear слышать _slih_ • shaht'

hearing aid слуховой аппарат
sloo • khah • voy ah • pah • raht

heart сердце *syer • tseh*

heart attack сердечный приступ
seer • dyech • niy prees • toop

heart condition
заболевание сердца
*zah • bah • lee • vah • nee • yeh
syer • tsah*

heater обогреватель
ah • bah • gree • vah • teel'

heating *n* отопление
ah • tahp • lyeh • nee • yeh

heavy тяжёлый *tee • zhoh • liy*

height рост *rost*

helmet шлем *shlyem*

help *v* помогать *pah • mah • gaht'*

here здесь *zdyes'*

high высокий *vih • soh • keey*

high blood pressure высокое
давление *vih • soh • kha • yeh
dahv • lyeh • nee • yeh*

highlight *v* (hair) мелировать
mee • lee • rah • vaht'

highway шоссе *shah • seh*

hiking *n* поход *pah • khot*

hill холм *kholm*

hire [BE] взять напрокат *vzyaht'
nah • prah • kaht*

hobby хобби *khoh • bee*

hold on *v* подождать
pah • dah • zhdaht'

hole (in clothes) дырка *dihr • kah*

holiday [BE] отпуск *ot • poosk*

home дом *dom*

honeymoon медовый месяц
mee • doh • viy myeh • syahts

horse лошадь *loh • shahd'*

horseracing бега *bee • gah*

hospital больница
bahl' • nee • tsah

hot *adj* горячий *gah • ryah • cheey*

hotel гостиница
gahs • tee • nee • tsah

hotel room номер *noh • meer*

hour час *chahs*

house дом *dom*

hungry голодный *gah • lod • niy*

hurt *v* болеть *bah • lyet'*

husband муж *moosh*

I

icy гололёд *gah • lah • lyot*

identification документ
dah • koo • myent

ill [BE] больной *bahl' • noy*

illegal незаконный
nee • zah • koh • niy

immediately немедленно
nee • myeh • dlee • nah

in (place) в *v*; (time) через
cheh • rees

incredible невероятный
nee • vee • rah • yaht • niy

indigestion изжога
eezh • zhoh • gah

indoor закрытый *zah • krih • tiy*

inexpensive недорогой
nee • dah • rah • goy

infect заразить *zah • rah • zeet'*

infection инфекция
een • fyek • tsih • yah

inflammation воспаление
vahs • pah • lyeh • nee • yeh

information информация
een • fahr • mah • tsih • yah

injection укол *oo • kol*

injury травма *trahv • mah*

innocent невиновен
nee • vee • noh • veen

insect насекомое
nah • see • koh • mah • yeh

insert *v* вставлять *fstahv • lyat'*

inside внутри *vnoo • tree*

insist настаивать
nah • _stah_ • ee • vaht'

insomnia бессоница
bees • _soh_ • nee • tsah

instructions инструкция
een • _strook_ • tsih • yah

insulin инсулин een • soo • _leen_

insurance страховка
strah • _khof_ • kahh

insurance claim страховой иск
strah • khah • _voy_ eesk

insurance company
страховая компания
strah • khah • _vah_ • yah
kahm • _pah_ • nee • yah

interesting интересный
een • tee • _ryes_ • niy

internet интернет een • ter • _net_

internet cafe интернет-кафе
een • ter • _net_ kah • _feh_

interpreter переводчик
pee • ree • _vot_ • cheek

intersection перекресток
pee • ree • _kryos_ • tahk

invitation приглашение
pree • glah • _sheh_ • nee • yeh

invite приглашать
pree • glah • _shaht'_

iron утюг oo • _tyook_

itemized bill детальный счёт
dee • _tahl'_ • niy shchot

J

jacket куртка _koort_ • kah

jar банка _bahn_ • kah

jaw челюсть _cheh_ • _lyoost'_

jazz джаз dzhahs

jeans джинсы _dzhihn_ • sih

jeweler ювелирный магазин
yoo • vee • _leer_ • niy
mah • gah • _zeen_

job работа rah • _boh_ • tah

joke шутка _shoot_ • kah

journalist журналист
zhoor • nah • _leest_

journey поездка pah • _yest_ • kah

K

kettle чайник _chie_ • neek

key ключ klyooch

key card электронный ключ
eh • leek • _tron_ • niy klyooch

key ring брелок bree • _lok_

kiddie pool детский бассейн
dyets • keey bah • _seyn_

kidney почка _poch_ • kah

kind (pleasant) любезный
lyoo • _byez_ • niy

kiss v целовать tsih • lah • _vaht'_

kitchen кухня _kookh_ • nyah

knee колено kah • _lyeh_ • nah

knife нож nosh

kosher кошерный kah • _sher_ • niy

L

label n ярлык yahr • _lihk_

lace кружево _kroo_ • zhih • vah

ladder стремянка
stree • _myahn_ • kah

lake озеро _oh_ • zee • rah

lamp лампа _lahm_ • pah

land v приземляться
pree • zeem • _lyah_ • tsah

language course языковые
курсы yah • zih • kah • _vih_ • yeh
koor • sih

large большой bahl' • _shoy_

last adj последний
pahs • _lyed_ • neey

late adj поздний _poz_ • neey

laugh v смеяться
smee • _yah_ • tsah

launderette [BE] прачечная
prah • cheech • nah • yah

laundromat прачечная
prah • cheech • nah • yah

lawyer адвокат *ahd • vah • kaht*

leader (of group) руководитель
roo • kah • vah • dee • teel'

leaflet брошюра *brah • shoo • rah*

leak *v* (roof, pipe) течь *tyech*

learn (language) изучать
ee • zoo • chaht'

leather кожа *koh • zhah*

leave *v* уезжать *oo • eezh • zhaht'*

left *adj* левый *leh • viy*

left-luggage office [BE] камера
хранения *kah • mee • rah*
khrah • nyeh • nee • yah

leg нога *nah • gah*

legal законный *zah • koh • niy*

lend дать взаимы *daht' vzie • mih*

length длина *dlee • nah*

less меньше *myen' • sheh*

lesson урок *oo • rok*

letter письмо *pees' • moh*

library библиотека
bee • blee • ah • tyeh • kah

lifeboat спасательная лодка
spah • sah • teel' • nah • yah
lot • kah

lifeguard спасатель
spah • sah • teel'

lifejacket спасательный жилет
spah • sah • teel' • niy zhih • lyet

lift [BE] *n* лифт *leeft*

lift pass пропуск на
подъёмник *proh • poosk nah*
pahd • yom • neek

light *adj* (weight) лёгкий
lyokh • keey; (color) светлый
svyet • liy; (electric) свет *svyet*

light bulb лампочка
lahm • pahch • kah

lighter (cigarette) зажигалка
zah • zhih • gahl • kah

like *v* нравиться *nrah • vee • tsah*

line (subway) линия
lee • nee • yah

linen лён *lyon*

lip губа *goo • bah*

lipstick губная памада
goob • nah • yah pah • mah • dah

liquor store винный магазин
vee • niy mah • gah • zeen

little (small) маленький
mah • leen' • keey

liver печень *pyeh • cheen'*

living room гостиная
gahs • tee • nah • yah

lobby (theater, hotel) фойе
fah • yeh

local местный *mes • niy*

lock *n* замок *zah • mok*

login вход в систему *fhot f*
sees • tyem • moo

long длинный *dlee • niy*

long-distance bus
междугородний автобус
myezh • doo • gah • rod • niy
ahf • toh • boos

long-sighted [BE] дальнозоркий
dahl' • nah • zor • keey

loose (clothing) свободный
svah • bod • niy

lose потерять *pah • tee • ryaht'*

lost-and-found бюро находок
byoo • roh nah • khoh • dahk

loud громкий *grom • keey*

love v любить *lyoo • beet'*

luggage багаж *bah • gahsh*

lunch обед *ah • byet*

lung лёгкое *lyokh • kah • yeh*

M

magazine журнал *zhoor • nahl*

magnificent великолепный
vee • lee • kah • lyep • niy

mail n почта *poch • tah;*
v отправлять *aht • prahv • lyaht'*
mailbox почтовый ящик
pahch • toh • viy yah • shcheek
main главный *glahv • niy*
main course второе
ftah • roh • yeh
make-up макияж
mah • kee • yahsh
male мужской *moosh • skoy*
mall (shopping) торговый центр
tahr • goh • viy tsentr
man (male) мужчина
moo • shchee • nah
manicure маникюр
mah • nee • kyoor
manual n **(for smth)** руководство
roo • kah • vod • stvah
many много *mnoh • gah*
map карта *kahr • tah*
market рынок *rih • nahk*
married (man) женат
zhih • naht; **(woman)** замужем
zah • moo • zhem
mascara тушь *toosh*
mask (diving) маска *mahs • kah*
massage массаж *mah • sahsh*
match (sport) матч *mahch*
matches спички *speech • kee*
mattress матрас *maht • rahs*
meal блюдо *blyoo • dah*
mean v значить *znah • cheet'*
measure v измерить
eez • myeh • reet
measurement измерение
eez • mee • ryeh • nee • yeh
medication лекарство
lee • kahr • stvah
meet v встречаться
fstree • chah • tsah
message сообщение
sah • ahp • shcheh • nee • yeh

metal металл *mee • tahl*
microwave микроволновая печь
meek • rah • vahl • noh •
vah • yah pyech
migraine мигрень *meeg • ryen'*
mileage километраж
kee • lah • mee • trahsh
mine мой *moy*
minute минута *mee • noo • tah*
mirror зеркало *zyer • kah • lah*
miss v **(pass)** пропустить
prah • poos • teet'; **(get lost)**
пропасть *prah • pahst'*
mistake ошибка *ah • shihp • kah*
misunderstanding
недоразумение
nee • dah • rah • zoo • myeh •
nee • yeh
mobile phone [BE] мобильный
телефон *mah • beel' • niy*
tee • lee • fon
modern современный
sah • vree • myen • niy
money деньги *dyen' • gee*
month месяц *myeh • syahts*
mop швабра *shvahb • rah*
more больше *bol' • sheh*
mosque мечеть *mee • chet'*
mosquito bite комариный укус
kah • mah • ree • niy oo • koos
motion sickness морская
болезнь *mahr • skah • yah*
bah • lyezn'
motorboat моторка
mah • tor • kah
motorway [BE] шоссе *shah • seh*
mountain гора *gah • rah*
mouth рот *rot*
movie фильм *feel'm*
movie theater кинотеатр
kee • nah • tee • ahtr
Mr. господин *gahs • pah • deen*

Mrs. госпожа *gahs • pah • zhah*
much много *mnoh • gah*
mug *n* кружка *kroosh • kah*;
  v ограбить *ah • grah • beet'*
mugging *n* ограбление
  ah • grahb • lyeh • nee • yeh
museum музей *moo • zey*
music музыка *moo • zih • kah*
my мой *moy*
myself сам *sahm*

N

name (first name) имя *ee • myah*;
  (family name) фамилия
  fah • mee • lee • yah
napkin салфетка *sahl • fyet • kah*
nappy *[BE]* пелёнка
  pee • lyon • kah
narrow узкий *oos • keey*
national национальный
  nah • tsih • ah • nahl' • niy
nationality национальность
  nah • tsih • ah • nahl' • nahst'
nature reserve заповедник
  zah • pah • vyed • neek
near около *oh • kah • lah*
nearby рядом *ryah • dahm*
near-sighted близорукий
  blee • za • roo • keey
neck шея *sheh • yah*
necklace ожерелье
  ah • zhih • ryel' • yeh
nerve нерв *nyerf*
nesting doll матрёшка
  maht • ryosh • kah
never никогда *nee • kahg • dah*
new новый *noh • viy*
newspaper газета *gah • zyeh • tah*
newsstand газетный киоск
  gah • zyet • niy kee • osk
next следующий
  slyeh • doo • yoo • shcheey

nice хороший *khah • roh • shiy*
niece племянница
  plee • myah • nee • tsah
no нет *nyet*
no one никто *nee • ktoh*
noisy шумный *shoom • niy*
non-alcoholic безалкогольный
  beez • ahl • kah • gol' • niy
non-smoking некурящий
  nee • koo • ryah • shcheey
nonsense ерунда *ee • roon • dah*
normal нормальный
  nahr • mahl' • niy
nose нос *nos*
nothing ничего *nee • chee • voh*
notify сообщать
  sah • aph • shchaht'
number (phone) номер
  noh • meer
nurse сестра *sees • trah*

O

occupied занятый *zah • nee • tiy*
odds (betting) шансы *shahn • sih*
off-license *[BE]* винный магазин
  vee • niy mah • gah • zeen
office офис *oh • fees*
often часто *chahs • tah*
old старый *sta • riy*
on (day, date) на *v*; **(place)** на *nah*
once один раз *ah • deen rahs*
one-way ticket билет в один
  конец *bee • lyet v ah • deen
  kah • nyets*
open *adj* открытый *aht • krih • tiy*;
  v открывать *aht • krih • vaht'*
opening hours часы работы
  chah • sih rah • boh • tih
opera опера *oh • pee • rah*
operation операция
  ah • pee • rah • tsih • yah

opposite напротив
nah • _proh_ • teef

optician оптика _op_ • tee • kah

or или _ee_ • lee

orchestra оркестр ahr • _kyestr_

order v заказывать
zah • _ka_ • zih • vaht'

ordering заказ zah • _kahs_

Orthodox православный
prah • vah • _slahv_ • niy

other другой droo • _goy_

outdoor на открытом
воздухе nah aht • _krih_ • tahm
voz • doo • khee

outside на улице nah
_oo_ • lee • tseh

oven духовка doo • _khof_ • kah

overheat перегреться
pee • ree • _gryeh_ • tsah

overlook n смотровая площадка
smah • trah • _vah_ • yah
plah • _shchaht_ • kah

owner владелец vlah • _dyeh_ • leets

P

pacifier соска _sos_ • kah

pack v упаковывать
oo • pah • _koh_ • vih • vaht'

package посылка pah • _sihl_ • kah

packet пакет pah • _kyet_

paddling pool [BE] детский
бассейн _dyets_ • keey bah • _seyn_

pain боль bol'

painkiller болеутоляющее
boh • lee • oo • tah • _lyah_ •
yoo • shchee • yeh

painting картина kahr • _tee_ • nah

pair пара _pah_ • rah

palace дворец dvah • _ryets_

panorama панорама
pah • nah • _rah_ • mah

pants брюки _bryoo_ • kee

paper бумага boo • _mah_ • gah

paracetamol [BE] парацетамол
pah • rah • tsih • tah • _mol_

parents родители
rah • _dee_ • tee • lee

park парк pahrk

parking lot автостоянка
ahf • tah • stah • _yahn_ • kah

party (social) вечеринка
vee • chee • _reen_ • kah

pass v проезжать
prah • eezh • _zhaht'_

passport паспорт _pahs_ • pahrt

pastry store кондитерская
kahn • _dee_ • teer • skah • yah

patch v заштопать
zah • _shtoh_ • paht'

path тропинка trah • _peen_ • kah

patient n пациент pah • tsih • _yent_

pay v платить plah • _teet'_

pay phone телефон-автомат
tee • lee • _fon_ ahf • tah • _maht_

payment оплата ah • _plah_ • tah

peak пик peek

pearl жемчуг _zhem_ • chook

pedestrian crossing переход
pee • ree • _khot_

pedestrian zone пешеходная
зона pee • shih • _khod_ • nah • yah
zoh • nah

pedicure педикюр
pee • dee • _kyoor_

pen ручка _rooch_ • kah

pencil карандаш
kah • rahn • _dahsh_

people люди _lyoo_ • dee

perhaps может быть _moh_ • zhiht
biht'

period n **(historical)**
период pee • _ree_ • aht;
(menstrual) менструация
meen • stroo • _ah_ • tsih • yah

petrol [BE] бензин *been • zeen*

pharmacy аптека *ahp • tyeh • kah*

phone v звонить *zvah • neet'*

phone card
телефонная карточка
*tee • lee • foh • nah • yah
kahr • tahch • kah*

phone call звонок *zvah • nok*

photo фотография
fah • tah • grah • fee • yah

photocopier ксерокс
ksyeh • rahks

photography фотография
fah • tah • grah • fee • yah

phrase фраза *frah • zah*

phrase book разговорник
rahz • gah • vor • neek

pick up v (get) взять
vzyaht'; (collect) забирать
zah • bee • raht'

picnic пикник *peek • neek*

piece n кусочек *koo • soh • cheek*

pill таблетка *tahb • lyet • kah*

pillow подушка *pah • doosh • kah*

pipe (smoking) трубка *troop • kah*

piste [BE] трасса *trah • sah*

pizzeria пиццерия
pee • tsih • ree • yah

place (space) место *myes • tah*

plane самолёт *sah • mah • lyot*

plan план *plahn*

plant n растение
rahs • tyeh • nee • yeh

plastic bag пакет *pah • kyet*

plastic wrap продуктовая плёнка
*prah • dook • toh • vah • yah
plyon • kah*

plate тарелка *tah • rel • kah*

platform [BE] платформа
plaht • for • mah

platinum платина *plah • tee • nah*

play n игра *eeg • rah;* v (games,
etc.) играть *eeg • raht';*
(perform) исполнять
ees • pahl • nyaht'

playground детская
площадка *dyets • kah • yah
plah • shchaht • kah*

playpen манеж *mah • nyesh*

pleasant приятный
pree • yaht • niy

please пожалуйста
pah • zhahl • stah

plug штепсель *shtep • seel'*

plunger вантуз *vahn • toos*

point v (at) показывать (на)
pah • kah • zih • vaht' (nah)

poison n яд *yaht*

poles палки *pahl • kee*

police милиция
mee • lee • tsih • yah

police station
отделение милиции
*aht • dee • lyeh • nee • yeh
mee • lee • tsih • ee*

popular популярный
pah • poo • lyahr • niy

port (harbor) порт *port*

porter носильщик
nah • seel' • 'shcheek

portion порция *por • tsih • yah*

possible возможно
vahz • mozh • nah

post n почта *poch • tah;*
v отправлять *aht • prahv • lyaht'*

postbox [BE] почтовый ящик
pahch • toh • viy yah • shcheek

postcard открытка
aht • kriht • kah

pottery керамика
kee • rah • mee • kah

pound (sterling) фунт *foont*

pregnant беременная
bee • reh • mee • nah • yah
prescribe выписывать
vih • pee • sih • vaht'
prescription рецепт *ree • tsept*
present *n* (gift) подарок
pah • dah • rahk
press *v* гладить *glah • deet'*
pretty красивый *krah • see • viy*
print *v* печатать *pee • chah • taht'*
program *n* программа
prah • grah • mah
pronounce *v* произносить
prah • eez • nah • seet'
pump насос *nah • sos*
puncture прокол *prah • kol*
puppet show кукольный театр
koo • kahl' • niy tee • ahtr
pure (material) чистый *chees • tiy*
purpose цель *tsel'*
purse сумка *soom • kah*
pushchair [BE]
прогулочная коляска
*prah • goo • lahch • nah • yah
kah • lyas • kah*
put *v* поставить *pah • stah • veet'*

Q

quality качество
kah • chees • tvah
queue [BE] *v* стоять в очереди
stah • yaht' v oh • chee • ree • dee
quick быстрый *bihs • triy*
quiet тихий *tee • kheey*

R

racetrack ипподром *ee • pah • drom*
racket (tennis) ракетка
rah • kyet • kah
railroad железная дорога
*zhee • lyez • nah • yah
dah • roh • gah*

railway [BE] железная дорога
*zhee • lyez • nah • yah
dah • roh • gah*
rain *v* идёт дождь *ee • dyot
doshch*
raincoat плащ *plahshch*
rape *n* изнасилование
*eez • nah • see • lah • vah •
nee • yeh*
rapids пороги *pah • roh • gee*
rash сыпь *sihp'*
razor бритва *breet • vah*
read *v* читать *chee • taht'*
ready готовый *gah • toh • viy*
real (genuine) настоящий
nah • stah • yah • shcheey
receipt квитанция
kvee • tahn • tsih • yah
reception (desk) регистрация
ree • gee • strah • tsih • yah
receptionist портье *pahrt' • yeh*
recommend рекомендовать
ree • kah • meen • dah • vaht'
reduction (in price) скидка
skeet • kah
refrigerator холодильник
khah • lah • deel' • neek
refund вернуть деньги
veer • noot' dyen' • gee
region район *rah • yon*
regular *adj* (size) средний
sryed • neey
religion религия
ree • lee • gee • yah
remember помнить *pom • neet'*
rent *v* взять напрокат *vzyat'
nah • prah • kaht*
repair *v* чинить *chee • neet'*
repeat *v* повторять
pahf • tah • ryaht'
report *v* заявить *zah • yah • veet'*
reservation заказ *zah • kahs*

reserve v заказать zah • _kah_ • zaht'

rest v отдыхать aht • dih • _khaht'_

restaurant ресторан rees • tah • _rahn_

restroom туалет too • ah • _lyet_

retail торговля tahr • _gov_ • lyah

retired на пенсии nah _pyen_ • see • ee

return v (surrender) возвратить vahz • vrah • _teet'_

return ticket [BE] билет туда и обратно bee • _lyet_ too • _dah_ ee ahb • _raht_ • nah

revolting отвратительный aht • vrah • _tee_ • teel' • niy

rib ребро reeb • _roh_

right adj (correct) правильный _prah_ • veel • 'niy

ring кольцо kahl' • _tsoh_

river река ree • _kah_

road дорога dah • _roh_ • gah

road map карта дорог _kahr_ • tah dah • _rok_

robbery грабеж grah • _byosh_

romantic романтичный rah • mahn • _teech_ • niy

roof (house, car) крыша _krih_ • shah

room комната _kom_ • nah • tah

room service обслуживание номеров ahp • _sloo_ • zhih • vah • nee • yeh nah • mee • _rof_

rope веревка vee • _ryof_ • kah

round adj круглый _kroog_ • liy; n (of game) раунд _rah_ • oond

round-trip ticket билет туда и обратно bee • _lyet_ too • _dah_ ee ahb • _raht_ • nah

rubbish [BE] мусор _moo_ • sahr

ruble [rouble] рубль roobl'

Russia Россия rahs • _see_ • yah

Russian adj русский _roos_ • keey

Russian language русский язык _roos_ • kee yah • _zihk_

S

safe adj безопасный bee • zah • _pahs_ • niy; n сейф seyf

safety безопасность bee • zah • _pahs_ • nahst'

safety pin булавка boo • _lahf_ • kah

sailboat яхта _yahkh_ • tah

sales tax НДС en deh es

same тот же самый tot zheh _sah_ • miy

sand песок pee • _sok_

sandals сандалии sahn • _dah_ • lee

sandy beach песчаный пляж pee • _shchah_ • niy plyahsh

sanitary napkins гигиенические салфетки gee • gee • ee • _nee_ • chees • kee • yeh sahl • _fyet_ • kee

saucepan кастрюля kahs • _tryoo_ • lyah

sauna сауна _sah_ • oo • nah

say v говорить gah • vah • _reet'_

scarf шарф shahrf

scenic route живописный маршрут zhi • vah • _pees_ • niy mahrsh • _root_

schedule n расписание rahs • pee • _sah_ • nee • yeh

scissors ножницы _nozh_ • nee • tsih

screwdriver отвёртка aht • _vyort_ • kah

sea море _moh_ • ryeh

seat место _myes_ • tah

second class (train) купейный

вагон koo • _pey_ • niy vah • _gon_
second-hand подержанный
pah • _dyer_ • zhah • niy
secretary секретарь
seek • ree • _tahr'_
sedative успокаивающее
oos • pah • _kah_ • ee • vah •
yoo • shchee • yeh
see видеть _vee_ • deet'
self-service самообслуживание
sah • mah • ahp • _sloo_ • zhih
• vah • nee • yeh
sell продавать prah • dah • _vaht'_
send посылать pah • sih • _laht'_
senior citizen пенсионер
pyen • see • ah • _nyer_
separately отдельно
ahd • _del'_ • nah
serious серьёзный see • _ryoz_ • niy
service (religious)
служба _sloozh_ • bah; (in
restaurant) обслуживание
ahp • _sloo_ • zhih • vah • nee • yeh
shade тень tyen'
shallow мелкий _myel_ • keey
shampoo шампунь shahm • _poon'_
shape n форма _for_ • mah
share v (a room) делить dee • _leet'_
sheet (bedding) простыня
prahs • tih • _nyah_
ship корабль kah • _rahbl'_
shirt рубашка roo • _bahsh_ • kah
shoe repair ремонт обуви
ree • _mont_ oh • boo • vee
shoe store обувной магазин
ah • boov • _noy_ mah • gah • _zeen_
shoes туфли _toof_ • lee
shop магазин mah • gah • _zeen_
shop assistant продавец
prah • dah • _vyets_
shopping basket корзинка
kahr • _zeen_ • kah

shopping centre [BE] торговый
центр tahr • _goh_ • viy tsentr
short adj (height) низкий
nees • keey
short-sighted [BE] близорукий
blee • zah • _roo_ • keey
shorts шорты _shor_ • tih
shoulder плечо plee • _choh_
shovel совок sah • _vok_
show v показывать
pah • _kah_ • zih • vaht'
shower душ doosh
shut adj закрытый
zah • _krih_ • tiy; v закрываться
zah • krih • _vah_ • tsah
sick больной bahl' • _noy;_
side n (of road) сторона
stah • rah • _nah_
sightseeing tour обзорная
экскурсия ahb • _zor_ • nah • yah
eeks • _koor_ • see • yah
sign (road) знак znahk
silk шёлк sholk
silver серебро see • ree • _broh_
single (unmarried) холостой
khah • _lash_ • toy
single room одноместный номер
ahd • nah • _myes_ • niy noh • meer
single ticket [BE] билет в один
конец _bee_ • lyet v _ah_ • deen
kah • _nyets_
sink раковина
rah • kah • vee • nah
sit v сесть syest'
size размер rahz • _myer_
skates коньки kahn' • _kee_
ski boots лыжные ботинки
lihzh • nih • yeh bah • _teen_ • kee
skin кожа _koh_ • zhah
skirt юбка _yoop_ • kah
skis лыжи _lih_ • zhih
sleep v спать spaht'

sleeping bag спальный мешок
spahl' • niy mee • _shok_

sleeping pill снотворное
snaht • _vor_ • nah • yeh

sleeve рукав roo • _kahf_

slippers тапочки _tah_ • pach • kee

slow adj медленный
myed • lee • niy

small (in size) маленький
mah • leen' • keey

smell n запах _zah_ • pakhh

smoke v курить koo • _reet'_

smoking adj курящий
koo • _ryah_ • shcheey

snack bar буфет boo • _fyet_

sneakers теннисные туфли
teh • nees • nih • ee _toof_ • lee

snorkel n трубка _troop_ • kah

snow снег snyek

soap мыло _mih_ • lah

soccer футбол food • _bol_

socket розетка rah • _zyet_ • kah

socks носки nahs • _kee_

sole (shoes) подошва
pah • _dosh_ • vah

some какой-то kah • _koy_ tah

someone кто-то _ktoh_ • tah

something что-то _shtoh_ • tah

sometimes иногда
ee • nahg • _dah_

soon скоро _skoh_ • rah

soother [BE] соска sos • _kah_

sore throat ангина
ahn • _gee_ • nah

souvenir сувенир soo • vee • _neer_

souvenir store магазин
сувениров _mah_ • gah • _zeen_
soo • vee • _nee_ • rahf

spa спа spah

space место _myes_ • tah

spare (extra) лишний _leesh_ • neey

speak v говорить gah • vah • _reet'_

specialist специалист
spee • _tsih_ • ah • _leest_

spell v называть по буквам
nah • _zih_ • _vaht'_ pah _book_ • vahm

spend v тратить _trah_ • teet'

spine позвоночник
pahz • vah • _noch_ • neek

spoon ложка _losh_ • kah

sport спорт sport

sports club спортклуб
sport • _kloop_

sporting goods
store спорттовары
spor • _tah_ • _vah_ • rih

sprain n растяжение
rahs • tee • zheh • nee • yeh

square adj квадратный
kvahd • _raht_ • niy; n площадь
ploh • shchaht'

stadium стадион stah • dee • _on_

staff персонал peer • sah • _nahl_

stainless steel нержавеющая
сталь nee • rzhah • _vye_ • yoo •
shchah • yah stahl'

stamp марка _mahr_ • kah

stand v стоять stah • _yaht'_

start v **(commence)** начинать
nah • chee • _naht'_; **(car)**
заводить zah • vah • _deet'_

station вокзал vahg • _zahl_

stationery канцелярские товары
kahn • tsih • _lyahr_ • skee • yeh
tah • _vah_ • rih

statue статуя _stah_ • too • yah

stay v остаться ah • _stah_ • tsah

sting укус oo • _koos_

stockings чулки chool • _kee_

stomach живот zhih • _vot_

stomachache болит живот
bah • _leet_ zhih • _vot_

stop n (bus, etc.) остановка
ah • stah • _nof_ • kah;
v останавливаться
ah • stah • _nahv_ • lee • vah • tsah
store магазин mah • gah • _zeen_
store guide перечень
отделов _pyeh_ • ree • cheen'
ahd • _dyeh_ • lahf
storm буря _boo_ • ryah
stove плита plee • _tah_
strange странный _strah_ • niy
stream ручей roo • _chey_
stroller прогулочная коляска
prah • _goo_ • lahch • nah • yah
kah • _lyas_ • kah
strong (potent) сильный
seel' • niy
student студент stoo • _dyent_
study v учиться oo • _chee_ • tsah
stunning ошеломляющий
ah • shih • lahm • _lyah_ • yoo
• shcheey
style стиль steel'
subtitled с субтитрами s
soop • _teet_ • rah • mee
subway метро meet • _roh_
subway station станция метро
stahn • tsih • yah meet • _roh_
suggest предлагать
preed • lah • _gaht'_
suit костюм kahs • _tyoom_
sunbathe v загорать
zah • gah • _raht'_
sunburn солнечный ожёг
sol • neech • niy ah • _zhok_
sunglasses солнечные очки
sol • neech • nih • ee ahch • _kee_
sunny солнечно _sol_ • nyech • nah
sunstroke солнечный удар
sol • neech • niy oo • _dahr_
superb превосходный
pree • vahs • _khod_ • niy

supermarket универсам
oo • nee • veer • _sahm_
supervision присмотр
pree • _smotr_
supplement доплата
dah • _plah_ • tah
surfboard доска для серфинга
dahs • _kah_ dlyah ser • feen • gah
surname фамилия
fah • _mee_ • lee • yah
suspicious подозрительный
pah • dah • _zree_ • teel' • niy
sweater пуловер poo • _loh_ • veer
sweatshirt байка bie • _kah_
swelling опухоль oh • _poo_ • khahl'
swim v плавать plah • vaht'
swimming плавание
plah • vah • nee • yeh
swimming pool бассейн
bah • _seyn_
swimming trunks плавки
plahf • kee
swimsuit купальник
koo • _pahl'_ • neek
symptoms симптомы
seemp • _toh_ • mih
synagogue синагога
see • nah • _goh_ • gah
synthetic синтетический
seen • teh • _tee_ • chees • keey

T

T-shirt майка _mie_ • kah
table столик _stoh_ • leek
take (carry) нести nyes • _tee_;
(medication) принимать
pree • nee • _maht'_; (time)
занимать zah • nee • _maht'_
talk v разговаривать
rahz • gah • _vah_ • ree • vaht'
tall высокий vih • _soh_ • keey
tampon тампон tahm • _pon_

tan загар *zah • gahr*

taxi такси *tahk • see*

taxi rank [BE] стоянка такси
stah • yahn • kah tahk • see

taxi stand стоянка такси
stah • yahn • kah tahk • see

team команда *kah • mahn • dah*

teaspoon чайная ложка
chie • nah • yah losh • kah

teddy bear мишка *meesh • kah*

telephone *n* телефон
tee • lee • fon

telephone bill счёт за телефон
shchot zah tee • lee • fon

telephone booth
телефон-автомат
tee • lee • fon • ahf • tah • maht

telephone call телефонный
звонок *tee • lee • foh • niy
zvah • nok*

telephone directory телефонный
справочник *tee • lee • foh • niy
sprah • vahch • neek*

telephone number номер
телефона *noh • meer
tee • lee • foh • nah*

tell *v* рассказывать
rahs • kah • zih • vaht'

temperature (body) температура
teem • pee • rah • too • rah

tennis теннис *teh • nees*

tennis court теннисный корт
teh • nees • niy kort

tent палатка *pah • laht • kah*

tent pegs колышки
koh • lihsh • kee

tent pole шест *shest*

terminal (bus) (авто) вокзал
(ahf • tah) vahg • zahl

terrible ужасный *ooh • zhahs • niy*

theater театр *tee • ahtr*

theft кража *krah • zhah*

then (time) затем *zah • tyem*

there там *tahm*

thermometer термометр
teer • moh • meetr

thermos термос *ter • mahs*

thick толстый *tols • tiy*

thief вор *vor*

thigh бедро *beed • roh*

thin тонкий *ton • keey*

think думать *doo • maht'*

throat горло *gor • lah*

through через *chyeh • rees*

thumb большой палец
bahl' • shoy pah • leets

ticket билет *bee • lyet*

ticket office билетные кассы
bee • lyet • nih • yeh kah • sih

tie галстук *gahls • took*

tight (loose) тесно *tyehs • niy*

tights колготки *kahl • got • kee*

time время *vryeh • myah*

timetable [BE] расписание
rahs • pee • sah • nee • yeh

tin [BE] банка *bahn • kah*

tin opener [BE] консервный нож
kahn • serv • niy nosh

tire *n* шина *shih • nah*

tired усталый *oos • tah • liy*

tissue бумажная салфетка
*boo • mahzh • nah • yah
salh • fyet • kah*

to (place) в *v*

tobacco табак *tah • bahk*

toe палец ноги *pah • leets
nah • gee*

together вместе *vmyes • tee*

toilet [BE] туалет *too • ah • lyet*

toilet paper туалетная бумага
*too • ah • lyet • nah • yah
boo • mah • gah*

tongue язык *yah • zihk*

too слишком *sleesh • kahm*

tooth зуб *zoop*
toothache зубная боль
  zoob • nah • yah bol'
toothbrush зубная щётка
  zoob • nah • yah shchot • kah
toothpaste зубная паста
  zoob • nah • yah pahs • tah
top крышка *krihsh • kah*
tour экскурсия
  eeks • koor • see • yah
tour guide экскурсовод
  eeks • koor • sah • vot
tourist турист *too • reest*
tourist office
  туристическое бюро
  too • rees • tee • chees • kah • yeh byoo • roh
tow truck буксир *book • seer*
tow v отбуксировать
  aht • book • see • rah • vaht'
towel полотенце
  pah • lah • tyen • tseh
tower башня *bahsh • nyah*
town город *goh • raht*
town hall горсовет *gor • sah • vyet*
toy игрушка *eeg • roosh • kah*
track платформа *plaht • for • mah*
traditional традиционный
  trah • dee • tsih • oh • niy
traffic дорожное движение
  dah • rozh • nah • yeh dvee • zheh • nee • yeh
traffic jam пробка *prop • kah*
traffic lights светофор
  svee • tah • for
trail трасса *trah • sah*
trailer трейлер *trey • leer*
train поезд *poh • eest*
train station вокзал *vahg • zahl*
tram трамвай *trahm • vie*
transit n проездом
  prah • yez • dahm

translate v переводить
  pee • ree • vah • deet'
translation перевод
  pee • ree • vot
translator переводчик
  pee • ree • vot • cheek
trash мусор *moo • sahr*
trash can мусорный бак
  moo • sahr • niy bahk
travel agency бюро путешествий
  byoo • roh poo • tee • shest • veey
travel sickness [BE] морская
  болезнь *mahr • skah • yah bah • lyezn'*
traveler's check дорожный чек
  dah • rozh • niy chehk
tray поднос *pahd • nos*
tree дерево *dyeh • ree • vah*
trim (hair) постричь *pah • streech*
trip (journey) поездка
  pah • yest • kah
trolley [BE] тележка
  tee • lyesh • kah
trousers [BE] брюки *bryoo • kee*
true правда *prahv • dah*
tunnel тунель *too • nel'*
turn down (volume, heat)
  уменьшать *oo • meen' • shaht'*
turn off выключать
  vih • klyoo • chaht'
turn on включать *fklyoo • chaht'*
turn up (volume, heat)
  увеличивать
  oo • vee • lee • chee • vaht'
turning поворот *pah • vah • rot*
TV телевизор *teh • leh • vee • zahr*
typical типичный *tee • peech • niy*

U

ugly некрасивый
  nee • krah • see • viy
ulcer язва *yahz • vah*

umbrella зонт *zont*

uncle дядя *dyah • dyah*

unconscious без сознания *byes*
sahz • nah • nee • yah

under под *paht*

underground [BE] метро
meet • roh

underground station [BE]
станция метро *stahn • tsih • yah*
meet • roh

understand понимать
pah • nee • maht'

uneven (ground) неровный
nee • rov • niy

unfortunately к сожалению *k*
sah • zhih • lyeh • nee • yoo

uniform форма *for • mah*

unit (for phonecard, etc.)
единица *ee • dee • nee • tsah*

unleaded (gas) без свинца *bees*
sveen • tsah

unlock отпирать *aht • pee • raht'*

unpleasant неприятный
nee • pree • yaht • niy

upper (berth) верхний
vyerkh • neey

urgent срочно *sroch • nah*

urine моча *mah • chah*

use v пользоваться
pol' • zah • vah • tsah

V

vacant свободный *svah • bod • niy*

vacation отпуск *oht • poosk*

vacuum cleaner пылесос
pih • lee • sos

vaginal infection
вагинальная инфекция
vah • gee • nahl' • nah • yah
een • fyek • tsih • yah

valid действителен
deey • stvee • tee • len

valley долина *dah • lee • nah*

valuable ценный *tseh • niy*

value стоимость *stoh • ee • mahst'*

VAT [BE] НДС *en deh es*

vegetarian вегетарианец
vee • gee • tah • ree • ah • neets

vein вена *vyeh • nah*

very очень *oh • cheen'*

village деревня *dee • ryev • nyah*

visa виза *vee • zah*

visit n визит *vee • zeet;*
v посещать *pah • see • shchaht'*

visiting hours часы
посещений *chee • sih*
pah • see • shcheh • neey

vitamins витамины
vee • tah • mee • nih

volleyball волейбол
vah • leey • bol

voltage напряжение
nah • pree • zheh • nee • yeh

vomit тошнить *tahsh • neet'*

W

wait ждать *zhdaht'*

waiter официант
ah • fee • tsih • ahnt

waiting room зал ожидания *zahl*
ah • zhih • dah • nee • yah

wake (someone) разбудить
rahz • boo • deet'

walk v идти *eet • tee*

walking route пешеходный
маршрут *pee • shih • khod • niy*
mahrsh • root

wallet кошелёк *kah • shih • lyohk*

want хотеть *khah • tet'*

war memorial мемориал
mee • mah • ree • ahl

ward (hospital) палата
pah • lah • tah

warm тёплый *tyop • liy*

washing machine стиральная
машина stee • _rahl'_ • nah • yah
mah • _shih_ • nah
watch часы chah • _sih_
water вода vah • _dah_
water skis водные лыжи
vod • nih • yeh lih • zhee
waterfall водопад vah • dah • _paht_
waterproof водонепроницаемый
voh • dah • nee • prah • nee •
tsah • ee • miy
wave волна vahl • _nah_
wear v одевать ah • dee • _vaht'_
weather погода pah • _goh_ • dah
weather forecast прогноз
погоды prahg • _nos_
pah • _goh_ • dih
wedding свадьба _svahd'_ • bah
week неделя nee • _deh_ • lyah
weekend выходные
vih • khahd • _nih_ • yeh
weigh вес vyes
wheelchair инвалидное кресло
een • vah • _leed_ • nah • yeh
kryes • lah
wide широкий shih • _roh_ • keey
wife жена zhih • _nah_
windbreaker ветровка
veet • _rof_ • kah
window окно ahk • _noh_
window seat место у окна
myes • tah oo ahk • _nah_
windscreen ветровое стекло
vee • trah • _voh_ • yeh steek • _loh_
windsurfer виндсерфер
veend • _syer_ • fyer
windy ветер _vyeh_ • teer
wireless internet
беспроводной интернет
bees • prah • vahd • _noy_
een • ter • _net_
with c s

withdraw снимать snee • _maht'_
without без bes
wood лес lyes
wool шерсть sherst'
work v работать rah • _boh_ • taht'
wound n рана _rah_ • nah
wrong неправильный
nee • _prah_ • veel' • niy

X
_____

X-ray рентген reen • _gyen_

Y
_____

yacht яхта _yahkh_ • tah
yellow жёлтый _zhol_ • tiy
young молодой mah • lah • _doy_
youth hostel общежитие
ahp • shchee • _zhih_ • tee • yeh

Z
_____

zebra crossing переход
pee • ree • _khot_
zipper молния _mol_ • nee • yah
zoo зоопарк zah • ah • _pahrk_

RUSSIAN–ENGLISH

А

аванс ah • <u>vahns</u> deposit

аварийный выход
ah • vah • <u>reey</u> • niy vih • <u>khaht</u>
emergency exit

автобус ahf • <u>toh</u> • boos bus

автобусная остановка
ahf • <u>toh</u> • boos • nah • yah
ahs • tah • <u>nof</u> • kah bus stop

автобусная станция
ahf • <u>toh</u> • boos • nah • yah
<u>stahn</u> • tsih • yah bus station

автовокзал ahf • tah vahg • <u>zahl</u>
terminal (bus)

автостоянка
ahf • tah • stah • <u>yahn</u> • kah
parking lot [car park BE]

адаптер ah • <u>dahp</u> • ter adapter

адвокат ahd • vah • <u>kaht</u> lawyer

адрес <u>ah</u> • drees address

адрес электронной почты
<u>ah</u> • drees ee • leek • <u>tron</u> • nie
<u>poch</u> • tih e-mail address

аккумулятор
ah • kah • moo • <u>lyah</u> • tahr
battery

аллергия ah • leer • <u>gee</u> • yah
allergy

американский
ah • mee • ree • <u>kahn</u> • skeey adj
American

ангина ahn • <u>gee</u> • nah sore throat

английский ahn • <u>gleey</u> • skeey
English

антибиотики
ahn • tee • bee • <u>oh</u> • tee • kee
antibiotics

антикварный
ahn • tee • <u>kvahr</u> • niy antique

антисептик ahn • tee • sep • <u>teek</u>
antiseptic

аппендикс ah • <u>pyen</u> • deeks
appendix

аптека ahp • <u>tyeh</u> • kah pharmacy
[chemist BE]

аспирин ah • spee • <u>reen</u> aspirin

астматик ahst • <u>mah</u> • teek
n asthmatic

аэропорт ah • eh • rah • <u>port</u>
airport

Б

багаж bah • <u>gahsh</u> luggage
[baggage BE]

багажная квитанция
bah • <u>gahzh</u> • nah • yah
kvee • <u>tahn</u> • tsih • yah baggage
check

багажная тележка
bah • <u>gahzh</u> • nah • yah
tee • <u>lyesh</u> • kah luggage cart
[trolley BE]

байка bie • kah sweatshirt

балет bah • <u>lyet</u> ballet

балкон bahl • <u>kon</u> balcony

банк bahnk bank

банка <u>bahn</u> • kah jar; can [tin BE]

банкомат bahn • kah • <u>maht</u> ATM

бар bahr bar (hotel, etc.)

баскетбол bahs • keet • <u>bol</u>
basketball

бассейн bah • <u>seyn</u> swimming
pool

башня <u>bahsh</u> • nyah tower

бега bee • <u>gah</u> horse racing

бедро beed • <u>roh</u> thigh

без *byez* without
без сознания *byes sah • znah • nee • yah* unconscious
безопасность *bee • zah • pahs • nahst'* safety
безопасный *bee • zah • pahs • niy adj* safe
бензин *been • zeen* gas [petrol BE]
беременна *bee • ryeh • mee • nah* pregnant
беспокоить *bees • pah • koh • eet'* disturb
беспроводной интернет *bees • prah • vahd • noy een • ter • net* wireless internet
бессонница *bees • soh • nee • tsah* insomnia
библиотека *bee • blee • ah • tyeh • kah* library
бизнес *beez • nees* business
бикини *bee • kee • nee* bikini
билет *bee • lyet* ticket
билет в один конец *bee • lyet v ah • deen kah • nyets* one-way [single BE] ticket
билет туда и обратно *bee • lyet too • dah ee ahb • raht • nah* round-trip [return BE] ticket
билетная касса *bee • lyet • nah • yah kah • sah* ticket office
бинокль *bee • noh • kahl'* binoculars
близорукий *blee • zah • roo • keey* near-sighted [short-sighted BE]
блузка *bloos • kah* blouse
болеть *bah • lyet' v* hurt
болеутоляющее *boh • lee • oo • tah • lyah • yoo • shchee • yeh* painkiller

боль *bol'* pain
больница *bahl' • nee • tsah* hospital
большой *bahl' • shoy* big
большой палец *bahl' • shoy pah • leets* thumb
ботанический сад *bah • tah • nee • chees • keey saht* botanical garden
бояться *bah • yah • tsah* frightened
браслет *brahs • lyet* bracelet
брат *braht* brother
брильянт *breel' • yahnt* diamond
британский *bree • tahn • skeey* British
бритва *breet • vah* razor
бронхит *brahn • kheet* bronchitis
брошь *brosh* brooch
брошюра *brah • shoo • rah* brochure
брюки *bryoo • kee* pants [trousers BE]
будильник *boo • deel' • neek* alarm clock
буксир *book • seer* tow truck
буксировать *book • see • rah • vaht'* tow
булавка *boo • lahf • kah* safety pin
булочная *boo • lahch • nah • yah* bakery
бумага *boo • mah • gah* paper
бумажная салфетка *boo • mahzh • nah • yah sahl • fyet • kah* tissue
буря *boo • ryah* storm
буфет *boo • fyet* snack bar
бухгалтер *boo • gahl • teer* accountant
быстрый *bihs • triy* quick
быть *biht'* be

бюро находок byoo • _roh_ nah • _khoh_ • dahk lost-and-found [lost property office BE]

бюстгальтер byoost • _gahl_ • ter bra

В

вагинальная инфекция vah • gee • _nahl'_ • nah • yah een • _fyek_ • tsih • yah vaginal infection

вагон vah • _gon_ car [coach BE] (train)

вагон-ресторан vah • _gon_ rees • tah • _rahn_ dining car

валюта vah • _lyoo_ • tah currency

вантуз _vahn_ • toos plunger

вата _vah_ • tah cotton

вегетарианец vee • gee • tah • ree • _ah_ • neets vegetarian

ведро veed • _roh_ bucket

Великобритания vee • lee • kah • bree • _tah_ • nee • yah Great Britain

великолепный vee • lee • kah • _lyep_ • niy magnificent

велосипед vee • lah • see • _pyet_ bicycle

велосипедный маршрут vee • lah • see • _pyed_ • niy mahrsh • _root_ cycle route

велоспорт vyeh • lah • _sport_ cycling

вена _vyeh_ • nah vein

вентилятор veen • tee • _lyah_ • tahr fan (air)

веревка vee • _ryof_ • kah rope

верхний _vyerkh_ • neey upper

вес vyes weight

веселье vee • _syel'_ • yeh fun

ветер _vyeh_ • teer wind

ветровка veet • _rof_ • kah windbreaker

ветровое стекло vee • trah • _voh_ • yeh steek • _loh_ windscreen

вечеринка vee • chee • _reen_ • kah party (social)

вешалка _vye_ • shahl • kah peg

взлом vzlom break-in

взрослый _vzros_ • liy adult

взять напрокат vzyat' nah • prah • _kaht_ v rent [hire BE]

видеть _vee_ • deet' see

виза _vee_ • zah visa

визит vee • _zeet_ n visit

вилка _veel_ • kah fork

виндсерфер veend • _syer_ • fyer windsurfer

винный магазин _vee_ • niy mah • gah • _zeen_ liquor store [off-license BE]

витамины vee • tah • _mee_ • nih vitamins

витрина vee • _tree_ • nah window (in store)

владелец vlah • _dyeh_ • leets owner

вместе _vmyes_ • tee together

внутри vnoo • _tree_ inside

вовремя _voh_ • vryeh • myah on time

вода vah • _dah_ n water

водитель vah • _dee_ • teel' driver

водительские права vah • _dee_ • teel' • skee • yeh _prah_ • vah driver's license

водная экскурсия _vod_ • nah • yah eks • _koor_ • see • yah boat trip

водные лыжи _vod_ • nih • yeh _lih_ • zhih water skis

водонепроницаемый voh • dah • nee • prah • nee • _tsah_ • ee • miy waterproof

водопад vah • dah • _paht_ water fall

воздух _voz_ • dookh air

возраст _voz_ • rahst n age

вокзал vahg • _zahl_ train [railway BE] station

волдырь vahl • _dihr'_ blister

волейбол vah • leey • _bol_ volleyball

волна vahl • _nah_ n wave

волосы _voh_ • lah • sih hair

вор vor thief

воспаление vahs • pah • _lyeh_ • nee • yeh inflammation

врач vrahch doctor

время _vryeh_ • myah time

все fsyoh all

все еще vsyoh ee • _shchoh_ still

всегда fseeg • _dah_ always

вставлять fstahv • _lyat'_ v insert

встречаться fstree • _chah_ • tsah meet

второй ftah • _roy_ second

вход в систему fkhot f sees • _tyeh_ • moo n login

входная плата fkhahd • _nah_ • yah _plah_ • tah entrance fee

въездная виза vyezd • _nah_ • yah _vee_ • zah entry visa

вывихнуть _vih_ • veekh • noot' v twist

выезжать vih • eezh • _zhaht'_ check-out (hotel)

вызывать _vih_ • zih • vaht' v call (the police)

выписывать vih • _pee_ • sih • vaht' prescribe

высокий vih • _soh_ • keey high

высокий vih • _soh_ • keey tall

высокое давление vih • _soh_ • kah • yeh dahv • _lyeh_ • nee • yeh high blood pressure

выход _vih_ • khaht n exit

выходные vih • khahd • _nih_ • yeh weekend

Г

гавань _gah_ • vahn' harbor

газета gah • _zyeh_ • tah newspaper

газетный киоск gah • _zyet_ • niy kee • _osk_ newsstand

галлон gah • _lon_ gallon

галстук _gahls_ • took tie

гандикап gahn • dee • _kahp_ handicap (golf)

гараж gah • _rahsh_ garage

гарантия gah • _rahn_ • tee • yah guarantee

гардероб gahr • dee • _rop_ coatcheck

гигиенические салфетки gee • gee • ee • _nee_ • chees • kee • yeh sahl • _fyet_ • kee sanitary napkins [pads BE]

гид geet guide (tour)

гинеколог gee • nee • _koh_ • lahk gynecologist

гитара gee • _tah_ • rah guitar

главный _glahv_ • niy main

глаз glahs eye

глубокий gloo • _boh_ • keey deep

глухой gloo • _khoy_ deaf

говорить gah • vah • _reet'_ speak

голова gah • lah • _vah_ head

головная боль
gah • lahv • nah • yah bol'
headache

голодный *gah • lod • niy* hungry

гололёд *gah • lah • lyot* icy

гольф *gol'f* golf

гора *gah • rah* mountain

горло *gor • lah* throat

город *goh • raht* town

горсовет *gor • sah • vyet* town hall

горячий *gah • rya • cheey* hot

гостиная *gahs • tee • nah • yah*
living room

гостиница *gahs • tee • nee • tsah*
hotel

готовить *gah • toh • veet'* prepare

готовый *gah • toh • viy* ready

грабеж *grah • byosh* robbery

градус *grah • doos* degree
(temperature)

грамм *grahm* gram

графин *grah • feen* carafe

грипп *greep* flu

громче *grom • chee* louder

грудная клетка *grood • nah • yah
klyet • kah* chest (body)

грудь *groot'* breast

группа *groo • pah* group

группа крови *groo • pah
kroh • vee* blood group

грязный *gryahz • niy* dirty

губа *goo • bah* lip

губная памада *goob • nah • yah
pah • mah • dah* lipstick

Д

давать *dah • vaht'* give

далеко *dah • lee • koh* far

дальнозоркий
dahl' • nah • zor • keey far-
sighted [long-sighted BE]

дать взаймы *daht' vzie • mih* lend

дача *dah • chah* summer cottage

дверь *dvyer'* door

движение *dah • rozh • nah • yeh
dvee • zheh • nee • yeh* traffic

дворец *dvah • ryets* palace

двухместный *dvookh • myes • niy*
double

девочка *dyeh • vahch • kah* girl

дезодорант
dee • zah • dah • rahnt deodorant

действителен
deey • stvee • tee • lyen valid

делать ставку *dyeh • laht'
stahf • koo* place a bet

день *dyen'* day

день рождения *dyen'
rahzh • dyeh • nee • yah* birthday

деньги *dyen' • gee* money

деревня *dee • ryev • nyah* village

дерево *dyeh • ree • vah* tree

десна *dees • nah* gum

детальный счёт *dee • tahl' • niy
shchot* itemized bill

дети *dyeh • tee* children

детская площадка
*dyets • kah • yah
plah • shchaht • kah* playground

детское сиденье
dyets • kah • yeh see • dyen' • yeh
child seat (in car)

дешевле *dee • shev • lee* cheaper

дешёвый *dee • shoh • viy* cheap

джаз *dzhahs* jazz

джинсовый *dzhihn • soh • viy adj*
denim

джинсы *dzhihn • sih* jeans

диабет *dee • ah • byet* diabetes

диабетик *dee • ah • byeh • teek*
diabetic (person)

диагноз dee • _ahg_ • nahs
diagnosis

диета dee • _yeh_ • tah n diet

дизельное топливо
dee • zeel' • _nah_ • yeh
top • lee • vah diesel

директор dee • _ryek_ • tahr director
(of company)

дирижёр dee • ree • _zhor_
conductor (orchestra)

длина dlee • _nah_ length

длинный _dlee_ • niy long

дневное представление
dneev • _noh_ • yeh
preet • stahv • _lyeh_ • nee • yeh
matinée

до dah until

добавочный номер
dah • _bah_ • vahch • niy
noh • meer extension

добираться dah • bee • _rah_ • tsah
get (to destination)

дождь doshch n rain

долина dah • _lee_ • nah valley

дом dom house

допуск _doh_ • poosk n access

дорога dah • _roh_ • gah road

дорогой dah • rah • _goy_ expensive

дорожная пробка
dah • _rozh_ • nah • yah prop • kah
traffic jam

дорожный чек dah • _rozh_ • niy
chehk traveler's check [cheques
BE]

доска для серфинга dahs • _kah_
dlyah _ser_ • feen • gah surfboard

доставлять dah • stahv • _lyat'_
deliver

достаточно
dah • _stah_ • tahch • nah enough

дрова drah • _vah_ firewood

друг drook friend

другие droo • _gee_ • yeh others

другой droo • _goy_ other

дружеский _droo_ • zhees • keey
friendly

дублирован
doob • _lee_ • rah • vahn dubbed

думать _doo_ • maht' think

духовка doo • _khof_ • kah oven

душ doosh shower

дырка _dihr_ • kah hole (in clothes)

дышать dih • _shaht'_ breathe

дюжина _dyoo_ • zhih • nah dozen

дядя _dyah_ • dyah uncle

Е

Европейский союз
yev • rah • _pey_ • skeey sah • _yoos_
European Union (EU)

ежедневно
ee • zhee • _dnyev_ • nah daily

ерунда ee • roon • _dah_ nonsense

есть yest' eat

ехать _yeh_ • khaht' drive

ещё ee • _shchoh_ extra (additional)

Ж

жалоба _zhah_ • lah • bah complaint

жар zhahr fever

ждать zhdaht' wait

жёлтый zhol • tiy yellow

жемчуг zhem • chook pearl

жена zhih • _nah_ wife

женат zhih • _naht_ married (man)

живописный маршрут
zhih • vah • pees • niy
mahrsh • root scenic route

живот zhih • _vot_ stomach

животное zhi • _vot_ • nah • yeh
animal

журнал zhoor • nahl magazine

З

забирать zah • bee • <u>raht'</u> collect
заблокирован
  zah • blah • <u>kee</u> • rah • vahn
  blocked
заболевание сердца
  zah • bah • lee • <u>vah</u> • nee • yeh
  <u>syer</u> • tsah heart condition
заболеть zah • bah • <u>lyet'</u> get sick
  [ill BE]
забывать zah • bih • <u>vaht'</u> forget
загар zah • <u>gahr</u> tan
загорать zah • gah • <u>raht'</u>
  sunbathe
заграницей
  zah • grah • <u>nee</u> • tsey abroad
задержка zah • <u>dyersh</u> • kah
  n delay
зажигалка zah • zhih • <u>gahl</u> • kah
  lighter (cigarette)
заказывать zah • <u>kah</u> • zih • vaht'
  v order
законный zah • <u>kon</u> • niy legal
закрываться
  zah • krih • <u>vah</u> • tsah v close
  (store, etc.)
закрытый zah • <u>krih</u> • tiy adj shut
закрытый бассейн zah • <u>krih</u> • tiy
  bah • seyn indoor pool
зал вылета zahl <u>vih</u> • lee • tah
  departure lounge
зал ожидания zahl
  ah • zhih • <u>dah</u> • nee • yah waiting
  room
замок <u>zah</u> • mahk castle
замок zah • <u>mok</u> n lock
замужем zah • moo • zhihm
  married (woman)
занят <u>zah</u> • nyaht busy
занятый <u>zah</u> • nee • tiy occupied

запах <u>zah</u> • pahkh smell
заповедник
  zah • pah • <u>vyed</u> • neek nature
  reserve
заправочная станция
  zah • <u>prah</u> • vahch • nah • yah
  <u>stahn</u> • tsih • yah gas station
затем zah • <u>tyem</u> then (time)
захватывающий
  zah • <u>khvah</u> • tih • vah • yoo •
  shcheey breathtaking
заштопать zah • <u>shtoh</u> • paht'
  patch
звонить zvah • <u>neet'</u> v call (phone)
здание <u>zdah</u> • nee • yeh building
здесь zdyes' here
зелёный zee • <u>lyoh</u> • niy green
зеркало zyer • kah • lah mirror
знак znahk sign (road)
значить znah • <u>cheet'</u> v mean
золото zoh • lah • tah gold
зонт zont umbrella
зоопарк zah • ah • <u>pahrk</u> n zoo
зуб zoop tooth
зубная боль zoob • <u>nah</u> • yah bol'
  tooth-ache
зубная паста zoob • <u>nah</u> • yah
  <u>pahs</u> • tah toothpaste
зубная щётка zoob • <u>nah</u> • yah
  <u>shchot</u> • kah toothbrush
зубной врач zoob • noy vrahch
  dentist

И

игра eeg • <u>rah</u> game
играть eeg • <u>raht'</u> v play (games,
  etc.)
игрушка eeg • <u>roosh</u> • kah n toy
идти за покупками eet • <u>tee</u>
  zah pah • <u>koop</u> • kah • mee go
  shopping

идти пешком eet • tee
peesh • kom v walk

из-за eez • zah because of

измерение
eez • mee • ryeh • nee • yeh
measurement

измерить eez • myeh • reet'
v measure

изнасилование
eez • nah • see • lah • vah • nee •
yeh n rape

изумруд ee • zoom • root emerald

изучать ee • zoo • chaht' learn
(language)

имя ee • myah name (first name)

инвалид een • vah • leet
n handicapped [disabled BE]

инвалидное кресло
een • vah • leed • nah • yeh
kryes • lah wheelchair

иногда ee • nahg • dah
sometimes

иностранная валюта
ee • nah • strah • nah • yah
vah • lyoo • tah foreign currency

инструкция
een • strook • tsih • yah
instructions

инсулин een • soo • leen insulin

интересный een • tee • ryes • niy
interesting

интернет een • ter • net internet

интернет-кафе een • ter • net
kah • feh internet cafe

инфекция een • fyek • tsih • yah
infection

информация
een • fahr • mah • tsih • yah
information

ипподром ee • pah • drom
racetrack

исполнять ees • pahl • nyaht'
perform

К

к сожалению k
sah • zhih • lyeh • nee • yoo
unfortunately

к счастью k shchahst' • yoo
fortunately

каждый kahzh • diy every

казино kah • zee • noh casino

какой-либо kah • koy • lee • bah
any

какой-то kah • koy tah some

календарь kah • leen • dahr'
calendar

камера хранения
kah • mee • rah
khrah • nyeh • nee • yah luggage
locker

канцелярские товары
kahn • tsih • lyahr • skee • yeh
tah • vah • rih stationery

карандаш kah • rahn • dahsh
pencil

карта kahr • tah map

карта дорог kahr • tah dah • rok
road map

картина kahr • tee • nah painting

картинная галерея
kahr • teen • nah • yah
gah • lee • ryeh • yah art gallery

карты kahr • tih cards

кассета kah • syeh • tah cassette

кассир kah • seer cashier

кастрюля kahs • tryoo • lyah
saucepan

качество kah • chees • tvah
quality

кашель kah • shihl' n cough

кашлять kahsh • lyaht' v cough

каюта kah • <u>yoo</u> • tah cabin

квадратный kvahd • <u>raht</u> • niy adj square

квартира kvahr • <u>tee</u> • rah apartment [flat BE]

кемпинг <u>kyem</u> • peenk camping

керамика kee • <u>rah</u> • mee • kah pottery

километраж kee • lah • mee • <u>trahsh</u> mileage

кинотеатр kee • nah • tee • <u>ahtr</u> movie theater [cinema BE]

кишечник kee • <u>shech</u> • neek bowel

класс klahs class (type of seat, etc.)

ключ klyooch key

клюшка <u>klyoosh</u> • kah club (golf)

книга <u>knee</u> • gah book

книжный магазин <u>kneezh</u> • niy mah • gah • <u>zeen</u> bookstore

кнопка <u>knop</u> • kah button

ковер kah • <u>vyor</u> carpet (rug)

код kot area code

кожа <u>koh</u> • zhah leather (material); skin (body)

колготки kahl • <u>got</u> • kee tights

колено kah • <u>lyeh</u> • nah knee

кольцо kahl' • <u>tsoh</u> n ring

команда kah • <u>mahn</u> • dah team

командировка kah • mahn • dee • <u>rof</u> • kah business trip

комариный укус kah • mah • <u>ree</u> • niy oo • <u>koos</u> mosquito bite

комиссионный сбор kah • mee • see • <u>oh</u> • niy zbor n commission

комната <u>kom</u> • nah • tah room (house)

компакт-диск kahm • <u>pahkt</u> deesk CD

компания kahm • <u>pah</u> • nee • yah company (companionship)

конверт kahn • <u>vyert</u> envelope

кондитерская kahn • <u>dee</u> • teer • skah • yah pastry store

кондиционер kahn • dee • tsih • ah • <u>nyer</u> conditioner

консервный нож kahn • <u>syerv</u> • niy nosh can [tin BE] opener

консульство kon • sool' • stvah consulate

консультироваться kahn • sool' • <u>tee</u> • rah • vah • tsah consult

контактные линзы kahn • <u>tahkt</u> • nih • yeh <u>leen</u> • zih contact lenses

концерт kahn • <u>tsert</u> concert

концертный зал kahn • <u>tsert</u> • niy zahl concert hall

кончаться kahn • <u>chah</u> • tsah v end

коньки kahn' • <u>kee</u> skates

копия <u>koh</u> • pee • yah copy

корабль kah • <u>rahbl'</u> ship

корзина kahr • <u>zee</u> • nah basket

кормить kahr • <u>meet'</u> feed

коронка kah • <u>ron</u> • kah cap (dental)

косметика kahs • <u>myeh</u> • tee • kah cosmetics

костыли kahs • tih • <u>lee</u> crutches

кость kost' bone

костюм kahs • <u>tyoom</u> n suit

кошелёк kah • shih • <u>lyok</u> wallet

кошерный kah • <u>sher</u> • niy kosher

кража <u>krah</u> • zhah theft

крайний случай _krie_ • _neey_ _sloo_ • _chie_ emergency

кран _krahn_ faucet [tap BE]

красивый _krah_ • _see_ • _viy_ beautiful

кредитная карточка _kree_ • _deet_ • _nah_ • _yah_ _kahr_ • _tahch_ • _kah_ credit card

крем для загара _kryem dlyah_ _zah_ • _gah_ • _rah_ sun-tan cream

кровать _krah_ • _vaht'_ bed

кровотечение _krah_ • _vah_ • _tee_ • _cheh_ • _nee_ • _yeh_ bleeding

кровь _krof'_ blood

кровяное давление _krah_ • _vee_ • _noh_ • _yeh_ _dahv_ • _lyeh_ • _nee_ • _yeh_ blood pressure

кроме _kroh_ • _mee_ except

круглый _kroog_ • _liy_ round

кружево _kroo_ • _zhih_ • _vah_ lace

кружка _kroosh_ • _kah_ n mug

круиз _kroo_ • _ees_ cruise

крыша _krih_ • _shah_ roof (house, car)

ксерокс _ksyeh_ • _rahks_ photocopier

кто-нибудь _ktoh_ • _nee_ • _boot'_ anyone

кто-то _ktoh_ • _tah_ someone

кукла _kook_ • _lah_ doll

кукольный театр _koo_ • _kahl'_ • _niy_ _tee_ • _ahtr_ puppet show

купальник _koo_ • _pahl'_ • _neek_ swimsuit

купе _koo_ • _peh_ compartment (train)

курить _koo_ • _reet'_ v smoke

курс обмена _koors_ _ahb_ • _myeh_ • _nah_ exchange rate

курящий _koo_ • _ryah_ • _shcheey_ adj smoking

кусочек _koo_ • _soh_ • _cheek_ piece

Л

лавина _lah_ • _vee_ • _nah_ avalanche

лазерный проигрыватель _lah_ • _zeer_ • _niy_ _prah_ • _eeg_ • _rih_ • _vah_ • _teel'_ CD-player

лак для волос _lahk dlyah_ _vah_ • _los_ hair spray

лампа _lahm_ • _pah_ lamp

лампочка _lahm_ • _pahch_ • _kah_ light bulb

лёгкий _lyokh_ • _keey_ light (opp. heavy); easy

лёгкое _lyokh_ • _kah_ • _yeh_ lung

лезвие _lyez_ • _vee_ • _yeh_ razor blade

лекарство _lee_ • _kahr_ • _stvah_ medication

лес _lyes_ forest

линия _lee_ • _nee_ • _yah_ line (metro)

лифт _leeft_ elevator [lift BE]

лицо _lee_ • _tsoh_ face

лишний _leesh_ • _neey_ spare (extra)

лодка _lot_ • _kah_ boat

ложка _losh_ • _kah_ spoon

лосьон после бритья _lahs'_ • _yon_ _pos_ • _lee breet'_ • _yah_ after-shave

лошадь _loh_ • _shahd'_ horse

лучше _looch_ • _sheh_ better

лыжи _lih_ • _zhih_ skis

лыжные ботинки _lizh_ • _nih_ • _yeh_ _bah_ • _teen_ • _kee_ ski boots

любезный _lyoo_ • _byez_ • _niy_ kind (pleasant)

любимый _lyoo_ • _bee_ • _miy_ favorite

любить _lyoo_ • _beet'_ v love

люди _lyoo_ • _dee_ people

M

магазин mah • gah • <u>zeen</u> store

майка <u>mie</u> • kah T-shirt

макияж mah • kee • <u>yash</u> n make-up

маленький <u>mah</u> • leen' • keey little (small)

мало <u>mah</u> • lah few; little

мальчик <u>mahl'</u> • cheek boy

манеж mah • <u>nyesh</u> playpen

маникюр mah • nee • <u>kyoor</u> manicure

марка <u>mahr</u> • kah stamp

маска <u>mahs</u> • kah mask (diving)

массаж mah • <u>sahsh</u> n massage

матрас maht • <u>rahs</u> mattress

матрёшка maht • <u>ryosh</u> • kah nesting doll

матч mahch match (sport)

машина mah • <u>shih</u> • nah car

мебель <u>myeh</u> • beel' furniture

медленный <u>myed</u> • lee • niy slow

медовый месяц mee • <u>doh</u> • viy myeh • syats honeymoon

медсестра myet • sees • <u>trah</u> nurse

медь myet' copper

междугородний автобус meezh • doo • gah • <u>rod</u> • niy ahf • <u>toh</u> • boos coach (long-distance bus)

мелировать mee • <u>lee</u> • rah • vaht' v highlight (hair)

мелкий <u>mel</u> • keey shallow

мемориал mee • mah • ree • <u>ahl</u> war memorial

менять mee • <u>nyaht'</u> v change

местный <u>myes</u> • niy local

местный наркоз <u>myes</u> • niy nahr • <u>kos</u> local anesthetic

место <u>myes</u> • tah place (space)

место багажа <u>myes</u> • tah bah • gah • <u>zhah</u> piece of luggage

место назначения <u>myes</u> • tah nahz • nah • <u>cheh</u> • nee • yah destination

место у окна <u>myes</u> • tah oo ahk • <u>nah</u> window seat

место у прохода <u>myes</u> • tah oo prah • <u>khoh</u> • dah aisle seat

месяц <u>myeh</u> • syahts month

металл mee • <u>tahl</u> metal

метро meet • <u>roh</u> subway [underground BE]

мечеть mee • <u>chet'</u> mosque

мигрень meeg • <u>ryen'</u> migraine

микроволновая печь meek • rah • vahl • <u>noh</u> • vah • yah pyech microwave

милиция mee • <u>lee</u> • tsih • yah police

минута mee • <u>noo</u> • tah minute

мобильный телефон mah • <u>beel'</u> • niy tee • lee • <u>fon</u> cell [mobile BE] phone

мой moy my

молния <u>mol</u> • nee • yah zipper

молодой mah • lah • <u>doy</u> young

монета mah • <u>nyeh</u> • tah coin

море <u>moh</u> • ryeh sea

мороз mah • <u>ros</u> frost

морозильная камера mah • rah • <u>zeel'</u> • nah • yah kah • mee • rah freezer

морская болезнь mahr • <u>skah</u> • yah bah • <u>lyezn'</u> motion [travel BE] sickness

мост most bridge

моторка mah • <u>tor</u> • kah motorboat

мотоцикл *mah • tah • tsihkl* motorbike

моча *mah • chah* urine

мочевой пузырь *mah • chee • voy poo • zihr'* bladder

моющее средство *moh • yoo • shchee • yeh sryet • stvah* detergent

муж *moosh* husband

мужчина *moo • shchee • nah* man (male)

музей *moo • zyey* museum

музыка *moo • zih • kah* music

мусор *moo • sahr* trash [rubbish BE]

мусорный бак *moo • sahr • niy bahk* trash can [dustbin BE]

мы *mih* we

мыло *mih • lah* soap

мышца *mihsh • tsah* muscle

мяч *myahch* ball

Н

на открытом воздухе *nah aht • krih • tahm voz • doo • khee* outdoor

на пенсии *nah pyen • see • ee* retired

на улице *nah oo • lee • tseh* outside

называть по буквам *nah • zih • vaht' pah book • vahm* v spell

наконец *nah • kah • nyets* at last

наличные *nah • leech • nih • yeh* n cash

нападение *nah • pah • dyeh • nee • yeh* n attack

направление *nah • prahv • lyeh • nee • yeh* direction

направлять *nah • prahv • lyaht'* v direct

например *nah • pree • myer* for example

напротив *nah • proh • teef* opposite

напряжение *nah • pree • zheh • nee • yeh* voltage

народная музыка *nah • rod • nah • yah moo • zih • kah* folk music

народное искусство *nah • rod • nah • yeh ees • koos • tvah* folk art

насекомое *nah • see • koh • mah • yeh* insect

насос *nah • sos* n pump

настаивать *nah • stah • ee • vaht'* insist

настоящий *nah • stah • yah • shcheey* real (genuine)

национальность *nah • tsih • ah • nahl' • nahst'* nationality

национальный *nah • tsih • ah • nahl' • niy* national

начинать *nah • chee • naht'* begin

начинаться *nah • chee • nah • tsah* v start

НДС *en deh es* sales tax [VAT BE]

невероятный *nee • vee • rah • yaht • niy* incredible

невиновен *nee • vee • noh • veen* innocent

неделя nee • _deh_ • lyah week

недоразумение
nee • dah • rah • zoo • _myeh_ •
nee • yeh misunderstanding

недорогой nee • dah • rah • _goy_
inexpensive

незаконный nee • zah • _kon_ • niy
illegal

некрасивый nee • krah • _see_ • viy
ugly

некурящий
nee • koo • _ryah_ • shcheey adj
non-smoking

немедленно
nee • _myeh_ • dlee • nah
immediately

неплохо nee • _ploh_ • khah not bad

неправильный
nee • _prah_ • veel' • niy wrong

неприятный nee • pree • _yaht_ • niy
unpleasant

нерв nyerf nerve

нержавеющая сталь
nee • rzhah • _vyeh_ • yoo •
shchah • yah stahl' stainless
steel

неровный nee • _rov_ • niy uneven
(ground)

несложный nyeh • _slozh_ • niy
easy

несчастный случай
nee • _shchahs_ • niy sloo • chie
accident

низкий _nees_ • keey short (height)

никогда nee • kahg • _dah_ never

никто nee • _ktoh_ no one

ничего nee • chee • _voh_ nothing

новый _noh_ • viy new

нога nah • _gah_ foot; leg

нож nosh knife

ножницы _nozh_ • nee • tsih
scissors

номер _noh_ • meer number
(telephone)

нормальный nahr • _mahl'_ • niy
normal

нос nos nose

носильщик nah • _seel'_ • shcheek
porter

носки nahs • _kee_ socks

ночной nahch • _noy_ all-night

ночью _noh_ • chyoo at night

нравиться _nrah_ • vee • tsah
v enjoy

нырять nih • _ryat'_ v dive

О

обед ah • _byet_ lunch

обезболивающее
ah • beez • _boh_ • lee • vah • yoo •
shchee • yeh anaesthetic

обзорная экскурсия
ahb • _zor_ • nah • yah
eeks • _koor_ • see • yah
sightseeing tour

облачно _ob_ • lahch • nah cloudy

обмен валюты ahb • _myen_
vah • _lyoo_ • tih currency
exchange office

обменивать
ahb • _myeh_ • nee • vaht'
exchange

обогреватель
ah • bah • gree • _vah_ • teel' heater

обслуживание номеров
ahp • _sloo_ • zhih • vah • nee • yeh
nah • mee • _rof_ room service

обувной магазин ah • boov • _noy_
mah • gah • _zeen_ shoe store

общежитие
ahp • shchee • <u>zhih</u> • tee • yeh
youth hostel

обязательный
ah • bee • <u>zah</u> • teel' • niy
necessary

огнетушитель
ahg • nee • too • <u>shih</u> • teel' fire
extinguisher

ограбление
ah • grahb • <u>lyeh</u> • nee • yeh
mugging; robbery

одевать ah • dee • <u>vat'</u> put on;
wear

одежда ah • <u>dyezh</u> • dah clothes

одеяло ah • dee • <u>yah</u> • lah blanket

один <u>ah</u> • deen alone

один раз ah • <u>deen</u> rahs once

одноместный номер
ahd • nah • <u>myes</u> • niy <u>noh</u> • meer
single room

одолжить ah • dahl • <u>zhit'</u> borrow

ожерелье ah • zhih • <u>ryel'</u> • yeh
necklace

ожог ah • <u>zhok</u> n burn

озеро <u>oh</u> • zee • rah lake

окно ahk • <u>noh</u> window

около <u>oh</u> • kah • lah about
(approximately); near

опаздывать ah • <u>pahz</u> • dih • vaht'
be delayed

опасный ah • <u>pahs</u> • niy
dangerous

опера <u>oh</u> • pee • rah opera

операция
ah • pee • <u>rah</u> • tsih • yah
operation

описывать ah • <u>pee</u> • sih • vaht'
describe

оплата ah • <u>plah</u> • tah payment

оправа ah • <u>prah</u> • vah n frame
(glasses)

оптика <u>op</u> • tee • kah optician

оркестр ahr • <u>kyestr</u> orchestra

осмотр ahs • <u>motr</u> examination
(medical)

основной ahs • nahv • <u>noy</u>
essential

останавливаться
as • stah • <u>nahv</u> • lee • vah • tsah
v stop

остановка ah • stah • <u>nof</u> • kah
n stop (bus, etc.)

остаться ah • <u>stah</u> • tsah v stay

осторожный ahs • tah • <u>rozh</u> • niy
careful

отбеливатель
aht • <u>byeh</u> • lee • vah • teel'
bleach

отвёртка aht • <u>vyort</u> • kah
screwdriver

отвратительный
aht • vrah • <u>tee</u> • teel' • niy
revolting

отдавать в химчистку
aht • dah • <u>vaht'</u> f
kheem • <u>cheest</u> • koo v dry clean

отдел aht • <u>dyel</u> department (in
store)

отделение милиции
aht • dee • <u>lyeh</u> • nee • yeh
mee • <u>lee</u> • tsih • ee police station

отдельно ahd • <u>del'</u> • nah
separately

отдыхать aht • dih • <u>khat'</u> v rest

открывать aht • krih • <u>vaht'</u>
v open

открытка aht • <u>kriht</u> • kah
postcard

открытый aht • <u>krih</u> • tiy adj open

отменять aht • mee • <u>nyaht'</u>
cancel (reservation)

отопление
ah • tahp • lyeh • nee • yeh
heating

отпирать *aht • pee • raht'* v unlock

отправляться
aht • prahv • lyah • tsah depart
(train, bus)

отпуск *ot • poosk* vocation
[holiday BE]

официант *ah • fee • tsih • ahnt*
waiter

очень *oh • cheen'* very

очередь *oh • chee • reet'* n queue

очки *ahch • kee* glasses (optical)

ошеломляющий
*ah • shih • lahm • lyah • yoo •
shcheey* stunning

ошибка *ah • shihp • kah*
n mistake

П

пакет *pah • kyet* carton; packet

палата *pah • lah • tah* ward
(hospital)

палатка *pah • laht • kah* tent

палаточный лагерь
pah • lah • tahch • niy lah • geer'
campsite

палец *pah • leets* finger

палец ноги *pah • leets nah • gee*
toe

пальто *pahl' • toh* coat

панорама *pah • nah • rah • mah*
panorama

пара *pah • rah* pair

парацетамол
pah • rah • tsih • tah • mol
acetaminophen [paracetamol
BE]

парикмахер
pah • reek • mah • kheer
hairdresser

парк *pahrk* park

паром *pah • rom* ferry

паспорт *pahs • pahrt* passport

пассажирский класс
pah • sah • zhihr • skeey klahs
economy class

пациент *pah • tsih • yent* n patient

пачка сигарет *pahch • kah
see • gah • ryet* packet of
cigarettes

педикюр *pee • dee • kyoor*
pedicure

пелёнка *pee • lyon • kah* diaper
[nappy BE]

пепельница
pyeh • peel' • nee • tsah ashtray

перевес багажа *pee • ree • vyes
bah • gah • zhah* excess luggage

перевод *pee • ree • vot* translation

переводить *pee • ree • vah • deet'*
translate

переводчик
pee • ree • vot • cheek translator
(text); interpreter (speech)

перегреться
pee • ree • gryeh • tsah overheat

перед *pyeh • reet* before

переделывать
pee • ree • dyeh • lih • vaht' alter

перекрёсток
pee • ree • kryos • tahk crossroad

перелом *pee • ree • lom* fracture
(of a bone)

переход *pee • ree • khot*
pedestrian crossing

период *pee • ree • aht* period
(historical)

персонал *peer • sah • nahl* n staff

перчатка *peer • chaht • kah* glove

песок *pee • sok* sand

песчаный пляж
pee • <u>shchah</u> • niy plyahsh sandy beach

печатать pee • <u>chah</u> • taht' v print

печень <u>pyeh</u> • cheen' liver

пешеходная зона
pee • shih • <u>khod</u> • nah • yah <u>zoh</u> • nah pedestrian zone [precinct BE]

пешеходный маршрут
pee • shih • <u>khod</u> • niy mahrsh • <u>root</u> walking route

пешком peesh • <u>kom</u> on foot

пещера pee • <u>shcheh</u> • rah cave

пикник peek • <u>neek</u> picnic

письмо pees' • <u>moh</u> letter

пить peet' v drink

пиццерия pee • tsih • <u>ree</u> • yah pizzeria

плавание <u>plah</u> • vah • neeh • yeh swimming

плавать <u>plah</u> • vaht' swim

плавки <u>plahf</u> • kee swimming trunks

план plahn n plan

пластырь <u>plahs</u> • tihr' adhesive bandage

плата <u>plah</u> • tah n charge

платина <u>plah</u> • tee • nah platinum

платить plah • <u>teet'</u> v pay

платок plah • <u>tok</u> handkerchief

платформа plaht • <u>for</u> • mah n track [platform BE]

платье <u>plaht'</u> • yeh dress

плащ plahshch raincoat

плёнка <u>plyon</u> • kah n film (camera)

плечо plee • <u>choh</u> shoulder

плита plee • <u>tah</u> stove [cooker BE]

пломба <u>plom</u> • bah filling (dental)

плохой plah • <u>khoy</u> bad

пляж plyahsh beach

по делу pah <u>dyeh</u> • loo on business

по крайней мере pah <u>kray</u> • neey <u>myeh</u> • ryeh at least

по почте pah <u>poch</u> • tyeh by mail

побережье pah • bee • <u>ryezh</u> • yeh coast

повар <u>poh</u> • vahr n cook

поворот pah • vah • <u>rot</u> n turning

повредить pah • vree • <u>deet'</u> v damage

повторять pahf • tah • <u>ryaht'</u> v repeat

погода pah • <u>goh</u> • dah weather

под pahd under

подарок pah • <u>dah</u> • rahk n present (gift)

подвал pahd • <u>vahl</u> basement

подвозить pahd • vah • zeet' give a lift

подержанный
pah • <u>dyer</u> • zhah • niy second-hand

поднос pahd • <u>nos</u> tray

пододеяльник
pah • dah • dee • <u>yahl'</u> • neek duvet

подозрительный
pah • dah • <u>zree</u> • teel' • niy suspicious

подошва pah • <u>dosh</u> • vah sole (shoes)

подробности
pahd • <u>rob</u> • nahs • tee details

подруга pahd • <u>roo</u> • gah girlfriend

подтвердить paht • tveer • <u>deet'</u> confirm (reservation)

подушка pah • <u>doosh</u> • kah pillow

поезд <u>poh</u> • eest train

поездка pah • <u>yest</u> • kah trip (journey)

пожар pah • <u>zhahr</u> fire

пожарная лестница
pah • zhahr • nah • yah lyes • nee • tsah fire escape

позвоночник
pahz • vah • noch • neek spine

поздний *poz • neey adj* late

пойти по магазинам *pie • tee pah mah • gah • zee • nahm* go shopping

пойти потанцевать *pie • tee pah • tahn • tsih • vaht'* go dancing

показывать *pah • kah • zih • vaht' v* show

покупать *pah • koo • paht'* buy

полный *pol • niy* full

половина *pah • lah • vee • nah* half

полотенце *pah • lah • tyen • tseh* towel

получать *pah • loo • chaht'* get (receive)

пользоваться
pol' • zah • vah • tsah v use

помедленнее
pah • myed • lee • nee • yeh slow down

поменьше *pah • myen' • sheh* smaller

помнить *pom • neet'* remember

помогать *pah • mah • gaht' v* help

понимать *pah • nee • maht'* understand

популярный *pah • poo • lyahr • niy* popular

поразительный
pah • rah • zee • teel' • niy amazing

порез *pah • ryes n* cut (finger)

пороги *pah • roh • ğee* rapids

порт *port* port (harbor)

портье *pahrt' • yeh* receptionist

посадочный талон
pah • sah • dahch • niy tah • lon boarding card

посещать *pah • see • shchaht' v* visit

после *pos • lee* after (time/place)

последний *pahs • lyed • neey* last

посол *pah • sol* ambassador

посольство *pah • sol' • stvah* embassy

постельное бельё
pahs • tel' • nah • yeh beel' • yoh n bedding

постричь *pah • streech v* trim (hair)

построенный
pah • stroh • yeh • niy built

посуда *pah • soo • dah* crockery

посудомоечная машина
pah • soo • dah • moh • eech nah • yah mah • shih • nah dishwasher

посылать *pah • sih • laht'* send

посылка *pah • sihl • kah* package (mail)

потерять *pah • tee • ryaht' v* lose

потерять сознание
pah • tee • ryaht' sah • znah • nee • yeh v collapse

потише *pah • tee • sheh* quieter

потому что
pah • tah • moo • shtah because

похмелье *pahkh • myel' • yeh n* hangover

починить *pah • chee • neet' v* repair

почка *poch • kah* kidney

почта *poch • tah* post office

почта *poch • tah* mail (letters)

почти *pahch • tee* almost

почтовый ящик *pahch • toh • viy yah • shcheek* mailbox [postbox BE]

пошлина _posh_ • lee • nah duty

правда _prahv_ • dah true

правильный _prah_ • veel' • niy right (correct)

православный prah • vah • _slahv_ • niy Orthodox

прачечная _prah_ • cheech • nah • yah laundromat (launderette BE]

превосходный pree • vahs • _khod_ • niy superb

предлагать preed • lah • _gaht'_ suggest

предприятие preet • pree • _yah_ • tee • yeh company (business)

предъявлять preed • yahv • _lyaht'_ declare

презерватив pree • zeer • vah • _teef_ condom

преследовать pree • _slyeh_ • dah • vaht' follow (pursue)

приблизительно pree • blee • _zee_ • teel' • nah approximately

прибывать pree • bih • _vaht'_ arrive

привлекательный pree • vlee • _kah_ • teel' • niy attractive

приглашать pree • glah • _shaht'_ invite

приглашение pree • glah • _sheh_ • nee • yeh invitation

приземляться pree • zeem • _lyah_ • tsah v land

примерочная pree • _myeh_ • rahch • nah • yah fitting room

принадлежать pree • nahd • lee • _zhaht'_ belong

принадлежности pree • nahd • _lyezh_ • nah • stee accessories

принимать лекарство pree • nee • _maht'_ lee • _kahr_ • stvah take medication

присмотр pree • _smotr_ supervision

приходить pree • khah • _deet'_ come

причудливый pree • _chood_ • lee • viy bizarre

приятный pree • _yaht_ • niy pleasant

пробор prah • _bor_ parting (hair)

проверить prah • _vyeh_ • reet' v check [cheque BE]

провожать prah • vah • _zhaht'_ accompany

прогноз погоды prahg • _nos_ pah • _goh_ • dih weather forecast

программа prah • _grah_ • mah program

продавать prah • dah • _vaht'_ sell

продавец prah • dah • _vyets_ shop assistant

проездом prah • _yez_ • dahm in transit

проезжать prah • eezh • _zhaht'_ v pass

произносить prah • eez • nah • _seet'_ pronounce

прокол prah • _kol_ puncture

просить prah • _seet'_ ask for

просматривать prah • _smah_ • tree • vaht' v browse

простуда prah • <u>stoo</u> • dah cold; flu

простыня prahs • tih • <u>nyah</u> sheet (bedding)

протез prah • <u>tes</u> denture

противозачаточное средство proh • <u>tee</u> • vah • zah • <u>chah</u> • tahch • nah • yeh <u>sryet</u> • stvah n contraceptive

профессия prah • <u>fyeh</u> • see • yah line (profession)

прыщ prihshch acne

прямой pryah • <u>moy</u> adj direct (train)

птица ptee • tsah bird

пустой poos • <u>toy</u> adj empty

путеводитель poo • tee • vah • <u>dee</u> • teel' guide book

пылесос pih • lee • <u>sos</u> vacuum cleaner

пьяный <u>pyah</u> • niy adj drunk

Р

работа rah • <u>boh</u> • tah job

работать rah • <u>boh</u> • taht' v work

разбудить rahz • boo • <u>deet'</u> wake someone

разговаривать rahz • gah • <u>vah</u> • ree • vaht' v talk

разговорник rahz • gah • <u>vor</u> • neek phrasebook

размер rahz • <u>myer</u> size

район rah • <u>yon</u> region

ракетка rah • <u>kyet</u> • kah racket (tennis)

раковина <u>rah</u> • kah • vee • nah sink

рана <u>rah</u> • nah n wound

ранний <u>rahn</u> • neey early

раскладушка rahs • klah • <u>doosh</u> • kah camp bed

расписание rahs • pee • <u>sah</u> • nee • yeh n schedule [timetable BE]

рассвет rahs • <u>vyet</u> dawn

рассказывать rahs • <u>kah</u> • zih • vaht' tell

растение rahs • <u>tyeh</u> • nee • yeh n plant

растяжение rahs • tee • zheh • nee • yeh n sprain

расчёска rah • <u>shchos</u> • kah n comb

раунд <u>rah</u> • oond round (of golf)

ребёнок ree • <u>byoh</u> • nahk baby; child

ребро reeb • <u>roh</u> rib

регистрационная стойка ree • gee • strah • tsih • <u>on</u> • nah • yah stoy • kah check-in desk

регистрация ree • gee • <u>strah</u> • tsih • yah reception (desk)

регистрироваться ree • gees • <u>tree</u> • rah • vah • tsah v check-in

рейс reys flight

река ree • <u>kah</u> river

рекомендовать ree • kah • meen • dah • <u>vaht'</u> recommend

религия ree • <u>lee</u> • gee • yah religion

ремень ree • <u>myen'</u> belt

ремесла ree • myos • <u>lah</u> handicrafts

ремонт обуви ree • <u>mont</u> oh • boo • vee shoe repair

рентген *reen • gyen* X-ray

ресторан *rees • tah • rahn* restaurant

рецепт *ree • tsept* prescription

родители *rah • dee • tee • lee* parents

розетка *rah • zyet • kah* electric outlet

романтичный *rah • mahn • teech • niy* romantic

Россия *rah • see • yah* Russia

рост *rost* height

рот *rot* mouth

рубашка *roo • bahsh • kah* shirt

рубль *roobl'* ruble [rouble]

рука *roo • kah* arm; hand

рукав *roo • kahf* sleeve

руководитель *roo • kah • vah • dee • teel'* leader (of group)

руководство *roo • kah • vod • stvah* manual (car)

русский *roos • keey* adj Russian

русский язык *roos • keey yah • zihk* Russian language

ручей *roo • chey* n stream

ручка *rooch • kah* pen

ручная кладь *rooch • nah • yah klaht'* hand luggage

рыба *rih • bah* fish

рынок *rih • nahk* market

рюкзак *ryoog • zahk* rucksack

рядом *ryah • dahm* nearby

рядом с *ryah • dahm s* next to

С

с *s* with

с субтитрами *s soop • teet • rah • mee* subtitled

сад *saht* garden

салфетка *sahl • fyet • kah* napkin

самолёт *sah • mah • lyot* plane

самообслуживание *sah • mah • ahp • sloo • zhih • vah • nee • yeh* self-service

сандалии *sahn • dah • lee* sandals

сапоги *sah • pah • gee* boots

сауна *sah • oo • nah* sauna

сахар *sah • khahr* sugar

свадьба *svahd' • bah* wedding

свежий *svye • zhiy* fresh

свет *svyet* n light (electic)

светлый *svyet • liy* adj light (opp. dark)

светофор *svee • tah • for* traffic lights

свеча *svee • chah* candle

свидетельство *svee • dyeh • teel' • stvah* certificate

свитер *svee • teer* sweater

свободное время *svah • bod • nah • yeh vryeh • myah* free time

свободный *svah • bod • niy* available (unoccupied, free)

связаться *svyah • zah • tsah* v contact

сдача *zdah • chah* change (coins)

сейф *seyf* n safe (lock up)

секретарь *seek • ree • tahr'* secretary

семья *seem' • yah* n family

сенная лихорадка *see • nah • yah lee • khah • raht • kah* hay fever

сердечный приступ *seer • dyech • niy prees • toop* heart attack

сердце *syer • tseh* heart

серебро *see • ree • broh* n silver

серый *syeh • riy* gray

серьги <u>syer'</u> • gee earrings

серьёзный seer' • <u>yoz</u> • niy serious

сесть syest' sit

сигара see • <u>gah</u> • rah cigar

сигарета see • gah • <u>ryeh</u> • tah cigarette

сильный <u>seel'</u> • niy strong (potent)

симптомы seemp • <u>toh</u> • mih symptoms

синагога see • nah • <u>goh</u> • gah synagogue

синтетический seen • teh • <u>tee</u> • chees • keey synthetic

синяк see • <u>nyahk</u> bruise

скала skah • <u>lah</u> cliff

скидка <u>skeet</u> • kah discount

сковорода skah • vah • rah • <u>dah</u> frying pan

скорая помощь <u>skoh</u> • rah • yah <u>poh</u> • mahshch ambulance

скоро <u>skoh</u> • rah soon

слева <u>slyeh</u> • vah on the left

следующий <u>slyeh</u> • doo • yoo • shcheey next

словарь slah • <u>vahr'</u> dictionary

сломан <u>sloh</u> • mahn broken

сломать slah • <u>maht'</u> v break

сломаться slah • <u>mah</u> • tsah v break down (car)

служба <u>sloozh</u> • bah n service (religious)

слуховой аппарат sloo • khah • <u>voy</u> ah • pah • <u>raht</u> hearing aid

слышать slih • <u>shaht'</u> hear

смеяться smee • <u>yah</u> • tsah v laugh

смотровая площадка smah • trah • <u>vah</u> • yah plah • <u>shchaht</u> • kah overlook

снаряжение snah • ree • <u>zheh</u> • nee • yeh equipment (sports)

снаряжение для дайвинга snah • ree • <u>zheh</u> • nee • yeh dlyah <u>die</u> • veen • gah diving equipment

снег snyek n snow

снотворное snah • <u>tvor</u> • nah • yeh sleeping pill

собор sah • <u>bor</u> cathedral

событие sah • <u>bih</u> • tee • yeh event

совок sah • <u>vok</u> shovel

современный sah • vree • <u>myen</u> • niy modern

современный танец sah • vree • <u>myen</u> • niy tah • neets contemporary dance

содержать sah • deer • <u>zhaht'</u> contain

Соединенные Штаты sah • ee • dee • <u>nyoh</u> • nih • ee <u>shtah</u> • tih United States

соленый sah • <u>lyoh</u> • niy salty

солнечно <u>sol</u> • neech • nah sunny

солнечные очки <u>sol</u> • neech • nih • ee ahch • <u>kee</u> sunglasses

солнечный ожёг <u>sol</u> • neech • niy ah • <u>zhok</u> sunburn

солнечный удар <u>sol</u> • neech • niy oo • <u>dahr</u> sunstroke

сообщение sah • ahp • <u>shcheh</u> • nee • yeh message

соска <u>sos</u> • kah pacifier [soother BE]

сотрясение мозга sah • tree • <u>syeh</u> • nee • yeh <u>moz</u> • gah concussion спа *spah* spa

спальный мешок *spahl' • niy mee • shok* sleeping bag

спальня *spahl' • nyah* bedroom

спасатель *spah • sah • teel'* lifeguard

спасательная лодка *spah • sah • teel' • nah • yah lot • kah* lifeboat

спасательный жилет *spah • sah • teel' • niy zhih • lyet* lifejacket

спать *spaht' v* sleep

специалист *spee • tsih • ah • leest* specialist

спина *spee • nah* back

спички *speech • kee* matches

спорт *sport* sport

спортзал *sport • zahl* gym

спортклуб *sport • kloop* sports club

спорттовары *spor • tah • vah • rih* sporting goods store

справа *sprah • vah* on the right

срочно *sroch • nah* urgent

стадион *stah • dee • on* stadium

стакан *stah • kahn* glass

станция метро *stahn • tsih • yah meet • roh* subway [underground BE] station

старый *stah • riy* old

старый город *stah • riy goh • raht* old town

статуя *stah • too • yah* statue

стиль *steel'* style

стиральная машина *stee • rahl' • nah • yah mah • shih • nah* washing machine

стоимость *stoh • ee • mahst'* value

столик *stoh • leek* table

сторона *stah • rah • nah* side (of road)

стоянка *stah • yahn • kah* pitch (for camping)

стоянка такси *stah • yahn • kah tahk • see* taxi stand [rank BE]

стоять в очереди *stah • yaht' v oh • chee • ree • dee* stand in line

страна *strah • nah* country (nation)

странный *strah • niy* strange

страховка *strah • khof • kah* insurance

стремянка *stree • myahn • kah* ladder

стрижка *streesh • kah* haircut

строить *stroh • eet'* build

студент *stoo • dyent* student

сувенир *soo • vee • neer* souvenir

судороги *soo • dah • rah • gee* cramps

сумка *soom • kah* purse [handbag BE]

сумма *soo • mah* amount

сухая стрижка *soo • khah • yah streesh • kah* dry cut

счёт *shchot n* bill

счёт за телефон *shchot zah tee • lee • fon* telephone bill

США *seh sheh ah* U.S.A.

сыпь *sihp'* rash

сыро *sih • rah adj* damp

Т

табак *tah • bahk* tobacco

таблетка *tahb • lyet • kah* pill (tablet)

также *tahk • zheh* also

такси *tahk • see* taxi

там *tahm* there

таможенная декларация *tah • moh • zhih • nah • yah deek • lah • rah • tsih • yah* customs declaration

таможня *tah • mozh • nyah* customs

тампон *tahm • pon* tampon

танец *tah • neets n* dance (performance)

тапочки *tah • pahch • kee* slippers

тарелка *tah • ryel • kah* plate

театр *tee • ahtr* theater

телевизор *tee • lee • vee • zahr* TV-set

тележка *tee • lyesh • kah* cart [trolley BE]

телефон *tee • lee • fon n* phone

телефон-автомат *tee • lee • fon ahf • tah • maht* pay phone

телефонный *справочник tee • lee • foh • niy sprah • vahch • neek* directory (telephone)

тёмный *tyom • niy* dark

температура *teem • pee • rah • too • rah* temperature

теннис *teh • nees* tennis

теннисные туфли *teh • nees • nih • ee toof • lee* sneakers

теннисный корт *teh • nees • niy kort* tennis court

тень *tyen'* shade

тёплый *tyop • liy* warm

термометр *teer • moh • meetr* thermometer

термос *ter • mahs* thermos flask

тесно *tyes • nah* crowded

тесный *tyes • niy* tight (loose)

течь *tyech v* leak (roof, pipe)

типичный *tee • peech • niy* typical

тихий *tee • kheey* quiet

ткань *tkahn'* fabric (material)

толстый *tols • tiy* thick

тонкий *ton • keey* thin

тонуть *tah • noot'* drown

торговый центр *tahr • goh • viy tsentr* mall [shopping centre]

тот же самый *tot zheh sah • miy* same

трава *trah • vah* grass

традиционный *trah • dee • tsih • oh • niy* traditional

трамвай *trahm • vie* tram

трасса *trah • sah* trail [piste BE]

тратить *trah • teet'* spend

трейлер *trey • leer* caravan

тропинка *trah • peen • kah* path

трубка *troop • kah* pipe (smoking)

трудный *trood • niy* difficult

тряпка *tryahp • kah* dish cloth

туалет *too • ah • lyet* restroom [toilet BE]

туалетная бумага *too • ah • lyet • nah • yah boo • mah • gah* toilet paper

туман *too • mahn* fog

туннель *too • nel'* tunnel

турист *too • reest* tourist

туфли *toof • lee* shoes

тушь *toosh* mascara

ты *tih* you (informal)

тяжёлый *tee • zhoh • liy* heavy

У

угол *oo • gahl* corner

уголь *oo • gahl'* charcoal

удалять *oo • dah • lyaht'* extract (tooth)

удобства *oo • dops • tvah* facilities

удостоверение
oo • dah • stah • vee • ryeh • nee • yeh identification

уезжать *oo • eezh • zhaht'* v leave

ужасный *oo • zhahs • niy* terrible

уже *oo • zheh* already

ужин *oo • zhih* dinner

узкий *oos • keey* narrow

укол *oo • kol* injection

Украина *oo • krah • ee • nah* Ukraine

укус *oo • koos* sting (wasp); bite (dog)

универсам *oo • nee • veer • sahm* supermarket

упаковочная пленка
oo • pah • koh • vahch • nah • yah plyon • kah plastic wrap [cling film BE]

упаковывать
oo • pah • koh • vih • vaht' v pack

урок *oo • rok* lesson

успокаивающее
oos • pah • kah • ee • vah • yoo • shchee • yeh sedative

усталый *oos • tah • liy* tired

утюг *oo • tyook* n iron

ухо *oo • khah* ear

уходить *oo • khah • deet'* go away

учитель *oo • chee • teel'* teacher

Ф

факс *fahks* n fax

фамилия *fah • mee • lee • yah* surname

фен *fyen* blow-dry

ферма *fyer • mah* farm

фильм *feel'm* movie [film BE]

фильтр *feel'tr* filter

фойе *fei • yeh* foyer (hotel, theater)

фольга *fahl' • gah* aluminium foil

фонтан *fahn • tahn* fountain

форма *for • mah* uniform

фотоаппарат
foh • tah • ah • pah • raht camera

фотография
fah • tah • grah • fee • yah photograph

фраза *frah • zah* phrase

фунт *foont* pound (sterling)

футбол *food • bol* soccer [football BE]

Х

химчистка *kheem • cheest • kah* dry cleaner

хобби *khoh • bee* hobby (pastime)

холм *kholm* hill

холодильник
khah • lah • deel' • neek refrigerator

холодный *khah • lod • niy* adj cold

холост *khoh • lahst* single (unmarried)

хороший *khah • roh • shiy* good

хотеть *khah • tet'* want

хрусталь *khroos • tahl'* n crystal

хрустальная посуда
khroos • tahl' • nah • yah pah • soo • dah cut glass

художественный салон
khoo • doh • zhes • tvee • niy sah • lon craft shop

Ц

цвет *tsvyet* color

цветок *tsvee • tok* flower

цветочный магазин
tsvye • toch • niy mah • gah • zeen florist

целовать *tsih • lah • vaht'* v kiss

цель *tsel'* purpose

ценный *tseh • niy* valuable

центр (города) tsentr (goh • rah • dah) center (of town)

центральное отопление tsihn • trahl' • nah • yeh ah • tahp • lyeh • nee • yeh central heating

цепочка tsih • poch • kah chain

церковь tser • kahf' church

Ч

чайная ложка chie • nah • yah losh • kah teaspoon

чайник chie • neek kettle

чартерный рейс chahr • ter • niy reys charter flight

час chahs hour

час пик chahs peek rush hour

часто chahs • tah often

часы chah • sih clock (watch)

часы посещений chah • sih pah • see • shcheh • neey visiting hours

часы работы chah • sih rah • boh • tih opening hours

чашка chahsh • kah cup

чек chek receipt

челюсть cheh • lyoost' jaw

через cheh • rees across

чистить chees • teet' v clean

чистка лица cheest • kah lee • tsah facial

чистый chees • tiy adj clean

читать chee • taht' read

что-то shtoh • tah something

чулки chool • kee stockings

Ш

шампунь shahm • poon' shampoo

шапка shahp • kah hat

шарф shahrf scarf

шахматы shahkh • mah • tih chess

швабра shvahb • rah mop

шезлонг shez • lonk deck chair

шёлк sholk silk

шерсть sherst' wool

шея sheh • yah neck

широкий shih • roh • keey wide

шкаф shkahf cupboard

шлем shlyem helmet

шорты shor • tih shorts

шоссе shah • seh highway [motorway BE]

штепсель shtep • seel' n plug

штопор shtoh • pahr corkscrew

шторы shtoh • rih blinds

шумный shoom • niy noisy

шутка shoot • kah n joke

щётка для волос shchot • kah dlyah vah • los hair brush

Э

экскурсия eks • koor • see • yah guided tour

экскурсовод eeks • koor • sah • vot tour guide

экспресс eks • pres express

электричество eh • leek • tree • cheest • vah electricity

электронная почта ee • leek • troh • nah • yah poch • tah e-mail

электронный билет ee • leek • tron • niy bee • lyet e-ticket

электронный ключ eh • leek • tron • niy klyooch key card

эмаль ee • mahl' enamel

эпилептик ee • pee • lyep • teek n epileptic

эскалатор *ees • kah • lah • tahr*
  escalator
этаж *eh • tahsh* floor (level)

Ю

юбка *yoop • kah* skirt
ювелирный магазин
  yoo • vee • leer • niy
  mah • gah • zeen jeweler

Я

я *yah* I
яд *yaht* poison
язва *yahz • vah* ulcer
язык *yah • zihk* tongue
языковые курсы
  yah • zih • kah • vih • yeh
  koor • sih language course
ярлык *yahr • lihk* n label
ясли *yahs • lee* nursery
яхта *yahkh • tah* yacht